The Criminal Law of Competition in the UK and in the US

The Criminal Law of Competition in the UK and in the US

Failure and Success

Mark Furse

Professor of Competition Law and Policy, University of Glasgow, UK

Edward Elgar

Cheltenham, UK • Northampton, MA, USA

Published by
Edward Elgar Publishing Limited
The Lypiatts
15 Lansdown Road
Cheltenham
Glos GL50 2JA
UK

Edward Elgar Publishing, Inc.
William Pratt House
9 Dewey Court
Northampton
Massachusetts 01060
USA

A catalogue record for this book
is available from the British Library

Library of Congress Control Number: 2012941924

MIX
Paper from responsible sources
FSC® C018575

ISBN 978 0 85793 430 7

Typeset by Servis Filmsetting Ltd, Stockport, Cheshire
Printed and bound by MPG Books Group, UK

Contents

Preface

In 2004, writing with Susan Nash, I published the first book to deal with the UK's new Cartel Offence, set out in the Enterprise Act 2002. At that time, when there had not yet been any enforcement of the new law, we looked forward to an effective regime, and anticipated, following the Penrose Report, that there would be a significant number of cases. This book, for which I bear sole responsibility, is probably the last to be written dealing with the first phase of the Cartel Offence, and looks back on the operation of the regime over the intervening years with despair, and looks forward with pessimism to the immediate future. The cut-off date for inclusion in material in this book is April 1, 2012, by which time the Department for Business, Innovation and Skills ('BIS') had published the Government response to a consultation exercise looking at various aspects of the UK competition law regime, including the operation of the Cartel Offence. The consultation exercise, and its result, is dealt with in Chapters 4 and 7 of this book. In essence, the Cartel Offence has given rise to convictions only in respect of three persons, in relation to a single cartel. In that case enforcement was driven by the United States' authorities, and the UK convictions were secured on the back of a US plea agreement (this case is discussed in detail in Chapters 4 and 6). While more general failings in the work of the Office of Fair Trading in the last eight years have made it difficult to determine to what extent difficulties encountered in enforcing the Cartel Offence have been a result of the structure of the Offence itself, or the result of wider institutional failings, it is clear, and the consultation exercise confirms that the Government believe this to be the case, that matters have not gone well. My primary aim in writing this book has been to evaluate the operation of the UK's Cartel Offence to date.

After an introduction I start with a general review of the literature relating to cartels and to the criminalisation and imposition of personal sanctions in respect to cartelisation. As will become clear, I am persuaded that individual criminal sanctions have a role to play, and in Chapter 3 I draw on the US experience, setting out relevant US law and procedure in some detail, to demonstrate how such an approach can, in practice, work well. In Chapter 4 I focus on the UK experience, seeking in particular to clarify differences between this and the US experience. Given that a major difference between the US antitrust regime and the UK competition regime is that the UK operates in the shadow of a superior EU regime, in Chapter 5 I look at the experience in Ireland. A constitutional peculiarity in Ireland gives rise to a situation in which competition law sanctions are criminal. Ireland has prosecuted more cases with success than has the UK, but the nature of those cases has been somewhat different than has been the case in the UK: in Ireland cases have been brought against localised, domestic cartels; in the UK prosecutions have been mounted against international cartels. The Irish experience however is also not one of stunning success – penalties have been limited, and enforcement activity has been bedevilled by a lack of resources.

In Chapter 6 I set out the key details of three major cartel cases which have had a significant impact on enforcement policy in the US, and which have fed into wider discussions as to the approaches to be taken to cartelisation. These cases illustrate the sophistication of cartel arrangements, the harms that cartelisation gives rise to, and the difficulty of enforcing prohibitions on cartelisation.

In Chapter 7 I set out my broad conclusions, and explain the reason for my pessimism for the UK's soon-to-be-revamped Cartel Offence. I hope that the evidence I consider throughout the book has misled me, and that I am in fact too pessimistic here. The evidence that cartels are not rare, that they are very harmful, and that they are organised in knowing defiance of legal prohibitions is overwhelming, and I take the view that criminalisation and incarceration is an appropriate enforcement mechanism, but only where the conditions are appropriate.

If I have achieved what I set out to, readers of this book should find before them a fair and balanced review of much of the relevant literature, explaining clearly the key arguments relating to criminal enforcement of anti-cartel laws, a clear statement of the law in the US and Ireland, and of the law in the UK up to the point before the Offence is to be changed, and a reasonable conclusion. It is unlikely that all readers will agree with my conclusions, and in fact many may disagree. The BIS consultation exercise demonstrated clearly that this is not an area in respect of which there is consensus in the UK at present.

Work began on this book in April 2011, just after BIS published its consultation document, and finished in April 2012, just after the response to that exercise was published. At both times, but not in the intervening 12 months, I was based at Hong Kong University, and I am very grateful for the continued support that HKU has offered to my work over the years. Notwithstanding the Hong Kong sojourns I remain a full-time member of staff at Glasgow University, School of Law, and have benefited from the support of the School throughout the period in which I have worked on this book. I must in particular acknowledge the continued support of my colleague and friend, Professor Rosa Greaves, who has been an exceptional Head of School. Students on the LLM course, Competition Law Enforcement, have patiently sat through seminars in which the arguments made in this book have been worked out and rehearsed, and I am grateful both for their patience and for their questions, which have often been acute. Dr Kay Munro has provided invaluable help in tracking down a wide range of materials, and has gone well beyond the call of duty in doing so. Colin MacIver and Ioannis Apostolakis at the University of Glasgow provided helpful research assistance. A number of academic and professional colleagues have looked at either the complete draft manuscript of this book, or parts of it, and have given me their comments; some have given me access to their own draft work, and I am very grateful for this engagement. The staff at Edward Elgar have been professional and helpful throughout the publication process. Finally, I must thank the patience of my wife, Dr Xuya Huang, who, after watching *The Informant!* (which is based around Mark Whitacre's role in uncovering the lysine cartel) asked 'what's wrong with price fixing?' This was a question she came to regret, although if she reads Chapter 2 of this book (an unlikely prospect) she may find a fairly full answer to that question.

As always, all errors and omissions in this text are my own. Also as always, I would welcome any (reasonable) comments about this book, which may be addressed to me at: mark.furse@glasgow.ac.uk.

The law in this book is up to date as at April 1, 2012 (which, coincidentally, is the 26th anniversary of the formalisation of the marine hose cartel discussed in Chapters 4 and 6).

Mark Furse
Hong Kong

1. Introduction

Cartels 'undermine and destroy a fundamental economic and political philosophy of Western democracies, ie free market capitalism';[1] are 'cancers on the open market economy';[2] they are 'the supreme evil of antitrust, overcharging consumers many billions of dollars each year',[3] and 'serve only to rob consumers'.[4] Such condemnation invites strong action; cartelists face, if caught, extremely high fines in the European Union (although the argument is made that these fines are insufficiently high – see Chapter 2, below), and high fines and imprisonment in the United States. Citing the experience of the US as a positive one, the UK[5] introduced the Cartel Offence in 2002. The argument made in this book is that the decision to do so has, at the time of writing, resulted only in failure. When work began on this book I was not certain that I would reach this conclusion, but I *was* certain that the implementation of the law by the Office of Fair Trading ('OFT') had gone disastrously wrong, as evidenced in the collapse of the first prosecution to be taken 'independently'. Earlier convictions secured in the *Marine Hose* cartel were, as will be discussed later in this book, in effect coerced on the back of United States' enforcement activity – in the language of industrial economics and competition policy, the OFT was a

---

[1] Whelan, PM, 'A Principled Argument for Personal Criminal Sanctions as Punishment under EC Cartel Law' (2007) *Competition Law Review* 7 at 29.

[2] Monti, M, 'Why Should We Be Concerned with Cartels and Collusive Behaviour?', in Konkurrensverket (Swedish Competition Authority), *Fighting Cartels – Why and How?* (2001) Konkurrensverket at 14.

[3] Connor, JM and Lande, RH, 'Optimal Cartel Deterrence: An Empirical Comparison of Sanctions to Overcharges' (2011) AAI Working Paper No 11-08, at 1. In the context of an attack on a particular line of economics and law analysis, we find an even more robust language employed: 'efficient hard-core price-fixing is no more likely than efficient child molestation' (Werden, GJ, and Simon, MJ, 'Why Price Fixers Should Go to Prison' (1987) 32 *Antitrust Bulletin* 917 at 932).

[4] Werden, GJ, Hammond, SD, and Barnett, BA, 'Deterrence and Detection of Cartels: Using All the Tools and Sanctions' (2011) 56:2 *Antitrust Bulletin* 207 at 207.

[5] This book deals with UK, US, Irish and EU law. Although the term 'antitrust' is finding increasing favour in the European Union and in the United Kingdom, I shall use it here only when discussing the antitrust law of the United States.

'free rider'.[6] It is not possible to say whether the success in this case led to a sense of complacency that in part contributed to the collapse of the *British Airways* case, which is discussed very extensively in Chapter 4 below. As of 2012 the UK's Cartel Offence has been the dog that did *not* bark.

In reaching my somewhat robust conclusion I have considered four questions. (1) Is criminalisation of competition law ever a good idea? (2) Was the UK correct to criminalise certain (anti-)competitive behaviour, and to what extent would a consideration of the approach taken under EU competition law – at the 'centre', among the national competition authorities ('NCAs'), and in particular in the UK – impact on the answer to this question? (3) If the criminalisation of aspects of competition law could be an appropriate strategy in the UK, was the correct approach taken in the legislative detail? (4) If the correct approach was taken by the legislature, is it possible to identify specific failings in the enforcement of the law by, primarily, the OFT? In order to avoid unnecessary suspense, the answers to these questions, which flow through the rest of the book, although not perhaps as neatly as the systematisation above would suggest, are as follows: the arguments in favour of criminalisation are strong; the UK's attempt to create a criminal system that stands apart from, but must operate alongside, UK and EU civil law is a mistaken endeavour; the correct approach was not taken in the legislative detail (evidence of which can be found in the 2012 proposals for reform); and there have clearly been failings in enforcement, as has been acknowledged by the OFT. The answers to questions 1 and 4 were in my mind before I began writing this book, although I would have been prepared to follow the evidence had it pointed in a different direction. It matters that I was convinced that the criminalisation of competition law could, in an appropriate context, be a successful strategy. This is important to the scheme of this book in that I have accepted – as apparently did the Government at the time the Cartel Offence was being brought forward in Parliament (see Chapter 4, below) – that the US experience of criminalisation has been broadly successful. I have thus used the US experience as a reference point throughout this book, and Chapter 3, below, is an attempt to explain the genesis of this policy, shifts in the policy over the more than 120 years since it was introduced, and enough of the detail of the application of the law in practice

[6] For the Office of Fair Trading the *Marine Hose* prosecutions continue to be held up as an example of success. Thus, for example, the OFT has argued that 'it is essential that the . . . UK retains the ability to pursue criminal investigations into individuals . . . as the OFT did successfully in the Marine hose case' (OFT, *A Competition Regime for Growth: A Consultation on Options for Reform. The OFT's Response to the Government's Consultation* (OFT 1335, June 2011) at 5.3.

to serve as a useful guide to this area. In respect of question 4 my conclusion sadly lacks originality; one would be hard-pressed to find any UK competition law expert outside the OFT who did not take the view that serious mistakes had been made by the OFT, and indeed this much was acknowledged by the OFT in its public breast-beating after the trial of a number of persons with links to British Airways collapsed. It is very likely that this latter case will be the last to have been brought within the framework originally established in 2002. Shortly after work began on this book the Government announced a reform of aspects of the UK competition law system, and included discussion of the future of the Cartel Offence in the relevant materials. This reform process is discussed in some detail in Chapter 4. That this book is in part a work of legal history will not, I hope, deter the reader anxious for solutions to practical problems at the time of reading; the policy issues raised here will remain relevant.

I recognise in writing this book that I am swimming in dangerous waters. The bibliography of the criminal law of competition is, on both sides of the Atlantic, small when compared to the amount of discussion given over to analyses of substantive conduct and broader policy. The US antitrust lawyer may choose to focus on precisely that substance and policy, leaving civil and criminal procedure to specialists in these areas of law. In the UK, at least until the collapse of *R v Burns and others*, there was very little literature relating to the Cartel Offence.[7] I have in these pages plunged into the murky depths of certain aspects of criminal law and procedure in the UK, the US and Ireland, and hope that specialists will forgive me for doing so.

Prior to 2002, when the Enterprise Act introduced the Cartel Offence ('the Offence') into the law of the United Kingdom, the UK had not for a long time maintained a criminal law of competition.[8] Post-war, the UK competition law regime, introduced in an Act of 1948,[9] and modified heavily in the Fair Trading Act of 1973, was largely supervisory in nature, with little provision made for punishment, whether in the form of civil or criminal sanctions. There was the possibility, in exceptional circumstances,

---

[7] References to almost all of this are provided in the bibliography, although this does not include shorter pieces not published in reference or reviewed journals.

[8] It was noted, shortly after the enactment of the Offence, 'that only five years ago, the UK still had one of the feeblest anticartel regimes in the developed world, where cartels could be registered and penalties (for contempt of court) only applied if a company had broken a solemn undertaking to sin no more' (Joshua, JM, 'The UK's New Cartel Offence and Its Implications for EC Competition Law: A Tangled Web' (2003) *European Law Review* 620 at 620).

[9] Monopolies and Restrictive Practices (Inquiry and Control) Act 1948.

of some criminal enforcement, but this rarely happened.[10] The decision to introduce competition law into the UK in 1948 was a tentative one, and it was not until membership of the European Economic Community, now the European Union ('EU'), took effect in 1973 that anti-competitive conduct in the UK could give rise in the first instance to substantial financial penalties and remedial orders. The 1948 legislation was the first competition law in the UK since 1844. By that year the high tide of economic laissez faire had ensured that a raft of earlier legislation had, over time, been repealed in its entirety. This earlier legislation, which can be dated back to the reigns of the Saxon kings, and which was reinforced after the Norman conquest, did include criminal penalties, including ones we would now regard as 'cruel and unusual'. Thus, for example, in respect of one offence the punishment on a third conviction was that the offender would have his right ear cut off, and would forever after 'be known as a man infamous'. It is not known what impact this enforcement mechanism had on compliance with the law, nor how often the punishment was imposed.

In the 1990s, with the introduction of the Competition Act 1998 ('CA98'), the UK began a process of what has been termed 'Europeanisation' of its competition law.[11] The Fair Trading Act 1973, the Restrictive Trade Practices Act 1976, the Resale Prices Act 1976, and the Competition Act 1980 were largely swept aside (although the distinctive

---

[10] Although see *Director General of Fair Trading v Pioneer Concrete (UK) Ltd* [1995] 1 AC 456. Here the respondents were engaged in the supply of ready-mixed concrete. They were subject to an injunction restraining them from giving effect to certain unlawful agreements under the Restrictive Trade Practices Act 1976, s35(1). It was established that, without the knowledge of the respondents, and against their express instructions, certain local managers had continued the unlawful arrangements. The respondent companies were found to be in contempt of court. In this case it was only the companies who could be held responsible for the contempt of court, and the House of Lords 'dealt with the case as one of vicarious liability' (The Law Commission, *Criminal Liability in Regulatory Contexts: A Consultation Paper* (2010), Consultation Paper No 195 at 100). Lord Templeman stated:

> [a]n employee who acts for the company within the scope of his employment is the company. Directors may give instructions, top management may exhort, middle management may question and workers may listen attentively. But if a worker makes a defective product or a lower manager accepts or rejects an order, he is the company (at 465).

[11] See, for example, Rodger, BJ, 'The Competition Act and the Enterprise Act Reforms: Sanctions and Deterrence in UK Competition Law', in *Competition Law Sanctioning in the European Union: The EU-Law Influence on the National Law System of Sanctions in the European Area* No 46, pp. 101–32 (2004).

UK approach to merger control and market investigations was retained), and were replaced by an *ex ante* prohibition system based on arts 101 and 102 TFEU. The OFT was forced to change its culture and to become an enforcer of law, with the power to impose penalties on undertakings in breach of the Chapter I and Chapter II Prohibitions of the CA98, as well as in respect of breaches of arts 101 and 102 TFEU.

The late 1990s was a vital period in the development of the approach to cartels in general and international cartels in particular. In July 1999 the US for the first time sentenced to imprisonment a foreign national following a breach of s 1 of the Sherman Act. The fact that it was able to do so reflected wider growing consensus as to the vigour with which cartels should be pursued:

> [t]he Antitrust Division has been able to secure prison sentences for culpable non-US citizens because the leniency program and improved cooperation with competition and law enforcement agencies in other countries substantially enhanced the Division's ability to access evidence outside the US and secure jurisdiction over culpable individuals abroad. Our foreign counterparts began to cooperate and conduct parallel investigations resulting in sanctions. Changing attitudes toward cartels by authorities in other countries occurred gradually, but 1998 was a watershed year for Europe. The OECD for the first time formally supported aggressive cartel enforcement, the European Commission's Directorate General for Competition created a special unit to investigate cartels and decided its first cartel cases under its new leniency program, and the Commission issued its first fines guidelines.[12]

The apparent success of the US regime is seductive, but in few seductions is the entire truth revealed, and as Baker has made clear, 'the United States did not arrive at the point it has – with potential criminal liability and jail time as serious deterrents – quickly or easily';[13] elsewhere Baker has referred to the 'long slow road' travelled by US antitrust law.[14] Having embarked on a Europeanisation of its domestic competition law in 1998, the UK quickly followed on with a partial Americanisation in 2002.

The decision in 2002 to reintroduce a criminal offence extending to

---

[12] Werden, GJ, Hammond, SD, and Barnett, BA, 'Recidivism Eliminated: Cartel Enforcement in the United States since 1999' (2011) Georgetown Global Antitrust Enforcement Symposium, September 22, 2011 at 5, internal footnotes omitted.

[13] Baker, DI, 'The Use of Criminal Law Remedies to Deter and Punish Cartels and Bid-Rigging' (2000–2001) 69 *George Washington Law Review* 693 at 694.

[14] Baker, DI, 'Punishment for Cartel Participants in the US: A Special Model?', in Beaton-Wells, C, and Ezrachi, A (eds), *Criminalising Cartels: Critical Studies of an International Regulatory Movement* (2011) Hart Publishing at 29.

certain classes of anti-competitive conduct 'dishonestly' entered into must be taken as evidence of a view held by the Government, with presumably the support of the Office of Fair Trading ('OFT'), that the introduction of the Offence would increase the efficiency of the UK's competition law regime. Indeed there is clear evidence in the preparatory materials – the consultation documents, responses, and in the debates in Parliament – that this belief was held. The Government in particular cited the experience of criminal enforcement in the US in support of its position. The US has maintained criminal sanctions in respect of antitrust violations since the introduction of the Sherman Act in 1890. Both sections 1 and 2 of that Act state that their breach may constitute a 'felony', although there has been no criminal enforcement in respect of s 2 of the Act, which condemns monopolisation. The Organisation for Economic Co-operation and Development ('OECD') presses the case for strong enforcement action to be taken in respect of certain forms of anti-competitive conduct (so-called 'hard core cartels'), but does not privilege in its recommendation any particular approach.[15] The European Union, whose competition law has arguably been more effective than that of UK law since the former took effect, does not encompass criminal sanctions within its regime, although as will be discussed in Chapter 4, it does allow member states the leeway to maintain national criminal sanctions, but if these are 'the means whereby competition rules applying to undertakings are enforced' enforcement of this law must be fully compliant with Regulation 1/2003.[16] Other EU member states, but not a majority, include some form of criminal law within their competition law systems. The Irish system is discussed in Chapter 5, below.

The inclusion of the provisions establishing the Cartel Offence in the Enterprise Act 2002 ('EA02') was somewhat surprising. The UK's competition regime had been substantially overhauled only recently with the passing of the CA98, which took effect on March 1, 2000. The UK national competition authority, the OFT, was struggling with a changed enforcement role, and the new system had not yet had time to bed-in. The introduction of the Offence is discussed in more detail in Chapter 4. A preparatory report had provided a loose estimate, which has turned out to be wildly optimistic, of the number of prosecutions that might be brought forward each year, and had suggested that the number was 'likely

---

[15] OECD, *Recommendation of the Council Concerning Effective Action against Hard Core Cartels*, March 25, 1998 [C/M(98)7/PROV].

[16] Council Regulation (EC) No 1/2003 of 16 December 2002 on the implementation of the rules on competition laid down in Articles [101] and [102] of the Treaty (2003) OJ L1/1, recital (8).

to be near the bottom' of a range with six as a lower bound.[17] As of April 2012, with the Offence having been in force since June 20, 2003,[18] only *one* case has given rise to convictions, and that case, which flowed from cartel activity in relation to marine hose was atypical in that the US authorities were heavily involved in its investigation, and in that guilty pleas lodged by three defendants in the UK were part of a plea agreement negotiated in the US. In March 2011 the coalition UK Government published a consultation document, *A Competition Regime for Growth: A Consultation on Options for Reform*,[19] which included at Chapter 6, proposals to amend the Cartel Offence. Clearly, in the view of the Department for Business, Innovation and Skills, ('BIS') something had gone wrong with the Offence or with its operation.[20] It may be that the ten-year period since the Offence was first enacted has provided sufficient evidence of deficiencies in the original wording of the Offence, but the case experience on which such a conclusion is drawn is severely limited. One thing that clearly did go wrong, although it is not clear if the blame for this can be attributed to the wording of the Offence itself, was the abandonment by the OFT, on May 10, 2010, of what would have been its highest profile prosecution of the Offence at that time. The case of *R v Burns and others*, which flowed from an alleged price-fixing arrangement operated by Virgin Atlantic and British Airways, was abandoned when previously undisclosed evidence came to light just as the main trial, after various preliminary appeals had been settled, was underway. The OFT subsequently stated that this development led to 'adverse reputational impacts for the OFT and

---

[17] Office of Fair Trading, *The Proposed Criminalisation of Cartels in the UK – A Report Prepared for the Office of Fair Trading by Sir Anthony Hammond QC and Roy Penrose OBE QPM* (OFT 365, November 2001) [2002] UKCLR 97, at Para 3.7. In the course of the enactment of the EA02 the Under Secretary of State did not commit herself to any specific number of cases, stating instead that '[t]he point is not about how many people we send to prison. . . . We would rather that people did not end up operating cartels, but it is important if they do so that we send a message, both to the individual and to society, that that is unacceptable and a serious offence' (*Hansard*, HC, Standing Committee B (April 23, 2002), col 169.

[18] Enterprise Act 2002 (Commencement No 3, Transitional and Transitory Provisions and Savings) Order 2003, SI 2003/1397, art 2.

[19] Department for Business, Innovation and Skills, *Competition for Growth: Consultation on Options for Reform* (March 2011). See further Chapter 4, below.

[20] At Para 6.5 of the Consultation Document, it is stated that:

> [t]he deterrent effect of the cartel offence is weaker than was intended because there have been so few completed cases to date: only two cases so far have reached trial stage and only one of them resulted in convictions.

the competition regime'.[21] A more acerbic commentator referred to the Offence as 'a dead man walking'.[22]

In this book I aim to examine some of the issues surrounding the criminalisation of competition law in the UK. It would be almost impossible to do this effectively without frequent reference to the US experience, which has clearly formed a strong reference point for the international competition law community. There are however things which clearly differentiate the US and UK situations; one such factor may simply be that of the socio-legal culture, although assessing this is problematic. A more fundamental difference lies in the way in which the relevant competition laws are framed within the legal systems. The federal law of the US does not have to jostle for position with a competition law of general application which is supreme over it, whereas UK competition law does. In the US the federal authorities can make a choice early on between *either* a civil action *or* a criminal prosecution. In the UK, as EU law makes clear, and as is restated in Regulation 1/2003, EU competition law takes supremacy over domestic competition law in the event that the two should conflict, or in the event that both apply to the same set of facts. In particular the UK authorities may not be able to view civil and criminal enforcement as an *either/or* situation, and instead the same set of factual circumstances may give rise to two different actions – one on the basis of a violation of the CA98 or the TFEU, the other on the basis of a violation of the Cartel Offence. US law allows for criminal prosecution of *both* the sinful corporation *and* the individual wrongdoer – UK law does not. Only where action is taken in the context of an unlawful agreement which does not affect trade between member states of the EU (within the terms of the relevant Commission notice and EU case law) would there not need to be any consideration of the impact of EU obligations. This means that in the UK the link between civil and criminal leniency is more complicated, and the practitioner community would probably say *too* complicated, than is the case in the US or, following recent changes to its system, Canada.[23]

Another feature of the UK regime is that there has been a deliberate

---

21 OFT, *Project Condor Review Board* (2010) Annex, p 9.

22 Joshua, JM, 'Shooting the Messenger: Does the UK Criminal Cartel Offense Have a Future?' (2010) *theantitrustsource*, August (www.antitrustsource.com).

23 A new cartel provision came into force in Canada in March 2010. This differs from the previous position in that, as with the position in the UK, it does not require any showing of effect on competition in respect of competitor agreements that fix prices, allocate markets, or limit output. The first conviction occurred in January 2012, when two firms pleaded guilty to price-fixing in the market for polyurethane foam, and were fined C$12.5 million.

attempt to remove complex issues of economics from the framing of the Offence. Thus s 188 of the EA02 sets out a number of arrangements which, if entered into dishonestly, constitute the core of the Offence. As stated in the 2011 Consultation Document, this was intended to 'decrease the likelihood of defendants seeking to rely on complex economic evidence that juries will find difficult to understand'.[24] That the Government might take the view that the introduction of economic evidence into a jury proceeding would be potentially detrimental to conviction rates is perhaps reasonable. In the United States, however, where section 1 cases are fairly regularly brought before juries and grand juries, there has been no differentiation between the terms of the civil infringement and of the criminal offence. Both types of cases are brought on precisely the same wording of s 1 of the Sherman Act. It may be that the differentiation of categories of conduct by use of the *per se* and rule of reason approaches developed by the courts since the early 1900s, and still continuing into the 21st century, mitigates against defendants seeking to bamboozle juries with complicated economic analyses.

I also probe here, in Chapter 2 in particular, the economic arguments underpinning the case for the adoption of a criminal law. If the primary purpose of competition law is to facilitate economic efficiency, or at least to mitigate against the harms arising from economic inefficiency, it is surely reasonable to evaluate and critique laws aimed at ensuring that end against an efficiency standard. Chapter 2 is therefore heavily reliant on the literature of others, and my hope is that this chapter will serve, in effect, as a literature review of the area as of mid-2012. This includes literature relating to the economics of law, and the economics of the enforcement of criminal competition law in particular.

It is a truism that the direct rewards of cartel participation do not

---

[24] Chapter 6, introduction. This argument is acknowledged in the 2011 Consultation Document, where it is stated, at Para 6.9 that the dishonesty element:

> was included to reduce the likelihood that conviction would depend on judgments taken on detailed economic evidence. The requirement to prove 'dishonesty' would largely exclude potentially beneficial arrangements from the offence and there would usually be no need for juries to consider the economic effects of agreements. There was a concern that juries would find it difficult to understand such evidence and this would make the offence very difficult to prosecute (internal footnote omitted).

One could counter this concern with a hope, perhaps naïve, that an overworked competition authority and the Serious Fraud Office would not contemplate launching prosecutions in cases where an argument as to countervailing benefits would be viable, although of course this would not preclude a defendant from running with such an argument.

typically flow to an individual, but to the corporation joining the cartel.[25] At the same time there *must be* a reason for individuals to commission the acts which lead to the corporations they are employed by, or which they own, entering into cartels. These might include promotion and bonuses if their company, or their part of the company, improves its position as a result; and perhaps importantly the reward might simply be one of an easier life. It is often argued in the economic literature, and the evidence for this is strong, that uncertainty is damaging to businesses, and certainly participation in a cartel can be expected to reduce uncertainty as the number of pressures on the company is correspondingly reduced by the elimination of direct sources of competitive pressures. The most commonly made argument for the existence of a criminal offence directed towards individuals is that this recognises the split personality of the corporate world, and attributes blame and condemnation directly to the responsible actors, presumably thereby reducing the incentives for them to enter into such arrangements. Thus, for example, Hughes LJ stated in *R v B*[26] that

> the Offence created by s 188 is one arrow in the UK legislative quiver designed to prevent anti-competitive practices . . . There is no doubt whatever that it was created because it was thought to provide a stronger deterrent to such practices to threaten executives with imprisonment than was achieved by threatening undertakings with civil financial penalties, heavy as the latter may often be.

Similarly, in the 2011 consultation document, the Government states that the 'possibility that business people will face imprisonment if found guilty of the Offence should radically alter the incentives to engage in cartels'.

In Chapters 3 and 4 I set out the relevant legal framework of the operation of criminal competition law in the US and in the UK, alongside discussion of the experience of enforcement. These chapters should serve as a useful guide to the state of the criminal law of competition in each regime as of April 2012. In Chapter 5 I consider the experience of Ireland, which operates a regime which is wholly criminal in nature. Chapter 6 presents three case studies of the operation of cartels, and the application of enforcement efforts against them. Chapter 7 presents some conclusions.

My fundamental starting point in writing this book has been a suspicion that the Cartel Offence is failing in the UK, at least at the time of writing,

---

25 This point was made in the UK case of *R v Whittle* [2008] EWCA Crim 2560 [2009] UKCLR 247 where the Appeal Court noted that the profits generated by participation in the cartel 'did not, of course, go directly into the pockets of any of the applicants' (at [21]).

26 [2009] EWCA Crim 2575 [2010] UKCLR 1, at [22].

and that the *perception* is that the criminal policy applied in the US is broadly effective. This is not to suggest that the application of criminal law to cartelists in the US is without its problems, although these are more clearly demonstrated in relation to international cartels, in respect of which jurisdictional and procedural difficulties in securing convictions mount.[27] Clearly the lack of case law in the UK is diminishing any impact the Offence may have been intended to have. In the preparatory White Paper[28] it was noted at Para 7.33 that the new Offence would have to 'be actively applied so that its deterrent effect is genuinely felt'. It is however surprisingly difficult to ascertain whether a law has failed or succeeded, particularly when the law is a new one. If there are no, or only a handful of, cases, this might suggest that the law is being complied with such that enforcement action is unnecessary. It might also suggest that there was in fact never a problem, and that the law was unnecessary (and hence inefficient). One could also argue that the law was necessary, but that avoidance is rife, and detection efforts weak. Similarly, a substantial body of case law and a number of successful prosecutions might imply that the law was necessary, that breaches were rife, and that detection is strong (and hence, perhaps, that the law is efficient). What we would not know in either circumstance are the answers to two important questions: (1) what effect has the law had in reducing the number of instances of the commission of the relevant offence by virtue of its very existence? (ie, have firms that would have entered into illegal cartels taken compliance efforts to ensure that they did not do so following the introduction of the law?); and (2) how many instances of continuing violations of the law are going undetected? The questions I seek to answer are those of whether the law in the UK has actually failed so far, and, if it has, why this might be the case, and whether the law in the US is actually succeeding, and again, if it is, why this might be the case. In short, are there lessons to be learnt from the experience of the US, and perhaps from other states, that could be applied in the UK to improve the efficiency of competition law enforcement via the application of personal criminal sanctions?

---

27 See, for example, Connor, JM, 'Problems with Prison in International Cartel Cases' (2011) 56:2 *Antitrust Bulletin* 311.

28 Department of Trade and Industry, *Productivity and Enterprise: A World Class Competition Regime* (Cm 2533, July 2001).

2. Criminalisation of cartel activity: economics and law

INTRODUCTION

This chapter reviews the economic and legal literature relating to the criminalisation of competition law in general, and of cartel activity in particular,[1] with the aim of setting out the main themes that apply in this area.[2] I do not substantially rework the arguments raised in the relevant literature, and there is not space here to present a comprehensive review. The extensive footnotes and bibliography should assist interested readers in following the threads of this literature should they wish to do so. Literature particular to specific aspects of the UK regime is discussed in Chapters 4 and 7, below. One of the surprising elements in the UK context has been the relative lack of comment on the Cartel Offence, although this has been somewhat redressed in the last year and a half, following the collapse of the *British Airways* case (discussed in Chapter 4), and the publication in March 2011 of a Consultation Document suggesting changes to the formulation of the Cartel Offence.[3] I do not in this chapter discuss in any detail the general literature relating to the economics of competition law, and I proceed from the starting assumption that the maintenance of effective competition law is of benefit.[4] The focus here is on cartelisation,

---

1 For a recent discussion of the economics and policy of many of the issues addressed in this Chapter see Utton, MA, *Cartels and Economic Collusion: The Persistence of Corporate Conspiracies* (2011) Edward Elgar.

2 Although the term 'Cartel Offence' is found at the heading of Part 6 of the Enterprise Act 2002, and above ss 188, 189 and 190, the term 'cartel' is not found otherwise in UK primary legislation relating to competition law. Neither is it found in the relevant US or EU primary legislation, but it is regularly encountered in secondary materials, including guidelines, decisions and case law.

3 Department for Business, Innovation and Skills, *A Competition Regime for Growth: A Consultation on Options for Reform* (March 2011). This was followed by *Growth, Competition and the Competition Regime: Government Response to Consultation* (March 2012).

4 While it seems hardly necessary to justify this stance, see the analysis of the

although I include a discussion of the economics of law literature relating to enforcement in general, and deterrence and punishment in particular.[5] Under this approach, 'criminal behaviour becomes part of a much more general theory and does not require ad hoc concepts of differential association, anomie, and the like'.[6] I remain aware of the dangers of making simplistic comparisons across regimes. Indeed, one of the arguments that I make in this book is that the UK government itself acted in response to over-simplistic assumptions when it sought simply to transplant criminal cartel law, as operated in the US, into the UK, without paying sufficient regard to domestic circumstances. Comparative legal literature is replete with criticism of the dangers of inappropriate comparisons; in the context of legal responses to cartelisation no one has expressed the problem better than Shaffer and Nesbitt: '[t]he implementation of transnational legal norms will ultimately depend on local factors, and in particular, domestic political and social attitudes regarding cartel behaviour, and domestic institutional structures, capacities and legacies'.[7]

Other approaches may be taken to the analysis of crime and criminal policy than the economic one. One of the core questions dealt with in this book, that of whether conduct amounting to participation in a cartel should be criminalised within the UK, may be addressed by theoreticians of criminal law in a very different way than by reference to 'efficiency' and economic standards. An interesting alternative approach is that which 'begin[s] with the familiar, intuitively plausible thought that crimes should

---

impact of the vitamins cartel, undertaken by Clarke and Evenett (the vitamins cartel is discussed in Chapter 6, below):

> . . . the estimates presented here suggest that the annual reduction in overcharges in several European nations during the 1990s was equivalent to 96% of the total cost of enforcing competition policy in those nations (including the costs of running Brussels-based competition policy). Without suggesting that such calculations constitute a full cost-benefit analysis of competition policy, they do suggest that one important element of the latter has paid substantial dividends during the 1990s. (Clarke, JL, and Evenett, SJ, 'The Deterrent Effects of National Anticartel Laws: Evidence from the International Vitamins Cartel' (2003) 48 *Antitrust Bulletin* 689 at 725)

5 See in particular Becker, GS, 'Crime and Punishment: An Economic Approach' (1968) 76 *Journal of Political Economy* 169. See generally Garoupa, N (ed), *Criminal Law and Economics* (2009) Edward Elgar, and Benson, BL, and Zimmerman, PR (eds), *Handbook on the Economics of Crime* (2010) Edward Elgar.

6 Becker, GS, note 5, at 176.

7 Shaffer, GC, and Nesbitt, NH, 'Criminalizing Cartels: A Global Trend?' (2011) 12 *Sedona Conference Journal*; *Minnesota Legal Studies Research Paper No 11-26* (2011) University of Minnesota, School of Law at 24.

be moral wrongs . . . criminal law must at least claim to define as criminal only conduct that is morally wrong'.[8] There has been only a limited amount of work analysing the relationship between morality and competition law specifically,[9] and I leave the discussion of the (im)moral space within which cartelists operate to others. Although some have claimed otherwise, it is not straightforward to draw a clear boundary between

---

[8] Duff, RA, *Answering for Crime: Responsibility and Liability in the Criminal Law* (2007) Hart Publishing, at 81. Duff continues to argue that:

> [t]his is, after all, what distinguishes criminal punishment from other measures. Criminal convictions and punishments do not merely penalise; they condemn. A tax may be intended to discourage the conduct taxed, but it does not condemn that conduct; a fine, by contrast, when imposed as a punishment, condemns the conduct as wrongful. A system of 'administrative regulations' . . . attaches penalties to breaches of the regulations – penalties designed to discourage disobedience. What distinguishes it from a system of criminal law and criminal punishments is that it does not condemn the conduct it penalises as wrongful; they have simply broken the rules and must pay the appropriate penalty. . . . what is distinctive of criminal law is still that it purports to define, and provide for the condemnation of, certain kinds of moral wrong; to justify the criminal law's content we must therefore show that what it defines as crimes are indeed wrongs of the appropriate kind' (ibid).

Within the context of the analytical framework provided by economics and law, the distinctions drawn by Duff and others who adopt a similar approach (even if the approaches lead to very different conclusions) are significantly discounted. A tax, a penalty payment, a fine, and a term in jail, may all simply be represented as a cost of acting in a particular way (see Becker: 'The cost of different punishments to an offender can be made comparable by converting them into their monetary equivalent or worth, which, of course, is directly measured only for fines' (note 5, above, at 179)). The question is not whether an action is 'moral' or 'immoral' (although moral opprobrium – stigma – may also be characterised as a cost) but becomes that of determining the most efficient way to deter an action that is considered to be harmful, or the most efficient way to redistribute income if an action is beneficial to some, but harmful to others. It is nevertheless possible to find reflections of a wider argument in economics and law literature generally, and in relation to cartel activity specifically. I do not deny the interest that might lie in taking other analytical approaches to the criminalisation of cartel conduct, and I may take other approaches elsewhere, but I do not do so in this book.

[9] See Stucke, ME, 'Morality and Antitrust' (2006) *Columbia Business Law Review* 443, and MacCulloch, A, 'The Cartel Offence: Defining an Appropriate "Moral Space"' (2012) 8:1 *European Competition Journal* 73. See also the discussion of 'Moral wrongdoing and harm' in The Law Commission, *Criminal Liability in Regulatory Contexts: A Consultation Paper* (2010) Consultation Paper No 195 at pp 67–72; Green, SP, 'Moral Ambiguity in White Collar Criminal Law' (2004) 18 *Notre Dame Journal of Law, Ethics and Public Policy* 501.

'criminal law' and 'regulation',[10] but this boundary, and on which side of it enforcement should lie, is central to the argument in this book, although the argument also relates to whether competition law enforcement should be targeted only at companies, or also at individuals (for corporations may also, as is the case in the US antitrust regime, face criminal sanctions).

At the outset however, it is necessary that we begin with a discussion of cartelisation, and the harms that are presumed to flow from its presence. If cartels are in fact relatively harmless, then the case for the maintenance of an enforcement regime becomes less sustainable. The evidence however strongly supports the view that cartels are harmful, and that the harms are considerable. There is an emerging consensus to this effect internationally, evidenced in part by the increasing prevalence of strong laws designed to curb and punish cartelisation.[11] The sanctions imposed in mature competition law regimes may be very substantial, such that some have argued that they lead to over-deterrence.[12] As stated in Chapter 1, I take as my starting point the principle that there exists an efficient level of law enforcement (whether this efficient level can be identified is a different matter[13]), and

---

[10] Thus, for example, Ogus has argued that: '[f]ew problems are encountered in delineating the scope of the criminal law since, as a matter of legal definition, it is the law prescribing liability for those offences which are prosecuted in the criminal justice system' (Ogus, A, 'Criminal Law and Regulation', in Garoupa, N (ed), *Criminal Law and Economics* (2009) Edward Elgar). This is an overly formalistic approach and under-inclusive. Thus, for example, it may be the amount of the penalty which determines, in the context of the operation of the European Convention on Human Rights, whether a procedure is criminal rather than civil in nature, rather than the categorisation of that procedure in the national legal system (see, for example, *Hüls v European Commission* case C-199/92P [1999] ECR 4287). Elsewhere Ogus has defined 'regulation' as 'that area of public law by which the state and its agents seek to induce individuals and firms to outcomes which, in the absence of such inducements, they would not freely reach' (Ogus, A, 'Enforcing Regulation: Do We Need the Criminal Law?', in Sjögren, H, and Skogh, G (eds), *New Perspectives on Economic Crime* (2004) Edward Elgar, at 42), yet this description would apply equally to criminal enforcement.

[11] See, for example, Shaffer, GC, and Nesbitt, NH, note 7: '[c]ountries around the world have increased sanctions against cartels, including in many cases adopting criminal sanctions for the first time, with the term cartels now commonly harnessed to the unsavoury epithet 'hard core' (at 2).

[12] See, for example, Lopatka, JE, and Page, WH, 'Indirect Purchaser Suits and the Consumer Interest' (2003) 48 *Antitrust Bulletin* 531: '[w]e are sceptical that the sum of all federal penalties for illegal antitrust overcharges is suboptimal' (at 567).

[13] See Connor, JM, and Lande, RH, 'Optimal Cartel Deterrence: An Empirical Comparison of Sanctions to Overcharges' (2011) AAI Working Paper No 11-08 at 3: '. . . there has never been a satisfactory answer to the most important question concerning the antitrust treatment of cartels: overall, is the combined effects [*sic*] of

that it is not only reasonable, but essential, to clarify and explain the impact that particular laws are likely to have on particular behaviour, the harms prevented, and the costs incurred. This does not necessarily require a fully quantified cost-benefit analysis, but it does require careful consideration of a number of complex and interrelated factors.

One of the difficulties encountered in assessing the efficiency of criminalisation in this area, and in assessing cartel enforcement in general, is that, as has been noted elsewhere, '[m]uch of the literature . . . is theoretical'.[14] While there is empirical economic work which examines cartels and their effects (and some work has been undertaken analysing the public's views as to the legitimacy of price-fixing, and support for various sanctions) conducting research into arrangements which are normally unlawful, and which are therefore perpetrated in secret, is difficult if not impossible. Public records relating to decisions by competition authorities, and cases heard by the courts, provide our best evidence, but clearly represent only those cartels in respect of which enforcement action is taken. An undetected cartel produces no public record.[15] There is, for example, no realistic prospect of obtaining useful evidence as to the amount of cartel activity by surveying firms and asking whether they are involved in cartels:[16] responses to any such questions are likely to be at best self-serving.[17] In 2003 the OECD made clear its assessment of the difficulty of

these sanctions optimal? Indeed, no one has ever before even seriously attempted to answer this crucial question, perhaps because of data constraints, complexity, and the number of factors involved.'

14 Stephan, A, 'Survey of Public Attitudes to Price-Fixing and Cartel Enforcement in Britain' (2008) *Competition Law Review* 123 at 124. See generally Harding, C, 'Cartel Deterrence: The Search for Evidence and Argument' (2011) 56 *Antitrust Bulletin* 345.

15 See, for example, Evenett, SJ, Levenstein, MC, and Suslow, VY, 'International Cartel Enforcement: Lessons from the 1990s' (2001) 24 *World Economy* 1221 at 1226: '[c]artels, being secretive organisations, rarely announce their formation. Empirical research on cartel formation is therefore limited to evidence gathered from cartels operating in a legal (or tolerant) environment or from evidence collected in antitrust prosecutions.'

16 There have, however, been some attempts to estimate the number of cartels that might exist. See, for example, Ormosi, P, 'How Big Is the Tip of an Iceberg? A Parsimonious Way to Estimate Cartel Detection Rate' (2011) Centre for Competition Policy, CCP Working Paper 11-6 (discussed below).

17 It may also be the case that senior management is unaware that personnel, even at senior levels, are engaging the firm in unlawful conduct. In the *Heavy Electrical Equipment* case, for example (discussed in Chapter 3, below), the Chairman of General Electric had testified before a Congressional Antitrust Subcommittee in May 1959 that GE was making '"earnest efforts" to comply with both the spirit and the letter of the antitrust laws'. He was reported to have reacted

establishing robust empirical links between sanctioning and deterrence in relation to cartelisation:

> [a]necdotal evidence exists that criminal sanctions against individuals can have deterrent effects. There is, however, no systematic empirical evidence available to prove such effects, and to assess whether the marginal benefit of introducing sanctions against individuals (in the form of less harm from cartel activity) exceeds the additional costs that in particular a system of criminal sanctions entails (including the costs of prosecution as well as of administrating a prison system). There appears to be agreement that it would be virtually impossible to generate the relevant data.[18]

Albeit that most of the literature is theoretical, and that much of the non-theoretical literature is highly technical, there is also literature (and other resources) in this area which may be described as populist. There have been at least three books published that provide non-expert, accurate, and engaging coverage of cartel activity (*The Informant!*,[19] *Rats in the Grain*,[20] and *The Art of the Steal*[21]). The first of these gave rise, in 2009, to a Steven Soderbergh film of the same name, starring Matt Damon as the eponymous 'hero'.[22] The BBC produced, in 2002, an exceptionally good documentary examining the art-auction market cartel,[23] which was also the subject of *The Art of the Steal*.[24] To a certain extent this material may be held up as evidence that the attitude to competition law changed substantially over the last half of the 20th century. Thorelli, HB, in his magisterial work *The Federal Antitrust Policy: Origin of an American Tradition*[25] wrote in his conclusion (at 607) that:

---

with 'shock and anger' when told by one of GE's Vice Presidents that GE was engaged in a price-fixing cartel (Smith, RA, 'The Incredible Electrical Conspiracy' (1961) *Fortune*, May, 161 at 161–62). When the firm began an internal investigation, conducted by company attorneys, '[m]ost of the guilty lied' (ibid, at 163).

18 *Cartel Sanctions against Individuals* (2003) DAF/COMP(2004)39 at 7.

19 Eichenwald, K, *The Informant: A True Story* (2000) Broadway.

20 Lieber, JB, *Rats in the Grain: The Dirty Tricks and Trials of Archer Daniels Midland, the Supermarket to the World* (2000) Basic Books.

21 Mason, C, *The Art of the Steal: Inside the Sotheby's–Christie's Auction House Scandal* (2004) Putnam. Note that for legal reasons this book was not published in the UK, but is readily available from the US.

22 Soderbergh, S, *The Informant!* (2009).

23 Rossiter, N, *Sotheby's and Christie's: A Crime amongst Gentlemen* (2002) BBC.

24 A search on Google in March 2011, with the search terms: 'Sotheby's – Christie's – price – fixing – scandal' gave rise to 5420 results (although many of these will have been duplicates).

25 (1955) Johns Hopkins University Press (this is, in my view, the best book ever written to deal with antitrust law).

> [a] weakness which antitrust shares with many other types of prohibitory legislation is that in form it is an instrument of social control rather than one of encouragement or promotion. It defines and condemns certain reprehensible phenomena, but ostensibly it does not operate in favour of any well-defined 'group interest'. Superficially it may even appear unimaginative. Certainly few people have found it as obviously desirable as, for instance, laws against larceny, bribery or fraud. Yet . . . given vigorous leadership and a favourable milieu antitrust may well possess as much popular appeal as any other public policy of importance.

By the 21st century the mood had undoubtedly changed. Werden's approach is more reflective of current thinking, at least in academic and practice literature:

> [c]artel activity is properly viewed as a property crime, like burglary or larceny, although cartel activity inflicts far greater economic harm. Cartel activity robs consumers and other market participants of the tangible blessings of competition. Cartel activity is never efficient or otherwise socially desirable; cartel participants can never gain more than the public loses. . . . Like other property crimes, cartel activity should be prohibited rather than merely taxed.[26]

CARTELS: FORMATION, FREQUENCY AND HARM

Stigler – a Theory of Oligopoly[27] and the Incentive Problem

Although much work had been published on oligopoly conduct by the time Stigler published a relatively short piece in *The Journal of Political Economy* in 1964, his contribution, which has had a very substantial influence on the literature, raises fundamental questions, and a discussion of it, and what has become known as the incentive problem, is a good place to start. When 'A Theory of Oligopoly' was published, Stigler, who became a Nobel laureate in 1982, was based at the University of Chicago School of Economics, and he has been strongly identified with the 'Chicago School' and its approach to the analysis of competitive processes and the application of competition law to them. In 'A Theory of Oligopoly' Stigler accepted as a starting position that oligopolists would 'wish to collude to maximise joint profits', but then sought to 'reconcile this wish with facts, such as that collusion is impossible for many firms and collusion is much

---

[26] Werden, GJ, 'Sanctioning Cartel Activity: Let the Punishment Fit the Crime' (2009) *European Competition Journal* 19 at 23.

[27] Stigler, GJ, 'A Theory of Oligopoly' (1964) 72:1 *Journal of Political Economy* 44.

more effective in some circumstances than in others'.[28] The standard theory that Stigler had to address took as its starting point the following assumption:

> [t]he combined profits of the entire set of firms in an industry are maximised when they act together as a monopolist. At least in the traditional formulation of the oligopoly problem, in which there are no major uncertainties as to the profit-maximising output and price at any time, this familiar conclusion seems inescapable. Moreover, the result holds for any number of firms.[29]

Stigler sought to modify this approach by 'simply presenting a systematic account of the factors governing the feasibility of collusion, which like most things in this world is not free'.[30] First he considered the issue of homogeneity, noting that not only sellers, but also the 'purchase commitments' would need to be homogenous for full homogeneity to apply. Stigler argued that in the real world purchase commitments in particular might not be homogenous. For example, different values might be placed on purchase commitments by sellers depending on the size of the purchase and the 'urgency' of the purchase; differences in the latter might give rise to different elasticities of demand, and might therefore invite sellers to impose price discrimination. The conclusion that flowed from this was that, to be truly effective, an oligopoly joint-profit maximising price structure would have to be complex.[31] The question then arises as to how such a complex structure might come into existence, and how it might be maintained. Setting to one side the issue of legal constraint, Stigler turns then to the key issue of enforcement of the oligopoly/cartel price(s). Stigler's focus on the incentive to cheat, and, in his argument, the inherent instability of cartels, is the most significant contribution he made to the study of this area of competitive activity. At page 46 Stigler presents the problem facing would-be cartelists in the following terms:

> [i]t is a well-established proposition that if any member of the agreement can secretly violate it, he will gain larger profits than by conforming to it. It is, moreover, surely one of the axioms of human behaviour that all agreements whose violation would be profitable to the violator must be enforced. The literature of collusive agreements, ranging from the pools of the 1880s, to the electrical conspiracies of recent times, is replete with instances of the collapse of conspiracies because of 'secret' price-cutting. This literature is biased:

28 At 44.
29 At 44.
30 At 44.
31 By page 46 Stigler is referring to 'almost infinitely numerous price classes'.

> conspiracies that are successful in avoiding an amount of price-cutting which leads to collapse of the agreement are less likely to be reported or detected. But no conspiracy can neglect the problem of enforcement.[32]

In other words, if a cartel sets a price of X, and X is above the competitive price Y, it is in the interests of any one member of the cartel to set a price below X, but above Y.[33] Crucially, every cartel member has precisely the same incentive. This argument is captured in the 'prisoners' dilemma' which emerges from game theory. A prisoners' dilemma is one in which the dominant strategy gives rise to a sub-optimal outcome. Thus the optimal outcome for the cartel as a whole would be for no-one to cheat, but the dominant strategy, in a world where detection of cheating was not possible, or where punishing cheating would not be possible, would be for *every* member to cheat. Stigler suggests that the most efficient way to avoid secret price reductions is to fix market shares.[34] In Stigler's words, 'this is the ideal method of enforcement'. It is also 'usually an easy form of collusion to detect, for it may require side payments among firms and it leaves indelible traces in the output records'.[35] Another effective way of avoiding secret price-cutting would be to assign individual purchasers to particular sellers. Where purchasers are numerous, and perhaps unidentifiable *ex ante*, such allocations could be effected by dividing markets along geographic lines, but these arrangements would be unlawful. Stigler argues however that the assignment of buyers to sellers will be difficult to sustain over time, as different sellers will fare differently. For some, purchasers will do well and expand their demand; for others, demand may shrink. Finally, if 'the turnover of buyers is large, the method is simply impractical'.[36] Detecting secret price cuts will be:

> as difficult as interested people can make it. The price-cutter will certainly protest his innocence, or, if this would tax credulity beyond its taxable capacity,

---

[32] The position also becomes rapidly more complicated as the numbers of participants in cartels grow. The number of paired relationships in any given situation is given by the formula: $pr = n(n - 1)/2$. Thus a cartel with 4 participants gives rise to 6 paired relationships, ($4 \times 3 = 12, \div 2 = 6$), and one with 8 participants gives rise to 28 paired relationships ($8 \times 7 = 56, \div 2 = 28$).

[33] Stigler notes that one way to reduce the incentive to cheat is to set the cartel price not significantly above the competitive price, such that the margin for manoeuvre available to any one seller is limited.

[34] This was, for example, one of the approaches taken in the *Marine Hose* cartel, discussed in Chapter 6, below.

[35] At 46.

[36] At 47.

> blame a disobedient subordinate. The price cut will often take the indirect form of modifying some non-price dimension of the transaction. The customer may, and often will, divulge price reductions, in order to have them matched by others, but he will learn from experience if each disclosure is followed by the withdrawal of the lower price offer. Indeed the buyer will frequently fabricate wholly fictitious price offers to test the rivals. Policing the collusion sounds very much like the subtle and complex problem presented in a good detective story.[37]

So, determining a cartel strategy is extremely complex, a cartel price that generates profits substantially above the competitive level incentivises everyone to cheat, and detecting cheating is very difficult, if not impossible. Stigler does not deal with the final part of the picture, which is to ask, how cheating, if detected, can be punished? The answer normally given to this is simply that other firms will lower their prices in response, thereby quickly eroding the now short-term benefits of cheating. That this may be so has created a difficulty to those seeking to analyse cartel conduct: the existence of a price war may be seen as evidence of the collapse of a cartel and the operation of the incentive problem; but a price war may also be evidence of the cartel asserting itself by punishing a cheat. This difficulty is well recognised, and it has been noted that 'empirical literature has struggled to distinguish between cartel punishments and cartel breakdowns'.[38]

Notwithstanding that Stigler recognised that in some circumstances collusive and cartel outcomes were possible, although these would be limited, the argument developed by Stigler, and adapted by others, may be used in support of the somewhat simplistic view that accepts both that cartels are harmful, and that they are unlikely to be successful such that over-enforcement should be avoided as being inefficient.[39] Unfortunately for those tempted to take this view, real world evidence suggests that companies are able both to arrive at and to maintain cartel outcomes; economic understanding too has advanced since 1964. This is particularly true in the case of game theory. Empirical evidence shows us that cartels have been able to put in place sophisticated and professionally managed arrangements to secure their functioning.[40] This was the case for example

37 At 47–48. A mathematical proof demonstrating the difficulty of detecting secret price-cutting is set out at pp 49–56.

38 Levenstein, MC, and Suslow, VY, 'What Determines Cartel Success?' (2006) 44 *Journal of Economic Literature* 43 at 44.

39 Ibid, at 44: '[f]ollowing Stigler (1964), many economists have argued that [attempts to form cartels] would inevitably fail as colluding firms succumbed to the temptation to shave prices secretly in order to increase their individual firm profits.'

40 See Evenett, SJ, et al, note 15, at 1221, who argue that the evidence

in relation to the *Marine Hose* cartel, discussed in Chapters 4 and 6, below, in which members each paid a fee to an independent consultant for his work in running the cartel.[41] In other cases firms have even been able to put in place mechanisms to allow a cheating member to compensate others when that cheating was detected. The work of Fraas and Greer, who surveyed antitrust actions taken against cartels in the United States, demonstrated clearly that as the number of members in a cartel increased, so too did the complexity and formality of the arrangements which were adopted to manage them.[42]

Game theory has moved on from the simple single-play games which were first developed. In a single game, such as is the case in the most simple forms of the prisoners' dilemma games, there is no possibility of retaliation by other players of the game if any one player cheats, such that cheating becomes probable. Even in games played over a number of periods it may also be shown that cheating is likely where participants know when the game will terminate. If we take as our example a cartel entered into by two participants, with a pre-determined end point, it is, even if retaliation were possible, virtually an inevitability that the cartel will collapse. This can be readily understood by applying backward induction. If in the last period the 'game' is played (let us call this t) B cheats, there is no retaliation that A can effectively apply (as the game by that point is over). Thus B has a

demonstrates that cartels do not 'always fall quickly under the weight of their own incentive problems. Even where cheating eventually undermines collusion, consumers may have been burdened by years of increased prices, and barriers to entry may have been created by strategic cartel behaviour'.

41 Indeed, interviewed after his incarceration one of the participants in the cartel stated, 'once you are in one of these things [cartels], it is virtually impossible to get out of it. How do you leave something like a cartel?' (O'Kane, M, 'Does Prison Work for Cartelists? The View from Behind Bars: An Interview of Bryan Allison by Michael O'Kane' (2011) 56 *Antitrust Bulletin* 483 at 489).

42 Fraas, AG, and Greer, DF, 'Market Structure and Price Collusion: An Empirical Analysis' (1977) 26 *Journal of Industrial Economics* 21. The authors surveyed 606 cases, with an average membership of 17 firms in each cartel. In the case of *DPP v Michael Flanagan and others*, February 9, 2007, Central Criminal Court, Ireland (unreported) it was argued that any cartel with more than eight members was hard to police and was unlikely to be successful. The judge in the case rejected this on the grounds that the cartel in question had over 50 members, and was policed in a sophisticated manner (see further Chapter 5, below). In 1961 Sutherland, in a work dealing with white collar crime generally, argued that '[f]ormal organisation for crimes of corporations is found most generally in restraint of trade, as illustrated by gentlemen's agreements, pools, many of the practices of trade associations, patent agreements, and cartels' (Sutherland, EH, *White Collar Crime* (1961) Holt, Rinehart and Winston, at 219 (it was Sutherland who originated the term 'white collar crime')).

clear incentive to cheat in that last period (as also does A). A knows that B has this incentive to cheat in the last period, such that A has an incentive to pre-empt this action by herself cheating in $t-1$. Given that A is going to cheat in $t-1$, B has an incentive to cheat in $t-2$, A in $t-3$, and so on. By working backwards from the cartel's end point, we quickly finish up in the situation where cheating the very first time the game is played is inevitable. However, in the real world cartels may not have a pre-defined end point. Where this is the case the backward-induction argument falls, and cartels become sustainable, even in the absence of sophisticated internal enforcement mechanism. It is also the case that as the game is repeated the players become more sophisticated, and more aware of the benefit of future profits (which will be reduced by cheating).[43]

Where cartels have been formed and then have collapsed, the evidence suggests that this is often in response to slumps in demand,[44] to the entry of new competitors into the cartelists' market, or in response to technological change. There is clear evidence however that cartels may successfully negotiate both slumps in demand and entry, adjusting to the former, and adapting to entrants by incorporating them into the cartel.

There have been many studies which have sought to identify the circumstances in which cartels do succeed, and which have sought to determine the duration of cartels once they have been formed. One conclusion which clearly flows is that the legal environment has an impact on the success of cartelisation in industries which are not concentrated. It is widely accepted that there is a positive relationship between cartel success and industry concentration, although there are examples of cartels being formed successfully in industries that are not concentrated. Where this has been the case, the evidence suggests that 'they almost always rely on industry associations',[45] and that in legal environments in which the activities of such associations are subject to effective control, cartel success is much less likely. Levenstein and Suslow analyse a significant number of empirical studies of cartels, in which the impact of a number of factors on the duration of cartels is considered. Perhaps surprisingly, the evidence does not point to a 'simple relationship between industry concentration and the

---

43 See, for example, Levenstein, MC, and Suslow, VY, note 38, at 46: 'Repeated interaction (over time or across markets) can, in principle, by providing the incentive of future collusive profits, deter firms from cheating, and allow them to escape the Prisoners' Dilemma.'

44 See, for example, Porter, RH, 'A Study of Cartel Stability: The Joint Executive Committee, 1880–1886' (1983) 14:2 *Bell Journal of Economics* 301 at 313.

45 Levenstein, MC, and Suslow, VY, note 38, at 44.

likelihood of collusion',[46] nor does it clearly suggest that there is a clear positive relationship between concentration and the duration of cartels' existence. Stigler had suggested that the presence of large customers would destabilise cartels as they would provide an incentive for a cartel member to defect. The evidence refutes this suggestion, and cartels are able to exist where there are very large customers (as was the case for example in the vitamins cartel discussed in Chapter 6, below). Indeed, in some cases 'customers were intimately involved in stabilising a cartel, providing information and punishment mechanisms not otherwise available'.[47] The number of studies of the relationship between price elasticities of demand and cartel success is limited, but the evidence suggests that, as would be expected, there is a positive relationship between demand elasticity and cartel success in raising prices. Above all, the learning process that cartels go through emerges as being particularly important, and it is this learning process that is primarily responsible for a resolution of the incentive problem:

> [t]hey learn how to monitor output and prices of individual cartel members in order to detect cheating. They learn how to structure incentives so that collusion is more profitable in the long run than cheating. Successful cartels fashion self-imposed penalties or other compensation schemes for firms that exceed cartel quotas. They learn how to structure cartel-imposed punishments and other disciplinary actions in response to cartel violations. They develop and implement exclusionary practices to prevent entry or expansion by non-members. Finally, they develop an elaborate internal hierarchy that allows communication on various levels . . . not only to provide flexibility in the details of the agreement, but to build trust as well.[48]

The evidence that emerges from cases in the US, and infringement decisions in the EU, amongst others, as to the mechanisms adopted by cartels to circumvent the incentive problem is impressive, with cartels putting in place very elaborate and carefully constructed schemes to manage their affairs. These include sophisticated information collation and dissemination schemes, procedures for detecting cheating (as was the case for example in *The Citroen Dealers' Association*[49] which employed 'mystery shoppers' to detect deviation from agreed prices), and even internal fining and compensation schemes which have been actively enforced. Cartel participants also learn to conceal the existence of the cartel, and may

46 Ibid, at 58.
47 Ibid, at 62.
48 Ibid.
49 *Director of Public Prosecutions v Patrick Duffy and Duffy Motors (Newbridge) Limited* [2009] IEHC 208 (discussed in Chapter 5, below).

learn not only from their own experiences, but also from those of others. The members of the heavy electrical equipment cartel, prosecuted by the US authorities in the early 1960s (discussed in Chapter 3, below), went to great efforts to conceal their activities from the Government, perhaps in part because one of the key participants, General Electric, had been taken to court nine times in the previous 50 years by the Department of Justice ('DOJ') for Sherman Act violations:

> . . . the corporate representatives resorted to devices that could be said to match the tactics of the notorious Appalachin gangsters. While the methods varied from one group to another, a common device was to assign each member of the group a code number or symbol. Communications were generally addressed to the homes, instead of the offices, of the several company representatives and mailed in envelopes bearing no return address or other means of identification. The rule prescribed was, without exception, to destroy all written communication.[50]

The Extent of Cartelisation, and the Duration of Cartels

Ormosi has pointed out that '[t]he main obstacle to establishing the harm caused by illegal collusion is the lack of knowledge on what proportion of cartels are discovered'.[51] The best evidence for the existence of cartels comes from cases in which cartels have been detected (and, perhaps, punished), but it is highly unlikely that this represents the totality of cartel activity. The mere fact that cartel conduct is prohibited and attracts sanction clearly does not deter all cartels. A pessimist might choose to suggest that the cartels which are detected are those which are most inefficiently and poorly run (although the evidence demonstrates clearly that many of those detected are in fact managed with great sophistication), or are those where the cartelists most overreach themselves in imposing overcharges, incentivising complaints and enforcement action. There have been a number of efforts, some based on survey methods, and some on various forms of quantitative analysis and modelling, to attempt to derive estimates as to the likelihood of a cartel being caught (and therefore of the number of cartels *not* caught).

---

[50] Watkins, MW, 'Electrical Equipment Antitrust Cases: Their Implications for Government and for Business' (1961) 29:1 *The University of Chicago Law Review* 97 at 104.

[51] Ormosi, P, note 16, at 2. Ormosi notes that: '[t]he number of detected cartels is a potentially biased indicator of the effectiveness of cartel enforcement. An increased number of observed cases could mean either an increase in the detection rate of cartels or a decrease in the deterrence rate of anti-cartel enforcement, or both' (at 2).

The trend in the early attempts to analyse detection rates was to rely upon survey evidence, as was the case for example in the work of Beckenstein and Landis-Gabel,[52] which was based on the survey responses of 859 members of the Antitrust Section of the American Bar Association. While the focus of the survey was on antitrust compliance programmes, the authors attempted to probe the causes of violations, and the enforcement environment. Asked whether the enforcement agencies were likely to detect a section 1 price-fixing violation, the mean average response suggested that around 50 per cent of such arrangements were likely to be detected.[53] Feinberg conducted similar work in the European Economic Community, and reported similar results to those of Beckenstein and Landis-Gabel in 1985.[54] These results appear to be somewhat higher than has emerged in most of the relevant literature, and it may be that the lawyer respondents have overestimated the risk of detection, perhaps in part because they underestimate the prevalence of cartelisation.[55]

A different approach was taken by Bryant and Eckard employing a statistical model based on cartel formation and collapse to estimate the duration of cartels,[56] suggesting that between 1961 and 1988 the probability of a cartel being caught was no more than 17 per cent in any year (or to put it another way, for each cartel caught in any given year at least another four went undetected that year). Similar figures have been suggested by others in the US context, and in the EU Combe et al estimated a detection rate of 12.9–13.3 per cent in any given year for the period 1969–2007.[57] Ormosi suggested in 2011 that capture-recapture ('CR') analysis, a statistical method used to estimate population sizes in ecology and epidemiology, could be employed to derive estimates of cartel

[52] Beckenstein, A, and Landis-Gabel, H, 'Antitrust Compliance: Results of a Survey of Legal Opinion' (1982) 52 *Antitrust Law Journal* 459.

[53] On a scale of 1 to 5, with 3 indicating 'neither agree nor disagree', and 5 indicating 'strongly agree', the mean response to the detection of a section 1 violation was 3.557 (at 464).

[54] Feinberg, R, 'The Enforcement and Effects of European Antitrust Policy: A Survey of Legal Opinion' (1985) 23 *Journal of Common Market Studies* 373.

[55] It cannot be assumed that independent counsel employed by a corporation to implement and monitor a compliance programme will be aware of all violations perpetrated by the corporation.

[56] Bryant, PG, and Eckard, EW, 'Price Fixing: The Probability of Getting Caught' (1991) 73.3 *Review of Economics and Statistics* 531.

[57] Combe, E, Monnier, C, and Legal, R, 'Cartels: The Probability of Getting Caught in the European Union' (2008) *Bruges European Economic Research Papers*, Paper 12.

detection rates.[58] Based on evidence relating to cartels detected in the EU by the EU Commission between 1984 and 2005, Ormosi suggests that the cartel detection rate was often under 10 per cent a year for the period, and only rose over 20 per cent in three years. These estimates are to be taken as an upper bound, suggesting perhaps that for every cartel detected in any given year, *at least* another nine go undetected. Very simplistically, all else being equal, any one cartel may be expected to survive, in the EU, for at least ten years.

Cartelisation and Harm

Recent studies have gone some way to 'overcoming the knowledge gap concerning the harm done by hard core cartels' identified by the OECD in 2000,[59] and have demonstrated that the harms that flow from cartelisation might be much more significant than had previously been thought. The OECD's concern was that the lack of information was hindering enforcement efforts, and, for example, allowed opponents of enhanced legislation to argue against its introduction on the grounds that the anti-competitive harms being targeted could not possibly justify such a robust approach. Recent work has responded to this concern. For example, a study published in 2006 suggested that the price surcharge that might be passed on to customers by a cartel could be as high as 40 per cent. It was also found that the average surcharge in respect of internationally operating cartels would likely be higher than in respect of domestic cartels.[60] However,

---

58 See Ormosi, P, note 16, at 3:

> [i]n the most simple form of CR analysis, the population size of a species is estimated by taking two successive random samples from the same population. The first sample is marked and replaced into the population. If the population does not change between the two independent sampling occasions, and all individuals are equally likely to be captured, then the proportion of marked subjects in the second sample should equal the ratio of the size of the first sample to population size.

This methodology depends on recidivism amongst cartelists. While work by Connor suggests that recidivism is prevalent among cartelists (Connor, JM, 'Recidivism Revealed: Private International Cartels 1990–2009' (2010) 6:2 *Competition Policy International* 101), this evidence has been challenged in the context of US enforcement (see Werden, GJ, Hammond, SD, and Barnett, BA, 'Recidivism Eliminated: Cartel Enforcement in the United States since 1999' (2011) Georgetown Global Antitrust Enforcement Symposium, September 22, 2011, discussed in Chapter 3, below).

59 OECD, *Hard Core Cartels* (2000) at 20.

60 Connor, JM, and Bolotova, Y, 'Cartel Overcharges: Survey and

overcharges and profits may vary significantly from cartel to cartel and within cartels, with different members benefiting at different rates.[61] It has been argued that this variance undermines a fining policy based on turnover percentages.[62]

OPTIMAL DETERRENCE

There is clear evidence to support the assertion that cartel formation diminishes in response to enhanced anti-competitive laws and enforcement.[63] Detection efforts and punishment may be directed either towards the corporate economic entities engaging in cartelisation, or to individual employees and company officers who take and implement decisions within those corporate entities, or to both the corporate entity *and* to the individual. By far the more common approach is for penalties to be directed exclusively towards the companies which engage in cartel conduct, and not towards individuals, which has the effect of placing those who actually engage in the unlawful conduct at one remove from the enforcement.[64] That this is the case probably flows in part from a false belief that the only beneficiaries of cartelisation are companies. In the case of the EU the law is directed, at present, solely to the corporate entity (in EU terminology, which is also applied in the UK, to 'undertakings'). A very small number of member states, of which the UK is the most obvious example, also act against individuals. The US targets both the corporations and the individual actors who are found to have engaged in antitrust violations.

Meta-analysis' (2006) 24 *International Journal of Industrial Organization* 1109. See also Levenstein, MC, and Suslow, VY, note 38, at 79–81.

61 See, for example, Rosati, F, and Ehmer, C, 'Science, Myth and Fines: Do Cartels Typically Raise Prices by 25%?' (2009) 4 *Concurrences* no 28832. It has been argued that this variance undermines a fining policy based on turnover percentages.

62 See Riley, A, 'Modernising Cartel Sanctions: Effective Sanctions for Price-fixing in the European Union' (2011) *European Competition Law Review* 551

63 See Connor, JM, 'Effectiveness of Antitrust Sanctions on Modern International Cartels' (2006) 6 *Journal of Industrial Competition and Trade* 195.

64 See Whelan, P, 'A Principled Argument for Personal Criminal Sanctions as Punishment under EC Cartel Law' (2007) *Competition Law Review* 7, at 27:

> [a]ctual condemnation, then, occurs at one level removed from the natural persons involved in the cartel. It is believed that the undertaking will discipline its own employees; a form of official condemnation by proxy is therefore assumed to exist. However . . . the ability of the undertaking to discipline its agents is not without serious drawbacks.

It has been suggested that, unlike other areas of competition law, cartel activity is unique in that *over-deterrence* is simply impossible. There are *no* economic arguments in favour of cartelisation, and a properly constructed and enforced cartel law *cannot* chill legitimate economically efficient cooperation.[65] If true,[66] this means that a much less nuanced approach can be taken towards the construction, enforcement and assessment of anti-cartel laws than can be taken to competition laws in general. The role of any anti-cartel law should simply be to deter cartel formation, which may be achieved by punishing those who engage in the proscribed conduct, and by doing so with sufficient frequency and sufficient severity to offer a credible threat of punishment to deter others from entering into the unlawful arrangements in the first place.[67] As noted towards the start of this chapter, arguments relating to punishment come in many hues, and I do not intend to deal here in detail with the more general literature relating to rationales for criminalisation. In essence however, general theories rest on 'just deserts' (retribution-based) approaches, and on deterrence. If society is morally outraged at the formation and operation of a cartel, and of the actions taken to achieve this by individuals, then punishment of those actors may be supported under a retribution theory.[68] Limited evidence relating to social attitudes to cartels and punishment is discussed below in relation to the UK – not to adduce support for a theory of retribution, but in the context of questioning whether an offence without support may struggle to establish its efficacy. The focus here is on arguments relating to deterrence, set specifically within the context of cartelisation.[69] This reflects in part the widely held assumption that the 'goal of prosecuting

---

[65] See, for example, Werden, GJ, note 26, at 26.

[66] It has been argued that the characterisation of unlawful horizontal anti-competitive conduct in the US remains too vague to, for instance, support the occasional use of the death penalty (see Block, M, and Sidak, JG, 'The Cost of Antitrust Deterrence: Why Not Hang a Price Fixer Now and Then?' (1980) 68 *Georgetown Law Journal* 1131).

[67] See, for example, Evenett, SJ, Levenstein, MC, and Suslow, VY, note 15, at 1234: '[a] group of firms will be *collectively* deterred from cartelising a nation's markets if that country's antitrust authority is expected to fine them more than the gains from participating in the cartel.'

[68] See Braithwaite's (disapproving) description of this approach: '[t]hey should be punished because they deserve to be punished. The quantum of their suffering should be in proportion to the seriousness of their crime, not according to any assessment of whether they are rehabilitated or when they no longer pose a threat to the community' (Braithwaite, J, 'Challenging Just Deserts: Punishing White-Collar Criminals' (1982) 73:2 *Journal of Criminal Law and Criminology* 723 at 723).

[69] For an excellent discussion of criminalisation in relation to cartelisation see Whelan, P, note 64.

cartels *is* deterrence'.[70] Deterrence is a consequentialist approach to criminalisation, which '[a]t its most basic . . . holds that punishment can only be justified if it leads to the prevention or reduction of future crime'.[71]

Crime, Punishment, and Becker

A prevalent, but not unanimous,[72] view in the literature relating to the enforcement of criminal law, following Becker,[73] is that a potential offender will be swayed by the cost of detection (penalty) discounted by the risk of detection.

The starting point for some who have examined this area is therefore that there must exist a level of penalty that can be imposed on firms or individuals that will deter cartel conduct, and that the most appropriate penalty is a fine. Becker thus argued more generally that 'social welfare is increased if fines are used *whenever feasible*'.[74] That illegal cartelisation is *not* currently deterred suggests to those taking this position only that penalties (fines) are not currently of sufficient severity. Thus, for example, it has been argued that:

> [a]n important insight is that even though cartel agreements are typically secret – and so the probability of detection and punishment p is low – so long as p is positive there exists a fine that will collectively deter cartelisation.[75]

This view has been most influentially and coherently advanced by Elzinga and Breit in *The Antitrust Penalties*.[76] The argument here is directed

---

70 Stucke, ME, note 9, at 457 (emphasis added). See, for example, Werden, GJ, note 26, at 24: '. . . deterrence is the only significant function of sanctions for cartel activity'.

71 Whelan, P, note 64, at 10.

72 See, for example, Parker, C, and Nielsen, VL, 'Deterrence and the Impact of Calculative Thinking on Business Compliance with Competition and Consumer Regulation' (2011) 56 *Antitrust Bulletin* 377, who, in the Australian context, argue that 'higher sanctions on their own are unlikely to lead to higher compliance with [competition law]' (at 378).

73 Becker, GS, note 5. As reformulated by Ogus: 'the inducement to comply with the law thus rests on the assumption that the costs incurred by offenders as a result of the liability (D), when discounted by the probability of being caught (p), will be sufficient to deter them from engaging in the undesired activity because pD exceeds the benefit (U) to the offender of the offence (Ogus, A, 'Criminal Law and Regulation', in Garoupa, N (ed), *Criminal Law and Economics* (2009) Edward Elgar at 91).

74 Becker, GS, note 5, at 193 (emphasis in original).

75 Evenett, SJ, Levenstein, MC, and Suslow, note 15, at 1235.

76 Elzinga, KG, and Breit, W, *The Antitrust Penalties: A Study in Law and Economics* (1976) Yale University Press.

more towards a comparison of the efficiency of a mixed public/private enforcement model than it is to a comparison of fines with imprisonment within the public enforcement model, but the authors do address the latter issue at an important passage in which efficiency arguments are developed within an economic framework to argue the case against incarceration as a punishment to be applied in relation to antitrust violations:

> [a] preliminary issue that [indifference analysis] can help illuminate is the inefficiency of incarceration as an antitrust weapon. . . . the indifference curves . . . represent a plausible trade-off between financial penalties and time to be served in jail. In other words, the geometry brings out clearly that there is some marginal rate of substitution between financial penalties and *any* other penalty, including jails, which means that the jail penalty, like any other penalty, can always be collapsed into its monetary equivalent. Thus the inefficiency of the jail penalty can be easily seen. For any given period of time spent in jail, there is some fine capable of securing the same deterrent effect. However, since the size of a fine can be changed without the expenditure of additional resources, while increased use of incarceration always involves greater costs to society, incarceration is an inferior penalty. Whenever any penalty can give the same amount of deterrence at less cost, or additional deterrence for the same cost, that option is economically superior.[77]

Lest it be argued that executives and corporate employees are *not* prepared to view incarceration and financial penalties as being matters for trade-off, the point has been forcefully and eloquently made that they are.[78] In at least one respect above, Elzinga and Breit may be mistaken. The imposition of financial penalties does not necessarily come without transactions costs. While it is to be expected that business executives will fiercely resist

---

[77] Ibid at 131. See also Evenett, SJ, Levenstein, MC, and Suslow, VY, note 15, at 1236: '. . . incarceration involves costly losses in and re-allocation of output: managers' productivity is less during their period of incarceration, and resources must be devoted to the construction and operation of prisons. If these were the sole considerations, then incarceration would be a less desirable alternative to fines.'

[78] See Connor, JM, and Lande, RH, note 13, at 24:

> [s]ome might contend that, because no corporate officer wants to spend any time in prison or under house arrest, they would be willing to pay virtually any amount of money to avoid the risk of prison. This is equivalent to placing an infinite (negative) value on prison time, and it implies that even a small probability of spending any time in prison or under house arrest has an infinite deterrence value. However, people do *not* act as if they infinitely disvalue the risk of getting put into prison or placed under house arrest for an antitrust offence. If they did, they would never try to form a cartel because this would put them at risk of going to prison. Rather, potential offenders act as if they tolerate the risk of prison to some extent.

jail sentences, and that they would be prepared to devote substantial resources to this end, it is also possible to contemplate that, faced with very high financial penalties, avoidance measures (such as, for example, the concealment of assets) will also give rise to substantial transaction costs. Elzinga and Breit *do* accept that there is some justification behind arguments that it might be efficient to impose financial penalties on individual managers, but ultimately are not persuaded by this approach due in part to the transactions costs that would arise in determining which individual managers were responsible for the unlawful acts.[79] Connor and Lande have attempted to quantify the cost of imprisonment on the offender, and have suggested that, in 2011, a year in prison for a corporate employee charged with price fixing would equate to a fine of approximately $2m. Given that it is argued that penalties addressed to individuals are widely considered to have more deterrent effect than penalties addressed to corporations, they suggest that the deterrent effect of this may be equivalent to approximately a $6m fine imposed on a company.[80] The rationality of the view advanced by Elzinga and Breit is seductive, but falls ultimately in the face of experience, which has grown significantly since 1976 when, notwithstanding a small number of high-profile prosecutions (see Chapter 3), the prospect of incarceration remained remote.

Building on the work of Becker, Lande suggested that in relation to competition law enforcement, optimal deterrence of cartelisation would be achieved where the cost of the violation (or the damages imposed on conviction) would be equal to the harms the cartel gives rise to, divided by the probability of detection.[81]

It has, however, been argued that 'Becker's model has no application to hard-core price-fixing'.[82] The attack on the Beckerian approach mounted by Werden and Simon is focussed on the fact that in assuming an efficient level of enforcement of criminal law, Becker assumes that there must be an efficient level of infringement. For Werden and Simon this is an unacceptable conclusion, as there is *no* efficient level of cartelisation, which is utterly without social benefit. At the same time, it is still possible, even accepting this, to apply Beckerian derived analysis: if the transaction costs of catching and punishing all cartelists at penalty Y would render absolute deterrence inefficient, the equation may be rebalanced by simply

---

79 Elzinga, KG, and Breit, W, note 76, at 132–33.

80 Connor, JM, and Lande, RH, note 13, at 28.

81 Landes, WM, 'Optimal Sanctions for Antitrust Violations' (1983) 50 *University of Chicago Law Review* 652.

82 Werden, GJ, and Simon, MJ, 'Why Price Fixers Should Go to Prison' (1987) 32 *Antitrust Bulletin* 917 at 919.

increasing the amount of the penalty to a level 'high enough to deter all hard-core price-fixing',[83] and there *must be* some such level (perhaps Y^2, or perhaps a significant term in jail?).

Compliance

The factors that encourage compliance[84] by corporations, and individuals within them, with legal standards are complex, and exacerbated by the fact that the relevant legal and natural persons may have somewhat different agendas, and may be subject to persuasion to compliance by different incentives; indeed, that this is the case is put forward by advocates of personal criminalisation of cartelists as a partial reason for the alleged efficacy of the policy.

The dynamics of decision-making within corporations, and in particular of decisions to comply, or not to comply, with legally required standards are incredibly complex, and the subject of increasing focus in the post-Enron world. There have been significant contributions flowing from work examining corporate crime and corporate corruption that are relevant to compliance with antitrust standards, and to unlawful cartelisation,[85] but, although 'effective legal policy concerning corporate crime must be founded on an understanding of the decision-making process underlying corporate action',[86] there is no straightforward answer to explain the interplay between *individual* and *corporate* decisions. Instead a number of different decision-making models have been developed, which broadly suggest that it may be appropriate to impose criminal sanctions (when these are desirable) on those in positions to prevent the offence that occurred (which would necessarily include, but might not be limited to, those who perpetrate the offence). Decision-making models are also, by their very nature, incapable of rendering with precision the

---

[83] Ibid at 933.

[84] 'Compliance' here is defined, following Fleming and Zyglidopoulos, as being 'not about punishment, but finding ways to persuade adherence to the rules in a business community' (Fleming, P, and Zyglidopoulos, SC, *Charting Corporate Corruption: Agency, Structure and Escalation* (2009) Edward Elgar, at 139).

[85] See, for example, Simpson, S, *Corporate Crime, Law and Social Control* (2002) Cambridge University Press; Ashforth, BE, and Anand, V, 'The Normalization of Corruption in Organizations' (2003) 25 *Research in Organizational Behaviour* 1; Fleming, P, and Spicer, A, *Contesting the Corporation: Power, Resistance and Struggle in Organizations* (2007) Cambridge University Press; Fleming, P, and Zyglidopoulos, SC, note 84.

[86] Kriesberg, SM, 'Decisionmaking Models and the Control of Corporate Crime' (1976) 85 *Yale Law Journal* 1091 at 1092.

decision-making process in any individual corporation. There is also a substantial literature dealing with corporate, as distinct from individual, deterrence, with work by Kagan and Scholz providing the key starting framework.[87] Whether it is in fact more appropriate to characterise corporations as amoral calculators, organisations prone to error, or political citizens is strongly contested, and the characterisation adopted will impact upon which approach to ensuring compliance with appropriate legal standards should be taken. The argument made in this book however does not focus on the corporation, and the interested reader may follow these arguments elsewhere.[88]

Whatever the precise dynamics of decision-making within corporations, Clarke and Evenett are almost certainly correct when they state that

> [c]artel members will weigh the gains from a further increase in prices in a given nation's market with the increase in the probability that such a price increase will result in enforcement action that, in turn, could lead to financial and other penalties.[89]

Similarly, Hammond argues that

> [r]egardless of whether a cartel is subject to criminal or administrative sanctions, it is axiomatic that cartel activity will not be adequately deterred nor reported if the potential penalties are perceived by firms and their executives as outweighed by the potential rewards.[90]

---

[87] Kagan, RA, and Scholz, JT, 'The Criminology of the Corporation and Regulatory Enforcement Strategies', in Hawkins, K, and Thomas, JM (eds), *Enforcing Regulation* (1984) Kluwer-Nijhoff.

[88] A good starting point, with the arguments made in the context of competition law compliance, may be found in Rodger, BJ, 'The Competition Act and the Enterprise Act Reforms: Sanctions and Deterrence in UK Competition Law', in Dannecker, G, and Jansen, O, *Competition Law Sanctioning in the European Union* (2004) Kluwer Law International at 118, and see the references therein.

[89] Clarke, JL, and Evenett, SJ, 'The Deterrent Effects of National Anticartel Laws: Evidence from the international vitamins cartel' (2003) 48 *Antitrust Bulletin* 689 at 691. Clarke and Evenett further argue that:

> [t]he constraint – if any – that a nation's cartel enforcement regime is likely to place on the pricing behaviour of cartel members will depend on a number of factors including the ability of the antitrust authorities to collect the relevant evidence, the incentives such an authority has to encourage private firms to come forward with evidence, the strength of any penalties for cartelisation that the nation's law allows for and, where relevant, the likelihood that a nation's courts will convict cartel conspirators.

[90] Hammond, SD, 'Cornerstones of an Effective Leniency Program', ICN

A consequence of this argument is that it may be anticipated that there exists an inverse relationship between strong cartel enforcement and cartel price rises: the less effective enforcement is in any given state, the more the cartel may seek to raise prices in that state. Evidence demonstrating that this is indeed the case would provide strong objective support for what appears to be a very sound intuitive approach, and analyses of price rises imposed by international cartels do indeed support this view. Thus, for example, Clarke and Evenett find that in the case of the vitamins cartel, countries in Latin America without an active cartel enforcement regime saw the value of imports of vitamins rise by over 50 per cent after the formation of the cartel, while those countries with an active cartel enforcement regime saw the value of imports rise by less than 40 per cent.[91] Some have found in these conclusions support for a very strong anti-cartel policy in the US, in effect positioning the US as a global police officer, whose enforcement efforts benefit not only the US. This argument has been tied in to private enforcement in the US, as well as to public enforcement.[92]

Executives who engage in cartel activity may do so in order to secure enhanced profits for their employer *and* rewards for themselves. Typically these might be higher salaries reflecting increased profitability, promotion, or simply the ability to bask in the warm glow of a superior's approval. Thus, for example, in the US *General Electric* case the sentencing judge remarked that the defendants 'were torn between conscience and an approved corporate policy, with the rewarding objective of promotion, comfortable security, and large salaries'.[93] Executives might in some cases hope to benefit from an easier working life if competitive pressures are reduced. Some have suggested that 'punishment has little deterrence power in the mindsets of managers',[94] although in relation to antitrust enforcement the evidence is strong that fines imposed against firms do not eliminate recidivism, whereas jail sentences imposed on individuals do (see Chapter 3, below). At the extreme it has been suggested

Workshop on Leniency Programs, November 22–23, 2004 (www.justice.gov/atr/public/speeches/206611.htm).

91 Clarke, JL, and Evenett, SJ, note 89, at 717.

92 See, for example, Schmidt, JT, 'Keeping US Courts Open to Foreign Antitrust Plaintiffs: A Hybrid Approach to the Effective Deterrence of International Cartels' (2006) 31 *Yale Journal of International Law* 211.

93 Judge J Cullen Ganey, reported in the *New York Times* (1961) February 7, quoted in Geis, G, 'Deterring Corporate Crime', in Ermann, MD, and Lundman, RJ, *Corporate and Governmental Deviance: Problems of Organizational Behavior in Contemporary Society* (1978) Oxford University Press.

94 Fleming, P, and Zyglidopoulos, SC, note 84, at 139.

that 'an organisation is *more likely* to engage in corporate crime if it has previously been investigated by a regulatory body than a firm which has not'.[95]

There has been little research published examining corporate competition law compliance in the UK. Work published in the US 'cannot be relied on because of the significant differences between the two jurisdictions relating to culture, legal process and the nature and content of the legislation'.[96] Frazer found in 1995 that the majority of companies surveyed agreed, or agreed strongly, with the statement that 'companies should always comply with competition laws'. In response to the statement 'companies should comply with competition laws where there is a likelihood of penalties', 43.6 per cent of respondents agreed strongly, and 28.7 per cent agreed. Frazer's work was conducted however at a time when the competition law regime in the UK was not *ex ante* prohibitory in nature (although EU law, which was prohibitory did apply), and the work would have to be repeated today to be a more reliable indicator as to the compliance culture in the UK at present.[97] It is therefore helpful that in 2010 the OFT published a study it had recently commissioned into the factors underpinning compliance with UK competition law.[98] However, it should be noted that the research focussed on only 'larger businesses having existing competition law compliance activities'[99] and that it is based on 22 detailed interviews. We cannot know, but might suspect, that responses given in such interviews would be somewhat self-serving and, under the terms of the research, companies which did not choose to operate competition law compliance programmes are not represented. The report notes that the general approach of companies was to focus compliance efforts on areas in which it was perceived that risks were presented, which is entirely as would be expected. The most important factors referred to by companies as encouraging compliance with competition law were reported to be 'the fear of reputational damage' and financial penalties.[100] The report states that an unspecified number of respondents were swayed by the threat of individual sanctions including the risk of criminal proceedings, and that these were useful in 'encouraging individuals to

[95] Ibid, at 139, emphasis added.

[96] Frazer, T, 'Monopoly, Prohibition and Deterrence' (1995) 58 *Modern Law Review* 846 at 853.

[97] Ibid, at 853–54.

[98] Office of Fair Trading, *Drivers of Compliance and Non-Compliance with Competition Law*, OFT 1227 (OFT, May 2010).

[99] Para 1.4.

[100] Para 1.10.

Table 2.1 Perceived importance of sanctions in deterring infringements of competition law

Ranking by businesses	Ranking by lawyers
1. Criminal penalties	1. Criminal penalties
2. Disqualification of directors	2. Fines
3. Adverse publicity	3. Disqualification of directors
4. Fines	4. Adverse publicity
5. Private damages actions	5. Private damages actions

focus on competition law compliance'.[101] An earlier report had also been prepared for the OFT by Deloitte in 2007,[102] which had more strongly emphasised the deterrent effect of sanctions targeted at individuals. Table 2.1 is drawn from the Deloitte report.

Later on in the 2010 report a slightly different, and stronger, emphasis is placed on individual criminal sanctions. Reference is made at Para 4.17 to the fact that *most* respondents expressed concern about the prospect of criminal sanctions:

> [m]ost respondents also said that they and individuals within their organisations were concerned about the implications of personal sanctions such as criminal penalties and [competition disqualification orders]. Most respondents said that discussion of personal sanctions was a helpful way to get the attention of individuals in the business when discussing competition law compliance. One respondent said that personal sanctions 'focus . . . the mind for an executive . . . at the end of the day, if they are going to think about what's in it for them . . .'

It appeared also from the OFT's research, as might be expected in the case of larger businesses, that it was not only criminalisation in the UK that would have an impact on compliance. Thus one respondent stated that the criminalisation of cartels in differing jurisdictions was a more important factor determining compliance than any one single investigation would be.[103] Even stronger support for the maintenance of criminalisation may be drawn from Para 4.2.14 of the report, where the following appears:

101 Para 1.10.
102 Office of Fair Trading, *The Deterrent Effect of Competition Enforcement by the OFT*, OFT 962 (OFT, November 2007).
103 At Para 4.1.24.

> [n]early all respondents said that within their organisations, most or even all businesspeople were aware that hard-core cartel activity, such as agreeing prices or sharing markets with competitors, was wrong and potentially criminal. Those respondents often did not find it difficult to gain a compliance commitment from employees with respect to hard-core cartels. What was more of a challenge was to drive compliance with regard to non-hard-core infringements that were less obviously 'wrong'. . . .

There is then, in this report, some support for the view that criminal sanctions are effective in focussing the minds of senior, and perhaps non-senior, staff (there is reference above to '*all* businesspeople') within companies towards compliance. The view stated in the report is that it provides an insight into 'the importance of sanctions against individuals' as a driver for compliance.[104] A larger report, based on responses from 809 firms, including 308 from small firms (defined as those with fewer than 200 employees) was published by the OFT in December 2011.[105] This had as its focus the extent to which enforcement action generally drives compliance, and does not specifically address criminalisation, although there is evidence presented to suggest that the threat of personal criminal sanctions drives compliance (but not uniquely). In Part 6 of the report, 'Sanctions and Enforcement', the authors state that 'the three most important factors deterring potentially anti-competitive behaviour are: the risk of reputational damage for the company; criminal sanctions for individuals; and financial penalties for the company'.[106] Thus, for example, 62 per cent of respondent large companies stated that the threat of criminal prosecution for the individual was a 'very important' deterrent; for small companies

---

[104] At Para 7.11 (although note that this comment includes reference to *all* forms of personal sanctions, including reputational damage, and does not just refer to criminal penalties).

[105] *The Impact of Competition Interventions on Compliance and Deterrence: Final Report* (OFT 1391, December 2011).

[106] At Para 6.5. At Para 6.14 the report's authors note that the findings of the Deloitte report are 'not completely consistent with our own findings as we find that reputational damage . . . and financial penalties for the firm are ranked as two of the most important sanctions by business'. See also Parker, C, and Nielsen, VL, 'Deterrence and the Impact of Calculative Thinking on Business Compliance with Competition and Consumer Regulation' (2011) 56 *Antitrust Bulletin* 377, who argue that:

> [i]t is not only the deterrence of formal legal sanctions that can provide calculative motivations for compliance. Informal economic and social sanctions applied by various third parties in the case of breach, such as stock price declines and social embarrassment among family and peers, may be even more effective at influencing compliance behaviour (at 381).

the figure was 51 per cent. Only 9 per cent of large companies stated that the threat of personal criminal sanctions was not very, or not at all, important. For small companies that figure rose to 14 per cent, with 4 per cent of respondents stating that they were unaware of this possibility.[107]

Corporate Liability and Fines

Irrespective of whether fines imposed on companies engaged in antitrust violations are imposed under civil/administrative law, or under criminal law procedures, they are substantial, but it has been argued that they are not substantial enough to deter cartelisation in international markets in particular.[108] In respect of the latter, the argument in effect is that firms engaged in international cartels may use the profits reaped in regimes with under-deterrence to pay the penalties incurred in regimes with more effective deterrence. As domestic regimes sets fines to align with their individual *domestic* enforcement needs, there will be under-deterrence unless all regimes in which international cartels operate are equally effective. The only alternative would be for domestic regimes with more effective enforcement regimes (the US and the EU in particular) to set penalties reflecting harm arising outwith their jurisdictions. Connor suggests that, '[b]ecause of the low penalties outside North America, global cartels incur only very small monetary penalties – about 4% of their world-wide affected commerce.'[109]

In the UK, adopting the practice of the EU, fines imposed on undertakings may be levied up to a maximum of 10 per cent of the turnover of the undertaking in the relevant market in the preceding business year.[110] In the US, fining limits are set in legislation, but the legislation also permits fines to be imposed that are up to twice the gain from, or twice the loss caused by, the cartel. A tendency to assume that the fines imposed under these regimes exceeded profits made by the punished cartel has been challenged

---

107 At Figure 6.1.

108 See, for example, Connor, JM, note 63: 'either greater sanctions ought to be applied, or . . . a multilateral approach implemented in order to approach optimal deterrence of international price fixing' (at 198). An alternative approach in the face of evidence that existing penalties are inadequate may be to focus on the competitive environments within which cartels are formed, and to advocate structural modifications to firms so as to change the environment; see, for example, Hay, GA, and Kelley, D, 'An Empirical Survey of Price Fixing Conspiracies' (1974) *Journal of Law and Economics* 13 at 27.

109 Connor, JM, note 63, at 214.

110 CA98, s 36. See also OFT *Guidance as to the Appropriate Amount of a Penalty* (2006).

in recent literature. Thus Connor argues that while 'officials frequently opine that cartel fines and settlements exceed a cartel's illegal profits . . . these claims are at best *ex post* assertions that say little about *ex ante* optimality'.[111]

Wils has used Bryant and Eckard's estimates as to the probability of detection as the basis for his conclusion that fines in the EU would need to be 'in the order of 150 percent of the annual turnover in the products concerned by the violation' in order to deter infringements in the EU.[112] While Wils's 150 per cent figure may seem high, Connor and Lande, basing analysis on estimated returns from cartels and all costs associated with subsequent conviction, produce results which show:

> that the combined level of United States cartel sanctions has been far too low. If mean average figures are used, the imposed sanctions have only been 16% to 21% as large as they should have been to protect victims of cartelisation optimally . . . This means that, in the aggregate, the overall level of the United States anti-cartel sanctions should be approximately five times as high as they are today.[113]

There is further support for this approach from Combe and Monnier, who conclude that 'fines imposed against cartels by the Commission are still far from optimal, even if we consider a 100% probability of detection'.[114]

Personal Liability and Incarceration

The view that cartelists should be subject to criminal law sanctions is not unanimously held. The majority of competition regimes of EU member states do *not* contain within them a criminal law element, and this narrow pattern is reflected more broadly in the relevant literature. However, the view of Scott D Hammond, who has extremely substantial experience of criminal enforcement, is one I find persuasive:

---

[111] Note 63, at 198.

[112] Wils, WPJ, 'Is Criminalization of EU Competition Law the Answer?' (2005) 28:2 *World Competition* 117 at 138; see also Wils, WPJ, 'Does the Effective Enforcement of Articles 81 and 82 EC Require Not Only Fines on Undertakings but Also Individual Penalties, in Particular Imprisonment?', in Ehlermann, CD, and Atanasiu, E (eds), *European Competition Law Annual 2001: Effective Private Enforcement of EC Antitrust Law* (2003) Hart Publishing.

[113] Connor, JM, and Lande, RH, note 13, at 4; see also Connor, JM, and Lande, RH, 'The Size of Cartel Overcharges: Implications for US and EU Fining Policies' (2006) 51:4 *Antitrust Bulletin* 983.

[114] Combe, E, and Monnier, C, 'Fines against Hard Core Cartels in Europe: The Myth of Overenforcement' (2011) 56 *Antitrust Bulletin* 235 at 260.

> ... all else being equal, a jurisdiction without individual liability and criminal sanctions will never be *as effective* at inducing amnesty applications as a programme that does. Individuals stand the most to lose and so avoiding jail sentences is the greatest incentive for seeking amnesty. Common sense suggests that the threat of individual exposure will tilt the balance at the margins such that some companies will report violations that they would not otherwise have reported if they were only facing financial penalties. However, this view is informed by more than common sense.
>
> We are observing first hand in some of our investigations how the threat of criminal prosecution in the United States has deterred a significant number of global cartels from extending their conspiracy into the United States. We have uncovered cartels that operated profitably and illegally in Europe, Asia, and elsewhere around the world, but did not expand their cartel activity to the United States solely because it was not worth the risk of US sanctions. I am referring to cartels that had every opportunity to target US consumers, because they sold in the US market. Indeed, in some cases the US market was the largest and potentially most profitable but the collusive conduct still ceased at the border. Why? The answer, from the mouths of the cartel members and verified by our investigators, is that the executives did not want to risk getting caught and going to jail in the United States.[115]

There are strong arguments from within the economics and law approach that support incarceration. First, the level of fines that would be required to deter cartelisation might be so high that individual companies or natural persons simply could not pay the required amount (they might even be protected by laws on bankruptcy). Thus it has been argued that 'the harm price-fixing causes is likely to be so great, and the likelihood of punishment so slight that Becker's optimal fine would be well beyond the ability of most defendants (including corporate defendants) to pay'.[116] Courts might be reluctant to fine individuals at the necessary levels, particularly where the impact of the fine would have serious consequences on family members and dependants. Given the reputational effects that flow from incarceration, and the clear aversion to incarceration held by executives (see below), a relatively short jail term may prove somewhat effective in sanctioning one individual, and in deterring another. Connor

[115] Hammond, SD, note 90.

[116] Werden, GJ, and Simon, MJ, note 82, at 924. See also Werden, GJ, Hammond, SD, and Barnett, BA, 'Deterrence and Detection of Cartels: Using All the Tools and Sanctions' (2011) 56 *Antitrust Bulletin* 207 at 211: 'fines at a level sufficient to deter can exceed the ability of cartel participants to pay'; and Craycraft, C, Craycraft, JL, and Gallo, JC, 'Antitrust Sanctions and a Firm's Ability to Pay' (1997) 12 *Review of Industrial Organization* 171, where it is argued that between 1955 and 1993, over 80 per cent of convicted firms would have been unable to pay optimal fines.

and Lande suggest that 'publicity about severe sentences for price fixing may help educate other corporate executives about the true individual and corporate legal risks of being caught'.[117] It has been recognised that the costs of imprisonment to the convicted offender may be substantially higher than are civil penalties, in part 'because stigma attaches to a criminal conviction much more than to other forms of condemnation',[118] and the costs of stigma may be substantial. A more subtle argument, in favour of incarceration in the specific context of cartelisation, has also been advanced by Evenett et al:

> . . . incarceration is needed to reduce or eliminate the expected harm caused by repeat offences. There may be legitimate concern that executives who have successfully arranged explicit agreements to carve up a market will, after the cartel is broken up, attempt more subtle forms of collusion (such as price leadership). The imposition of fines alone may not induce a firm's shareholders to replace the offending executives . . . a clean break with the past may be needed.[119]

The fact that the evidence demonstrates that recidivism is prevalent in cartelists, and that the EU and US have both felt compelled to adjust their fining policies to reflect this, adds weight to this argument.[120] Lever has based advocacy for the existence of individual criminal penalties in part on the fact that recidivism exists, arguing that while individuals may demonstrate a propensity towards certain forms of criminally proscribed conduct, corporations are simply incapable of this.[121] With some elegance Harding has argued that there came a point, following more effective enforcement, when cartelisation clearly moved into the shadows, and when cartelists accepted that their actions were illegal, but found the temptation to engage in cartelisation irresistible, and that this in itself may be advanced to justify criminalisation:

> [i]n dramatic terms, this was the point at which cartelists determined to persist in their conduct despite its dogmatic illegality, a conscious move into outlaw territory. It is that outlaw resolve that calls for our investigation, in order to

---

117 Connor, JM, and Lande, RH, note 13 at 13,

118 Ogus, A, note 73, at 94; and see Funk, P, 'On the Effective Use of Stigma as a Crime-Deterrent' (2004) 48 *European Economic Review* 715.

119 Evenett, SJ, Levenstein, MC, and Suslow, VY, note 15, at 1236.

120 See Connor, JM, note 58.

121 Lever J, 'Opinion: Whether and if so how, the EC Commission's 2006 guidelines on setting fines for infringements of Arts 81 and 82 EC are fairly subject to serious criticism', (2009) German Employers' Association, Law and Public Procurement Series.

> probe and understand its delinquency and hence the basis for any criminalisation. For it is that very outlaw determination, embodying a combination 'anti-trust awareness' and engagement in subterfuge . . . that provides the key to the contemporary condemnation of cartels, so that they become a matter not only of economic but also normative objection.[122]

The impact of criminalisation on the costs of enforcement has not been fully researched: as rights of the defence are increased when criminal sanctions are being imposed, and as higher standards of proof are typically required, it flows that enforcement costs may be increased. Defining offences simply, such that, for example, the need for sophisticated economic analysis is removed, may however reduce costs when compared with civil infringement decisions replete with economic analysis. It has been argued persuasively that individual criminalisation enhances enforcement in that it makes more information available to enforcement authorities, as Baker explains:

> [i]ndividuals have information; if they can be offered immunity from prosecution in return for cooperation, they can be encouraged to provide evidence against enterprises participating in a suspected cartel. Absent such evidence, leading antitrust enforcers [such as the EU] are forced to rely almost entirely on documentary evidence to prove the existence of a cartel.[123]

There are also those who advance arguments based around the sociology of the firm, recognising that while firms are the economic actors which engage in cartelisation, the decision to do so is made by and implemented by individuals. Some appear to find it unpalatable that individuals are not themselves subject to sanction when cartelisation takes place. Thus, for example, Massey condemns cartelisation, and then focuses on the individuals who implement cartels, 'who calculate that they stand to earn substantial profits from such behaviour'. These people, Massey argues, 'are not petty crooks; they are clever sophisticated business executives who have risen to senior management positions in their companies'.[124] Arguments based on such an approach are on their face attractive, but

---

122 Harding, C, 'The Anti-Cartel Enforcement Industry: Criminological Perspectives on Cartel Criminalisation', in Beaton-Wells, C, and Ezrachi, A (eds), *Criminalising Cartels* (2011) Hart Publishing at 372–73.

123 Baker, DI, 'The Use of Criminal Law Remedies to Deter and Punish Cartels and Bid-Rigging' (2000–2001) 69 *George Washington Law Review* 693 at 698.

124 Massey, P, 'Criminal Sanctions for Competition Law: A Review of Irish Experience', (2004) *Competition Law Review* 23 at 30.

conflate moral indignation with deterrence efficiency. In particular more work is needed to research how cartel decisions are made within firms, and how those who make and implement them are rewarded *and* punished within the closed environment of the firm. Unfortunately, as with so much in this area, there remains a lack of evidence as to the true impact of personal sanctions, including imprisonment, on individual conduct (although the US experience, discussed in the following chapter, is indicative that the policy *does* work).[125]

That the threat of imprisonment may have a significant impact on company executives, and that the actual experience is likely to be deeply unpleasant for them, would appear to be evident. The argument has been most effectively put forward by Gilbert Geis:

> [j]ail terms have a self-evident deterrent impact upon corporate officials, who belong to a social group that is exquisitely sensitive to status deprivation and censure. The white-collar offender and his business colleagues, more than the narcotic addict or the ghetto mugger, are apt to learn well the lesson intended by a prison term.[126]

---

[125] Thus the OECD has recognised that: '[t]here is no systematic evidence proving the deterrent effects of sanctions on individuals' (note 18, executive summary).

[126] Geis, G, note 93, at 278–79. There is no published research which is based on interviews with those imprisoned for antitrust violations, and it is not possible to comment in detail on the impact of such sentences on offenders. In *The Art of the Steal* Christopher Mason discusses some of the treatment accorded to the multimillionaire Alfred Taubman following his conviction in April 2002 for his role in the Sotheby's/Christie's fine art auction commission-fixing cartel. Taubman flew to prison in his private jet, where, on arrival, he 'was strip-searched and given a uniform of khaki shirt and pants' (at 372). Mason notes that: '[a]s a person accustomed to traveling on his private plane every three or four days – to Michigan, New York, Florida, Europe or wherever the fancy took him – it was extremely challenging to find himself cooped up in one place for months on end. He was used to calling the shots, and he found it hard to adapt to the prison's mind-numbing regulations' (at 375).

At page 376 Mason reports an exchange which demonstrates starkly the fall in status Taubman was subjected to:

> Parker Gilbert, the former chairman of Morgan Stanley Dean Witter and a director of the Taubman Company, was happy to receive a call from Taubman, whom he was planning to see the following week.
>
> 'Is there anything I can bring you?' Gilbert asked.
>
> 'Yes,' Taubman replied. 'Twenty dollars in quarters.'
>
> For a couple of legendary American businessmen accustomed to doing transactions in the hundreds of millions, it was quite an adjustment to get used to the daily currency of prison life.

Simester has stated with equal eloquence:

> [c]onvictions are official. They condemn D on behalf of society as a whole. To say that D has a criminal record is to say that he has been labelled as a reprehensible wrongdoer; that the state has made a formal adverse statement about *him*. Moreover, the statement marks D out in such a way that it becomes appropriate, within the community, for the regard in which he is held to be affected . . . [This] tends not only to censure D for the particular act that is proscribed, but also to undermine D's participation in the society itself.[127]

The fact that the application of criminal law does carry with it the full weight of state condemnation has compelled some to argue that decisions to criminalise certain forms of conduct should be taken carefully. This matter is discussed by the Law Commission in its 2010 consultation, *Criminal Liability in Regulatory Contexts*, although the discussion there relates primarily to the application of criminal law to companies, rather than to individuals, and there is no specific mention of the Cartel Offence. The reluctance of courts to impose custodial sentences on business executives has long been recognised, as has a general trend of criminal justice systems as a whole to be lenient to this constituency. The approach of judges in specific cases in the US, the UK and Ireland are referred to in following chapters. Conklin has pointed to the 'high degree of cultural homogeneity among the defendants . . . and the judges who determine guilt and mete out sentences'.[128] There is also a clear reluctance to impose sentences on first-time offenders, and persons of 'good character', and 'some judges prefer to view businessmen as having good intentions, even when there is evidence to the contrary'.[129] In the US a broad acceptance of the need to impose significant jail terms on antitrust violators has been created only over a long period of time, and was particularly facilitated by changes in sentencing guidelines in 1987; as late as 2006 Stucke was able

---

A further fascinating insight into the experiences facing convicted cartelists is provided in O'Kane, M, 'Does Prison Work for Cartelists? – the View from Behind Bars: An Interview of Bryan Allison by Michael O'Kane' (2011) 56 *Antitrust Bulletin* 483. Thus, for example, Allison describes his experience shortly after arrest: '[w]e were made to wear shackles around our ankles and one of the other guys whispered to me, "This is so extreme"' (at 486).

[127] Simester, AP (ed), *Appraising Strict Liability* (2005) Oxford University Press, at 35, quoted in The Law Commission, *Criminal Liability in Regulatory Contexts: A Consultation Paper* (2010), Consultation Paper No 195 at Para 4.11 (emphasis in original).

[128] Conklin, JE, *"Illegal but Not Criminal": Business Crime in America* (1977) Prentice-Hall, at 112.

[129] Ibid, at 117.

to point to the reluctance of the US courts to incarcerate individuals 'who have the earmarks of respectable business executives'.[130]

Leniency

Evidence gained from cases makes clear that cartels exist, that they may be very effectively managed, and that the problems identified by Stigler may be circumvented. If members are careful to avoid detection, and it is clear from the history of some cartels that members may be *very* careful, then detection of cartels becomes difficult. At the same time, cartels can function only where there is communication between members, and this communication leaves trails. Notwithstanding that members must anticipate investigation, and presumably seek to minimise record-keeping, it is remarkable how much evidence is often presented, included detailed notes and memoranda of meetings, when cartels have been investigated and prosecuted.[131]

Following the introduction of a leniency programme by the US in 1978 a clear strategy has emerged of exploiting uncertainties existing between the cartel members, by providing members, subject to limited conditions, with incentives to disclose the existence of the cartel to the relevant authorities, and to avoid penalties by so doing. In the US the leniency programme is operated by the Department of Justice, Antitrust Division (see Chapter 3),[132] and in the UK the OFT also operates a leniency programme, as does the EU Commission. There is also a model leniency programme promoted by the European Competition Network. In the case of the US there are separate programmes in respect of corporations and individuals, while in the EU, given that individuals are not subject to arts 101 and 102 TFEU, there is only a programme aimed at undertakings. The very existence of leniency programmes suggests that competition enforcement recognises efficiency objectives and prioritises these over moral condemnation; a successful leniency applicant, who by definition will have engaged in unlawful cartelisation, goes unpunished and escapes moral condemnation, the enforcement authority taking the view that to permit this enhances overall detection. Another view might be to accept that the guilty cartelist has

---

130 Stucke, ME, note 9, at 456. See also at 540: 'many federal judges have treated antitrust offenders as respectable executives who posed no danger to society'.

131 See, for example, the three case studies presented in Chapter 6, below.

132 See Hammond, SD, 'Lessons Common to Detecting and Deterring Cartel Activity', in Konkurrensverket (Swedish Competition Authority), *Fighting Cartels – Why and How?* (2001) Konkurrensverket at 191.

wiped the slate clean and atoned for her sins in confessing the existence of the cartel.

The UK authorities, accommodating the Cartel Offence, include a 'no-action letter' alongside the corporate leniency programme which applies in respect of art 101 TFEU and the corresponding Chapter I Prohibition. Corporations are not able to benefit from leniency in the US where they coerced another party into the unlawful conduct, or where they are 'clearly . . . the leader in, or originator of, the activity'.[133] In the EU an undertaking may not benefit from full leniency if it has 'compelled another enterprise to take part in the cartel'.[134] In the UK applicants may not benefit from leniency where they have coerced others into the cartel, but may benefit where they have played a leading role in the creation and management of the cartel.[135] All leniency programmes impose conditions which must be followed for full leniency to be granted – these typically require that the applicant be the first to apply, provides decisive evidence allowing the case to move forward, and provides full information and continuous cooperation during any proceedings which follow the application. While some have criticised the very concept of leniency, the better view is that the benefit of leniency programmes far outweighs any detriment. The OFT takes the view that:

> it is in the interests of the economic well-being of the United Kingdom to grant lenient treatment to undertakings or individuals who inform competition authorities of cartels and who then cooperate fully with any subsequent investigation. . . . The secret nature of cartels and their damaging effects justifies such a policy. . . . the interests of customers and end-consumers in ensuring that such practices are detected and brought to an end outweigh the policy objectives of imposing penalties (or doing so to the fullest extent possible) on those individuals and/or undertakings who have committed an infringement or

---

133 DOJ, Corporate Leniency Policy, Para A6.

134 EU Commission, *Commission Notice on Immunity from Fines and Reduction of Fines in Cartel Cases* (2006) OJ C298/17. In the EU the fact that an undertaking has played a leading role in the promotion of a cartel not only removes the benefit of leniency, but is also considered an 'aggravating factor' in the calculation of the penalty in the event that an infringement decision is made. The impact of excluding ringleaders from the benefit of leniency has recently begun to attract attention; see, for example, Bos, I, and Wandschneider, F, 'Cartel Ringleaders and the Corporate Leniency Program' (2011) Centre for Competition Policy, CCP Working Paper 11-13, and Leslie, CR, 'Antitrust Amnesty, Game Theory and Cartel Stability' (2006) 31 *Journal of Corporation Law* 453.

135 OFT, *Applications for Leniency and No-action in Cartel Cases. OFT's Detailed Guidance on the Principles and Process: A Consultation on OFT Guidance* (OFT 803con, October 2011), revised guidance, Paras 2.50–2.55.

offence but who report their conduct to the OFT and cooperate fully with the OFT and, where appropriate, any other relevant authorities.[136]

The role played by leniency programmes in the enforcement of competition laws has been highly significant in the previous 20 years. Schmidt is by no means alone in asserting that 'government amnesty policies are critical to identify and prosecute cartels'.[137] Klawiter stated that the DOJ's leniency programme is 'without any doubt, the single most effective tool in the detection and prosecution of cartels ever devised'.[138] Competition authorities have exploited the problems cartel-participants face in stabilising their arrangements (discussed in part above) by simultaneously increasing the cost of detection – the introduction of the UK's Cartel Offence is one example of this – while also increasing the benefits that may flow from successful leniency applications.

The dynamic in leniency programmes is clearly different when sanctions and leniency programmes apply not only to corporate violators, but also to individuals. Individuals may have different incentives than their employers, may act with very different motives, and may not be under the control of the corporate employer at a time when the leniency application is made. In practice, the effect is to increase the number of actors who may have an incentive to destabilise a cartel.[139] Thus Hammond has pointed to the risk that a company engaged in a cartel faces: any employee or officer participating in the cartel may also act as a whistle-blower, and could in that case be unique in securing leniency.[140] At the same time it has been

136 Ibid.

137 Schmidt, JT, note 92, at 213.

138 Klawiter, DC, 'Corporate Leniency after the Blockbuster Cartels: Are We Entering a New Era?', in Ehlermann, CD, and Atanasiu, I (eds), *European Competition Law Annual 2006: Enforcement of Prohibition of Cartels* (2007) Hart Publishing, at 489.

139 Baker has noted that the threat of individual criminal penalties may also increase the constituency of potential whistle-blowers: '[t]he desire for revenge is more picturesque, but is still very much present. In my experience, disgruntled current employees, fired employees, former trade association officials, and even ex-spouses and ex-lovers may be anxious to finger the individuals who they think have done them in' (Baker, DI, 'The Use of Criminal Law Remedies to Deter and Punish Cartels and Bid-Rigging' (2000–2001) 69 *George Washington Law Review* 693 at 708).

140 'The real value and measure of the Individual Leniency Programme is not in the number of individual applications we receive, but in the number of corporate applications it generates. It works because it acts as a watchdog to ensure that companies report the conduct themselves. . . . If the company self-reports the conduct under the Corporate Leniency Policy, then the company and

suggested that pure leniency, by itself, may be insufficient to deter collusion, and that enforcement authorities should contemplate the introduction of rewards for those who blow the whistle.[141]

The specifics of leniency programmes in the US and the UK are discussed in the following two chapters, and some of the consequences of their application in a small selection of cartel cases are further considered in Chapter 6.

SUPPORT FOR CRIMINALISATION IN THE UK

Given the harms of cartelisation outlined above, it might be supposed that it would be widely accepted that hard-core cartel activity should invite condemnation, and that criminalisation would satisfy the Law Commission, which argued that 'criminal law should only be employed to deal with wrongdoers who deserve the stigma associated with criminal conviction because they have engaged in seriously reprehensible conduct'.[142] Ogus is not alone in suggesting that 'risk averse' politicians are more likely to introduce *ex ante* prohibitions in respect of harms which are perceived by the public to result in 'very high losses'.[143] Thus the process of legal discourse, which is a complex one, may require that the public support laws if those laws are to be effective in changing conduct. While a law is more likely to be enforced effectively if it has public support, enforcing that law may have an impact on public attitudes; society may take from enforcement the message that the act which has invited condemnation and

---

all of its co-operating executives will avoid criminal prosecution. However, if the company delays or decides not to report, then the company puts itself in a race for leniency with its own employees. In this example, if the company does not report the conduct first, then the executive may come forward on his own and report the conduct for his own protection, thereby potentially leaving the company out in the cold' (Hammond, SD, note 90).

141 See, for example, Aubert, C, Rey, P, and Kovacic, WE, 'The Impact of Leniency and Whistle-blowing Programs on Cartels' (2006) 24 *International Journal of Industrial Organization* 1241.

142 The Law Commission, *Criminal Liability in Regulatory Contexts: A Consultation Paper* (2010) Consultation Paper No 195 at Para 1.28.

143 Ogus, A, 'Criminal Law and Regulation', in Garoupa, N (ed), note 10, at 93. Conklin has argued that a significant reason for leniency towards business offenders is 'the absence of an influential and well-organised public demand for the prosecution and punishment of business offenders. . . . As a result, little effective pressure is brought to bear on those who make the law or have the power to prosecute business offenders' (Conklin, JE, note 128, at 109).

punishment is wrong.[144] It has been suggested that the very use of the word 'dishonestly' in the Cartel Offence in the UK sends a signal as to the moral opprobrium that should be attached to cartelisation.[145] Indeed, the Undersecretary of State suggested as much in Parliament, stating that the language chosen would 'focus the attention of courts, juries and the wider public on the wrongful nature of hard-core cartels'.[146] It has been noted that competition authorities are deliberately employing 'highly emotive and moral language' to generate public support for strong condemnation of cartelisation.[147] Stephan has also analysed the extent to which public support for the criminalisation of cartelisation may be shaped by the

---

144 See von Hirsch, A, *Censure and Sanctions* (1993) Clarendon Press. Stucke, for example, has argued that '[o]ne aspect of criminal law is educational. As the harms of certain conduct are exposed or fully understood, society's moral condemnation may increase' (note 8, at 490). See also Werden, GJ, and Simon, MJ, note 82, at 933: '[i]t is one thing for us to assert that hard-core price-fixing is a serious crime and quite another for society to view it that way. The best tool we can think of for educating society is the prison sentence for antitrust felons that is imposed with some frequency'. The importance of cultural attitudes to specific crimes, while difficult to determine, has been highlighted by Shaffer and Nesbitt:

> [c]ultural attitudes may be the biggest hurdle to enforcement trends. Not all publics are convinced that cartel offences merit the criminal penalty of jail time, which is advocated most vocally by the United States. Criminalisation implies moral judgments that vary with socio-cultural context. US antitrust law has long exhibited a moral dimension which facilitates the use of criminal sanctions against individuals in cartel cases. In contrast, 'there appears to be (at least outside North America) no strong feeling on the part of the wider public about the inherent criminality of price fixing and like practices.' National competition authorities outside of North America recognise this uphill battle and thus view public education about the evils of cartel offences as a central component of their missions (note 7, at 24, internal references omitted).

In 2006 Stucke argued that 'there is *no* consensus on the morality of antitrust offences' (note 9, at 444, emphasis added).

145 Thus MacCulloch (citing Williams, R, 'Cartels in the Criminal Law Landscape', in Beaton-Wells, C, and Ezrachi, A (eds), note 122, at 289–312), notes that:

> [t]he cartel offence seeks to pull itself up by its own bootstraps in that it seeks to harden moral opprobrium by criminalising cartels, but 'dishonesty cannot *inculcate* collective moral censure for the cartel offence because it *presupposes* and relies upon such collective moral censure already existing' (MacCulloch, A, note 9, nyp, emphasis in original).

146 *Hansard*, April 18, 2002, para 1.

147 Note 14, at 141. See also Harding, C, 'Business Collusion as a Criminological Phenomenon: Exploring the Global Criminalisation of Business Cartels' (2006) 14 *Critical Criminology* 181.

media in general, but recognises that cartel cases are 'less newsworthy than conventional crimes such as theft and assault'.[148] However, a recent survey in the UK showed that attitudes towards cartelists are somewhat ambiguous.[149] Stephan's work presents the results of a survey of 1219 residents of Great Britain carried out by YouGov Plc in March 2007. In relation to price-fixing 69 per cent of respondents agreed with the statement that 'this is bad for . . . customers because it will result in much higher prices', with 25 per cent agreeing very strongly.[150] Results were less clear-cut when respondents were presented with a market-sharing scenario with a wide geographic dispersion of sellers, although the question still signalled a price rise as a result. Stephan concludes from this that 'where forms of collusion other than price-fixing bring some benefit to consumers, they are more likely to be acceptable'.[151] When asked expressly whether 'fixing prices' was harmful to customers and should be punished, 73 per cent of respondents agreed with only 9 per cent disagreeing.[152] Respondents who did not feel that price-fixing was harmless were then asked a series of questions relating to what the appropriate punishment for price-fixing should be. The responses are of interest, and are as follows: public naming and shaming, 55 per cent; bans from holding senior managerial positions,

---

148 Stephan, A, '"The Battle for Hearts and Minds": The Role of the Media in Treating Cartels as Criminal', in Beaton-Wells, C, and Ezrachi, A (eds), note 122, at 387.

149 Note 13. This work is cited in the 2011 Consultation Document. Commenting on the Enterprise Bill, Harding and Joshua noted that the intention was to criminalise 'a form of business behaviour hitherto regarded for the most part with a fair measure of moral ambivalence' (Harding, C, and Joshua, J, 'Breaking Up the Hard Core: The Prospects for the Proposed Cartel Offence' (2002) *Criminal Law Review* 933 at 933). Survey work published in the US in 1969 showed that 68 per cent of respondents supported incarceration for antitrust violators. Disappointingly 0 per cent of respondents were in favour of execution (Gibbons, DC, 'Crime and Punishment: A Study in Social Attitudes' (1969) 47 *Social Forces* 391 at 395).

150 At 129. Note that in the first question asked, to which these results relate, the term 'price fixing' was not used in the question.

151 At 129.

152 See 130. Stephan notes that:

> [e]ducation and newspaper readership appears to have little impact on attitudes towards price-fixing, suggesting that these two mediums are poor at disseminating information about its effects; current cartel laws; and prosecutions in the UK. On the other hand, age seems to have a big impact with only 50% of 18–24s feeling price-fixing is harmful and should be punished, compared to at least 79% of 45s and over. This suggests that an important source of knowledge about price-fixing may be experience as a consumer (internal reference omitted).

48 per cent; personal fines, 42 per cent; imprisonment, 11 per cent.[153] Given that these questions were not asked of some of the original sample, the figures in effect give a result of fewer than 10 per cent of respondents supporting incarceration for price-fixing cartelists. Public support is perhaps not a prerequisite for an effective policy of criminalisation (see also above),[154] but it has been noted elsewhere, half a century ago, that the 'first prerequisite for imposing heavier sanctions on corporate criminals involves the development of a deepening sense of moral outrage on the part of the public.'[155] At the time of writing, the evidence suggests that the wider UK public does not respond to cartelisation with deeply felt moral outrage.

CONCLUSION

Fundamentally the decision to introduce a criminal law of cartelisation into the UK rests on the assumption that penalties directed solely at undertakings are insufficient to ensure that individuals within those

---

[153] At 133.

[154] See, for example, Kovacic: '[c]onsumer groups and media organisations help inform the broader public about the purpose and content of the criminal enforcement regime' (Kovacic, WE, 'Criminal Enforcement Norms in Competition Policy: US Insights', in Beaton-Wells, C, and Ezrachi, A (eds), note 122, at 60). With reference to a number of interest groups, 'academic, business, consumer, media and professional organisations', Kovacic states that:

> [t]he roll-out and successful implementation of a successful criminal enforcement programme will depend partly on the competition agency's skill in building support within external communities of observers whose views can help sustain the application of criminal sanctions (ibid).

See also Baker:

> [f]or a majority of Americans, imbued with the 'robber barons' lore, price fixing is seen as *covert theft* – and thus sending antitrust conspirators to jail, like other white-collar thieves, is seen as the right remedy (Baker, DI, 'Punishment for Cartel Participants in the US: A Special Model?, in Beaton-Wells, C, and Ezrachi, A (eds), note 122, at 33 (emphasis in original)).

Stephan has argued that:

> public support is of central importance to the success of criminal cartelisation. A popular understanding of why cartels are harmful and should attract criminal penalties, lends legitimacy to the cartel offence and helps to ensure continued political backing for criminal prosecutions; reducing lobbying for soft enforcement (note 148, at 393).

[155] Geis, G, note 93, at 282.

undertakings comply with the standards imposed by competition law, and that these decisions by individuals are reflected in corporate conduct.[156] If the civil competition laws which pre-dated the introduction of the Cartel Offence (art 101 TFEU and the Chapter I Prohibition) were adequate to ensure an efficient level of deterrence, it would have been inefficient, and demonstrably irrational, to introduce the new legislation. The evidence and arguments discussed above suggest that the policy was *not* an irrational one.

At the same time it must be the case that an unrealistic threat of prosecution will be recognised for what it is, and may ultimately prove counter-productive. Thus, for example, the Law Commission has stated that there is little to be gained from creating criminal offences in regulatory contexts which are then rarely used, with the risk that 'ordinary people and businesses are being subject to ever increasing numbers of what, in all probability, will turn out to be illusory or empty threats of criminal prosecution'.[157] One of the central arguments I make in this book is that, at the time of writing, the threat of effective prosecutions being brought forward under the Cartel Offence is practically close to zero.

The focus of the argument in this book is on criminalisation of competition law, but there are ways in which individuals may be punished for engaging in anti-competitive conduct other than through criminal law. This is the case, for example, in respect of director disqualification orders which are available in the UK, and which are discussed in Chapter 4, below. It has been argued that the EU could adopt the right to impose personal fines under civil law without the need for a major legal adjustment.[158] I do not explore this possibility at any length in this book,

---

[156] Some have argued that financial penalties imposed on companies are not persuasive to the individual actors. See, for example, Stone, CD, 'Social Control of Corporate Behavior', in Ermann, MD, and Lundman, RJ, *Corporate and Governmental Deviance: Problems of Organizational Behavior in Contemporary Society* (1978) Oxford University Press, at 254:

> [a] second group of reasons to doubt the efficacy of the law's profit threats has to do with the fact that the calculations that will maximise the profit of 'the corporation' do not coincide with the calculations that encourage and restrain the key personnel, who have the most influence over corporate policies. Threats to the corporate treasury don't necessarily intimidate them.

[157] The Law Commission, *Criminal Liability in Regulatory Contexts: A Consultation Paper* (2010) Consultation Paper No 195 at Para 1.27.

[158] See Riley, A, note 62 at 561, n 62: '[i]t is contended here that civil fines and director disqualification can be adopted under existing instruments where criminal sanctions including imprisonment could not be adopted without a further significant expansion of jurisdiction under the Treaties'. See Chapter 7, below.

although I return to it in Chapter 7, but it must be recognised that such an approach, particularly where it resulted in fines being imposed on individuals, may raise many of the same difficulties as does criminal enforcement, with individuals vigorously resisting, and with the necessity of the full range of legal protections available under criminal law being applied.

3. Criminalisation in the United States

INTRODUCTION

The dual civil and criminal law nature of the US antitrust regime is explicit in the wording of the primary legislation of the Sherman Act, which was first enacted in 1890. At the time of writing, s 1 of the Sherman Act is in the following terms:

> Every contract, combination in the form of trust or otherwise, or conspiracy, in restraint of trade or commerce among the several States or with foreign nations, is declared to be illegal. Every person who shall make any contract or engage in any combination or conspiracy hereby declared to be illegal shall be deemed guilty of a felony, and, on conviction thereof, shall be punished by a fine not exceeding $100,000,000 if a corporation, or, if any other person, $1,000,000, or by imprisonment not exceeding 10 years, or by both said punishments, in the discretion of the court.[1]

The approach taken to enforcement of the Sherman Act has varied substantially over the 120 years since the Act entered into force on July 2, 1890. When first introduced the legislature did not focus on enforcement mechanisms, the power to enforce the new law simply being passed to the Attorney General with no additional funds or resources made available to support enforcement, and the first attempt to enforce the new legislation was a crushing failure for the Government.[2] In the contemporary period criminal enforcement is very much to the fore, and the DOJ, Antitrust Division, places great emphasis on the potency of criminal prosecutions

---

1 The penalties specified in s 1 have been increased over the years (see below).

2 See *United States v EC Knight Co*, 60 Fed 306 (CCED, Pa), affirmed on appeal 60 Fed 934 (3d Cir 1894), and by the Supreme Court at 156 US 1 (1895) (this judgment has been labelled 'supremely silly' (Lieber, JB, *Rats in the Grain: The Dirty Tricks and Trials of Archer Daniels Midland, the Supermarket to the World* (2000) Basic Books at 105); see also Letwin, WL, *Law and Economic Policy in America: The Evolution of the Sherman Act* (1967) Edinburgh University Press at 121–22.

targeted at individual company officers. Thus, in its *Grand Jury Manual* ('*GJM*'),[3] it explains that:

> [i]nternally, it is the Division's policy to prosecute corporations that have engaged in criminal activity and also their officers and agents when the evidence so warrants. Because a corporation cannot be sentenced to jail, *prosecution of individuals who commit the illegal acts is one of the most potent deterrents to antitrust violations*.[4]

In 2011, the Antitrust Division filed 90 criminal cases, the highest level in the past 20 years, and accepted $520m in criminal fines. The defendants included 27 corporations and 82 individuals, with 21 separate jail terms being imposed.[5] Given that a significant number of cases over the last 15 years have involved international cartels, and have resulted in personal sanctions imposed on non-US citizens, it may be fairly claimed that '[w]hen it comes to jail time for price fixers, the United States is virtually the world's policeman'.[6]

The system of competition law enforcement in the EU is substantially a self-contained one. Rules relating to the gathering of evidence, to procedures to be taken when decisions are made, to penalties and to rights have largely emerged within the closed context of the competition law process. The same is substantially true in respect of the civil competition law in the UK, but is not the case in respect of the Cartel Offence, which operates within the wider construct of domestic criminal law. In the US the Sherman Act operates entirely within a wider legal sphere, and the rules relating to its enforcement are found in federal law, including federal rules of civil and criminal procedure, and in interpretative case law. In this chapter the question of what conduct is condemned under s 1 of the Sherman Act will be considered first, followed by discussion of the enforcement of those provisions. Although the Sherman Act also states, in s 2, that 'monopolisation' may be a felony, this is not considered here. Effectively the felony aspect of monopolisation has fallen into desuetude. The Federal Trade Commission Act which, at s 5, outlaws some 'unfair' methods of competition, is administered entirely through administrative law procedures and will also be ignored here. One criminal antitrust

---

[3] (1991 1st edn). All references here to the *GJM* are to this edition.

[4] At VII-39, emphasis added.

[5] Sharis Pozen, Acting Assistant Attorney General, speech to the ABA Section of Antitrust Law, November 17, 2011. For a discussion of the US approach to cartel sanctioning, and changes over time, see Werden, GJ, 'Sanctioning Cartel Activity: Let the Punishment Fit the Crime' (2009) *European Competition Journal* 19.

[6] Connor, JM, 'Problems with Prison in International Cartel Cases' (2011) 56 *Antitrust Bulletin* 311 at 338.

law will also be ignored. This is the Robinson–Patman Act which makes price discrimination a criminal offence. This is a bizarre law, and one which the Department of Justice is not involved in enforcing.[7] The focus in this book then is on the criminal enforcement of s 1 of the Sherman Act by the Antitrust Division of the DOJ (hereafter 'DOJ', or 'Antitrust Division'). Given that one of the arguments made in this book is that the UK's pursuit of criminal sanctions in respect of cartel conduct is partly put at jeopardy because of the inherent links with the civil application of competition law, both by the OFT and by DG Competition (and indeed potentially by other members of the ECN), attention is also paid in this chapter to the relationship of civil and criminal enforcement. In this latter respect the relationship between private and public enforcement is also an important one. Any party charged with a breach of s 1 of the Sherman Act must anticipate that private actions for damages are likely to follow. The fact that damages in the US can be high, with statutory provision for treble damages, increases the costs to the defendant of detection and punishment of the offence. The DOJ has stated that 'because of the benefit to plaintiffs in civil damage actions of awaiting federal criminal convictions, most damage actions will follow federal prosecutions'.[8] While the Division does not 'promote' private actions, it does 'assist the public to obtain redress for damages suffered by antitrust violators'.[9]

THE DEVELOPMENT OF THE OFFENCE

One of the remarkable aspects of the criminal law of cartelisation in the US is the extent to which its supporters bridge the political spectrum. Thus

---

[7] Robert Bork has evocatively referred to the Robinson–Patman Act provisions as 'the misshapen progeny of intolerable draftsmanship coupled to wholly mistaken economic theory' (Bork, RH, *The Antitrust Paradox: A Policy at War with Itself* (1993) The Free Press).

[8] See DOJ, *GJM*, at VII-77. This dynamic may affect the criminal proceedings. The fact that when Grand Jury proceedings are concluded 'plaintiffs will frequently request access to grand jury materials such as documents and transcripts' undoubtedly puts pressure on defendants to consider carefully whether a plea agreement (see below) may minimise the amount of material that becomes available to civil claimants. The Division has indicated that it will inform a relevant court where disclosure 'does not interfere with any ongoing investigation or prosecution'. Further, the Division's policy is 'not to file matters under seal during pretrial criminal proceedings so that the public, including plaintiffs who believe that they have suffered damages, may have access to the public record' (ibid at 77–78).

[9] *GJM*, at VII-78.

Baker has stated that both '[a]ntitrust liberals and conservatives in the US agree that cartels are bad at any level . . . and that severely punishing the individuals who conspire is critical to discouraging potential conspirators in the future'.[10] This pattern is reflected also in the legislative history of US antitrust law. Thorelli has demonstrated the extent to which the legislature in the US enacted the Sherman Act in the belief that, to a substantial degree, it was merely codifying existing principles of common law inherited from the English.[11] The Antitrust Bill, as first introduced to Congress by Senator John Sherman,[12] provided in section 3:

> [t]hat all persons entering into any such arrangement, contract, agreement, trust, or combination described in section one of this Act, either on his own

---

[10] Baker, DI, 'Punishment for Cartel Participants in the US: A Special Model?', in Beaton-Wells, C, and Ezrachi, A (eds), *Criminalising Cartels: Critical Studies of an International Regulatory Movement* (2011) Hart Publishing at 27.

[11] Thorelli, HB, *The Federal Antitrust Policy* (1955) Johns Hopkins University Press. See also Letwin, WL, 'Congress and the Sherman Antitrust Law: 1887–1890' (1955–1956) 23 *University of Chicago Law Review* 221; Peritz, RJR, *Competition Policy in America 1888–1992: History, Rhetoric, Law* (1996) Oxford University Press at 9–58; and Clark, JD, *The Federal Trust Policy* (1931) Johns Hopkins University Press. Senator Sherman's Bill, introduced before the 51st Congress, 1st Session (December 4, 1889), provided, in its first clause, the following:

> *Be it enacted by the Senate and House of Representatives of the United States of America in Congress assembled,* That all arrangements, contracts, agreements, trusts, or combinations between persons or corporations made with a view, or which tend, to prevent full and free competition . . . or which tend, to advance the cost to the consumer of any of such articles, are hereby declared to be against public policy, unlawful and void.

Introducing his bill, Sherman stated that:

> [i]t declares that certain contracts are against public policy, null and void. It does not announce a new principle of law, but applies old and well-recognized principles of the common law to the complicated jurisdiction of our State and Federal Government ((1890) 21 *Cong. Rec.* 3: 2456, quoted in Thorelli, at 181).

Letwin does not contradict Thorelli, but does argue that the position with regard to the *intention* of Congress (rather than the form that intention took) is a complex matter:

> [t]he deceptive simplicity of the Sherman Act has led many historians to believe that the intention of Congress was equally simple. . . . But the process by which laws are made in the American democracy is not so direct and obvious. Congress does not merely enact its private dogmas, nor does it simply supply whatever the people order (at 221).

[12] Letwin, note 11, provides a pen-portrait of Senator Sherman at 249: '. . . he was aging, at times impatient and confused, but still the most prominent and esteemed Republican in Congress'.

> account or as agent or attorney for another . . . or in any capacity whatever, shall be guilty of a high misdemeanor, and, on conviction thereof in any district or circuit court of the United States, shall be subject to a fine of not more than ten thousand dollars, or to imprisonment in the penitentiary for a term of not more than five years, or to both such fine and imprisonment, in the discretion of the court. . . .

As originally enacted, this provision was amended to the extent that the maximum penalty was reduced to a fine of not more than $5000, or to imprisonment not exceeding one year.[13] The Offence, now a felony, was originally stated as being a 'misdemeanor'. The Bill was subject to strong attack, particularly from Senator George, who had introduced his own Bill to deal with combines, which did not make it out of the Committee on Finance. George attacked the constitutionality of the Sherman Bill, and argued further that it was too limited in being directed against agreements alone. There was also criticism of the way the illegality was to be framed:

> [h]e also pointed out the weakness inherent in the fact that to be unlawful the agreements would also have to be made with a certain specified intent. To prove such intent in criminal suits, where intent always must 'be proven to exist beyond a reasonable doubt,' might often present insurmountable difficulties.[14]

A revised version of the Bill, which contained no criminal provisions, was reported to Congress by the Finance Committee on March 18, 1890. Senator Sherman, supporting the Bill on March 21, 1890, stated that every 'corporation engaged in business must be responsible for the tendency of its business . . . but individuals can only be punished for criminal intentions'. The latter would be a 'difficult process' which 'might be well left to the future'.[15] Senator Hoar was in support of greater sanctions, pointing to

---

[13] The maximum penalty was not raised from $5000 to $50 000 until 1955. It has been calculated that fines levied against General Motors and DuPont before the limits were raised amounted to less than one ten-millionth of the net profits earned by them over the periods covered by the indictments (see 'Increasing Community Control over Corporate Crime – a Problem in the Law of Sanctions' (1961–1962) 71 *Yale Law Journal* 280 at 287).

[14] Thorelli, note 11, at 177.

[15] In the same speech Senator Sherman dealt with the issue of intent and the extent to which this could be ascribed to a corporation:

> In providing a remedy the intention of the combination is immaterial. The intention of a corporation can not be proven. If the natural effects of its acts are injurious, if they tend to produce evil results, if their policy is denounced by the law as against the common good, it may be restrained, be punished with a penalty or with damages, and in a proper case it may be deprived of its corporate

a significant disparity between the strong investigatory powers the government would have in its prosecution, and the fact that these could lead only to a civil suit.[16] Senator Reagan, a Texan democrat, had introduced his own Bill directed against trusts on August 14, 1888 which provided, *inter alia*, that any person convicted of the proscribed conduct would be 'guilty of a high misdemeanor', and would be liable to a jail term of 'not more than five years and not less than one year'.[17] This Bill disappeared into the bowels of Committee, but on March 25, 1890, following the debate of March 24, Reagan's Bill was treated as an amendment to the Sherman Bill. Sherman had argued unsuccessfully that Reagan's Bill should not be merged with his own as it was still before the Committee on the Judiciary, and that its criminal penalties were inappropriate. The amendment was adopted by the Senate in Committee of the Whole by a vote of 34 to 12. It was substantially this text, with further amendments, revisions and clarifications, that was reported to Senate on March 27, 1890, and which was then referred to the Judiciary Committee. On April 2, 1890, the Judiciary Committee reported back a version of the Bill which 'was in all respects identical with the measure which was finally enacted into law'.[18] Letwin describes the work in the Judiciary Committee as having been done largely by Senator George Edmunds. The approach taken by Reagan to punishment was maintained.[19] Sherman criticised the revised Bill as 'totally ineffective in dealing with combinations and trusts',[20] yet, along with the majority of his colleagues in Senate, he voted in favour of the Bill, which

---

powers and franchises. It is the tendency of a corporation, and not its intention, that the courts deal with.

16 March 24, 1890, the record of this day's debate is at 21 *Cong. Rec.* 3: 2556–2572.

17 See Thorelli, note 11, at 169–70.

18 Thorelli, note 11, at 199.

19 See Peritz, RJR, note 11, at 26:

> [t]he 1890 bill's combination of civil and criminal penalties passed both chambers without debate, despite its seeming trespass of property rights traditionally safeguarded in common-law doctrine and constitutional jurisprudence. Apparently, the statute presented a synthesis of sorts: common-law categories of liability joined to radically new remedies. The Sherman Act created a mechanism for socialising common-law liability beyond the contractarian limits of 'actual' injury seen in contract cases and of judicial refusals to enforce agreements in restraint of trade. In short, the statute authorised both public and private exercise of something akin to a 'police power' to enforce common-law standards of commercial conduct.

20 Quoted in Letwin, WL, note 11, at 255.

continues to bear his name. The Bill was signed into law by President Harrison, becoming law on July 2, 1890.

In 1974, a year in which a number of significant changes were made to the US antitrust regime, violations of the Sherman Act became felonies, rather than misdemeanours, and fines were increased to $1m for corporations, and $100 000 for individuals.[21] Section 14 of the Clayton Act 1914[22] set out the misdemeanour penalties applicable to corporate officers who are found to have participated in antitrust violations. Since 1974 this charge has not been used, and the policy of the DOJ Antitrust Division is that all criminal cases that it brings shall be prosecuted as felonies.[23] In 1984 the Criminal Fines Enforcement Act (which was repealed in 1987) increased the maximum fines payable by individuals to $250 000. The Sentencing Reform Act of 1984 gave rise to further amendments and led eventually to the introduction of new sentencing guidelines in 1987. Also in 1987 the Criminal Fines Improvement Act restated the 'alternative sentencing' provision, under which fines may be set in relation to profits gained or losses caused.[24] In 1990 the Antitrust Amendments Act raised penalties again and in 2004 the Antitrust Criminal Penalty Enhancement and Reform Act increased the penalties available for criminal antitrust violations, and also offered financial incentives for informants.[25] This

---

[21] See the Antitrust Procedures and Penalties Act, 1974. President Ford had called for the measure, and in Senate the Bill was passed by a vote of 92 to 0. Baker has suggested that this was in part a response to the operation of the OPEC cartel, and to public frustration with inflationary pressures, but has noted that there was 'very little public debate' at the time of the change (Baker, DI, 'The Use of Criminal Law Remedies to Deter and Punish Cartels and Bid-Rigging' (2000–2001) 69 *George Washington Law Review* 693 at 695). See Werden, GJ, Hammond, SD, and Barnett, BA, 'Deterrence and Detection of Cartels: Using All the Tools and Sanctions' (2011) 56:2 *Antitrust Bulletin* 207 at 220: '[t]he 1974 legislation began a long-term upward trend in the frequency with which convicted individuals have been sentenced to prison and in the average length of their sentences'.

[22] 15 USC §24.

[23] See, for example, DOJ, *GJM*, at VII-38.

[24] 18 USC §3571(d) provides that:

> If any person derives pecuniary gain from the offense, or if the offense results in pecuniary loss to a person other than the defendant, the defendant may be fined not more than the greater of twice the gross gain or twice the gross loss, unless imposition of a fine under this subsection would unduly complicate or prolong the sentencing process.

[25] See generally Harrison, G, and Bell, M, 'Recent Enhancements in Antitrust Criminal Enforcement: Bigger Sticks and Sweeter Carrots' (2005–2006) 6 *Houston Business and Tax Law Journal* 206. See also Bennett, DJ, 'Killing One Bird with Two Stones: The Effect of *Empagran* and the Antitrust Criminal Penalty

brought in the current maximum prison sentences of ten years, corporate fines of up to $100m, and personal fines of $1m. A revision of the sentencing guidelines was effected to reflect these higher penalties. One of the major changes introduced by the 2004 legislation was to remove the threat of treble-damages awards in subsequent civil litigation from those companies who benefited from full leniency under the DOJ amnesty programme (discussed below).[26]

THE FELONY

The text of section 1 of the Sherman Act has been set out above. In summary, every arrangement falling within its terms is a 'felony'.[27] However, Congress left a lot open to interpretation, and the courts have had to provide definitions of the various terms of s 1. Although s 1 makes reference to contracts, combinations and conspiracies, there is no substantial consequence that flows from these categories of form (thus for example indictments and informations may refer to a particular anti-competitive arrangement as proceeding by way of combination or conspiracy), although there has been substantial case law relating to the evidence required to establish a conspiracy in cases arising in oligopoly markets exhibiting parallelism.

The most significant development has been the creation of the 'rule of reason'[28] and the '*per se*' rule, which serve now to put a constraint on what

---

Enhancement and Reform Act of 2004 on Detecting and Deterring International Cartels' (2004–2005) 93 *Georgetown Law Journal* 1421.

[26] See section 213(a) of the 2004 Act. Those benefiting from amnesty remain liable to single damages payments.

[27] Although the UK's substantive law, discussed in the following chapter, is framed in a very different way to the US law, the end result in terms of determining what may be treated as a criminal violation is very similar. This much was acknowledged in discussions relating to the extent to which extradition could be effected from the UK into the US at the time the legislation was being enacted. Extradition requires 'dual criminality', which is to say that the offence alleged in the US would also have had to constitute an offence in the UK were the conduct to have been entered into in the UK. It was stated by the Undersecretary of State that following the introduction of the Cartel Offence the US would likely be able to extradite in respect of s 1 cases. For the US approach to extradition generally see Snow, TG, 'The Investigation and Prosecution of White Collar Crime: International Challenges and the Legal Tools Available to Address Them' (2002–2003) 11 *William & Mary Bill of Rights Journal* 209.

[28] The rule of reason was first set out in *Standard Oil Co v United States* 221 US 1 (1911), and was more fully clarified in *Chicago Board of Trade v United*

may be prosecuted as a criminal act. The treatment of specific categories of conduct, and their inclusion within or without the *per se* rule, has varied over time. In relation to infringements which may be characterised as 'hard-core': horizontal price-fixing; horizontal market-sharing; and bid-rigging,[29] there has been broad consistency, although even this is not true of the early period of enforcement. In general 'an unreasonable restraint is one that raises price, reduces output, diminishes quality, limits choice, or creates, maintains, enhances, or preserves market power'.[30]

A *per se* violation arises in respect of a practice that 'facially appears to be one that would always or almost always tend to restrict competition and decrease output'.[31] Where action is brought against a practice falling within the *per se* rule it is not necessary for there to be an analysis as to the effects of the practice in the particular case. The courts have held that such sensitive analysis is not required as there would be a sufficiently unlikely probability that mitigating benefits 'are not sufficiently common or important to justify the time and expense necessary to identify them'.[32] A further consequence of the treatment accorded to *per se* violations of the Sherman Act is that in order to establish that the offence has been committed, the prosecution has to show only that the defendant participated knowingly in a conspiracy to engage in the condemned activity, not that there was a specific intent to restrain trade. The courts have thus consistently held that proof that the defendant knowingly joined the relevant conspiracy is sufficient to establish that the purpose was to restrain trade.[33]

The categories of conduct falling within the terms of s 1 of the Sherman Act that are condemned *per se* have shifted over time, but have not always been coterminous with that conduct which may be subject to criminal

---

States 246 US 231 (1918) by Justice Brandeis: '[t]he true test of legality is whether the restraint imposed is such as merely regulates and perhaps thereby promotes competition or whether it is such as may suppress or even destroy competition.' The rule of reason is not dealt with further here, as no criminal prosecutions are brought in relation to conduct falling within the rule of reason.

29 For a very early treatment of bid-rigging in the US case law see *Swift & Co v United States* 196 US 375 (1905), in which a number of meat producers agreed not to underbid each other in relation to sales to wholesale stockyards.

30 ABA, Antitrust Section, *Antitrust Law Developments (Sixth)* (2007) American Bar Association, at 47.

31 *Broadcast Music, Inc. v CBS* 441 US 1 (1979), at 19.

32 *Continental TV Inc. v GTE Sylvania Inc.* 433 US 36 (1977) at 50. See ABA, Antitrust Section, note 30, at 52: '[w]hen a restraint is unambiguously in a category where the per se rule has been firmly established, the Supreme Court has not wavered from its application of the rule and has rejected defendants' attempts to proffer justifications for the particular practices at issue.'

33 See, for example, *United States v Koppers Co* 652 F.2d 290 at 294–95.

prosecution. It was only recently that the Supreme Court, in *Leegin*,[34] moved resale price maintenance ('RPM') from the *per se* prohibition to the rule of reason category, meaning that *no* vertical arrangements fall within the *per se* rule. Even while RPM was deemed to be unlawful *per se*, criminal cases were not being brought to enforce the rule, and in recent decades the DOJ has focussed its criminal enforcement efforts on hard-core cartel arrangements. The treatment and categorisation of these infringements has been, after an initial unsettled period, generally consistent. As noted above, the first case in which bid-rigging was condemned was dealt with as early as 1905, and while there was initial uncertainty as to how to deal with horizontal price-fixing and market-sharing, the fact that these would be prohibited became clear after 1911, and there was already in some cases condemnation before the *Standard Oil* judgment.[35]

Price-Fixing and Bid-Rigging

At the time of writing, the position is that the courts 'treat certain agreements as illegal per se with virtually no factual enquiry . . . naked price-fixing, bid-rigging, and market allocation'.[36] The leading case in relation to horizontal price-fixing is *Trenton Potteries*,[37] in which the Supreme Court held that irrespective as to the level of the fixed price, price-fixing agreements are to be treated as being *per se* illegal. The Court was emphatic in its denunciation:

> [t]he aim and result of every price-fixing agreement, if effective, is the elimination of one form of competition. The power to fix prices, whether reasonably exercised or not, involves power to control the market and to fix arbitrary and

---

[34] *Leegin Creative Leather Products v PSKS Inc.* 127 S Ct 763 (2006).

[35] It is relevant to the early development of the law that the distinction between horizontal and vertical forms of competition was not regarded as important. See for example Peritz, RJR, note 11, at 34:

> . . . classical political economy made no distinction between horizontal and vertical dimensions. Competition was understood as both vertical and horizontal, as involving rivalry not only among sellers but also between buyers and sellers. In the years surrounding the Sherman Act legislative debates, economist Francis Walker's *Political Economy*, well known and widely disseminated, defined competition as 'the operation of individual self-interest, among buyers and sellers.' This view, still respectable for the next three decades, was explicitly adopted in several influential dissenting opinions written by a well-informed Justice Holmes.

[36] ABA, Antitrust Section, note 30, at 55 (internal footnotes omitted).

[37] *United States v Trenton Potteries Co* 273 US 392 (1927).

> unreasonable prices. The reasonable price fixed today may through economic and business changes become the unreasonable price of tomorrow. Once established, it may be maintained unchanged because of the absence of competition secured by the agreement for a price reasonable when fixed. Agreements which create such potential power may well be held to be in themselves unreasonable or unlawful restraints, without the necessity of minute inquiry whether a particular price is reasonable or unreasonable as fixed and without placing on the government in enforcing the Sherman Law the burden of ascertaining from day to day whether it has become unreasonable through the mere variation of economic conditions.[38]

The rule applies in relation to all horizontal price-fixing unless the price-fixing takes the form of an 'ancillary restraint', operating as a necessary part of an agreement that falls within the rule of reason and is pro-competitive.[39] The courts have taken a wide view as to what constitutes a 'price', and the *per se* principle extends, *inter alia*, to agreements to restrict discounts,[40] to set standard trade-in conditions,[41] restrict advertising,[42] and to set credit conditions.[43] It is irrelevant whether the prices that are agreed horizontally are minimum prices or maximum prices. Thus, for example, in *Kiefer-Stewart Co v Joseph E Seagram & Sons*[44] the Supreme Court held, when dealing with maximum price-fixing agreements, that these 'no less than those to fix minimum prices, cripple the freedom of traders and thereby restrain their ability to sell in accordance with their own judgment'.[45] It is common practice for the DOJ to use its criminal prosecutorial powers when taking action against price-fixing agreements.

There are very limited circumstances in which horizontal price-fixing agreements have been held *not* to be caught by the *per se* rule.[46] In one case relating to the rules of a professional body, which included a restriction on its members from discussing prices with potential customers until such time as a service provider had been finally selected, the Court paid

---

38 At 397–98.

39 See, for example, *NCAA v Board of Regents* 468 US 85 (1984).

40 *United States v American Radiator & Standard Sanitary Corp* 433 F.2d 174 (3d Cir. 1970).

41 *Plymouth Dealers' Assn v United States* 279 F.2d 128 (9th Cir. 1960).

42 *Blackburn v Sweeney* 53 F.3d 825 (7th Cir. 1995).

43 *Catalano Inc. v Target Sales* 446 US 643 (1980) (*per curiam*).

44 340 US 211 (1951).

45 At 213.

46 This may provide support for the UK's position of making *all* such arrangements subject to the Cartel Offence, while recognising the role of prosecutorial discretion, and placing limits on those who can bring prosecutions forward (see Chapter 4, below) as an appropriate one.

careful attention to the context within which the rules operated, before determining that it *was* appropriate to apply the *per se* rule.[47] The Court *has* held that some agreements which clearly do fix prices are to be analysed carefully as the *per se* rule might not apply. This was the case, for example, in *Broadcast Music v CBS*[48] in which there was in place a blanket licence agreement under which holders of copyright in music accepted a commonly agreed fee for the use of their compositions. The Court held that this created a useful new mechanism, the efficiency of which took the agreement out of the *per se* category.[49]

The *per se* analysis is *not* applied to horizontal agreements to exchange price information, with such agreements being analysed under the rule of reason,[50] as was the case in *United States v Container Corp of America*,[51] and *United States v United States Gypsum Co.*[52] In the former case the Court emphasised that it was the competitive impact of the exchange that rendered the arrangement *per se* unlawful, holding that the exchange of such information in an oligopolistic industry 'had an anti-competitive effect in the industry, chilling the vigour of price competition'.[53] Only where the information exchange is part of a wider price-fixing arrangement is criminal enforcement and condemnation likely.

Bid-rigging is treated by the courts as a special category of price-fixing, and there are a large number of cases in which the courts have held that

---

47 *National Society of Professional Engineers v United States* 435 US 679 (1978). The Court held, at 692–93:

> [w]hile this is not price fixing as such, no elaborate industry analysis is required to demonstrate the anti-competitive character of such an agreement. It operates as an absolute ban on competitive bidding, applying with equal force to both complicated and simple projects and to both inexperienced and sophisticated customers. . . . On its face, this agreement restrains trade within the meaning of s 1 of the Sherman Act.

48 *Broadcast Music, Inc. v CBS* 441 US 1 (1979).

49 See also *United States v Brown University* 5 F.3d 658 (3d Cir. 1993) in which the Court rejected a Government attempt to prosecute as a *per se* violation an arrangement between a number of private universities relating to the scholarships which would be offered. The Court held that the agreement was not one whose purpose was to achieve 'pure profit maximization', and that a full rule of reason inquiry was appropriate.

50 The wording of s 188 of the Enterprise Act, which makes it a criminal offence to 'directly or *indirectly* fix a price' (emphasis added), may also extend to the exchange of price information, although this has not yet been tested.

51 393 US 333 (1969).

52 438 US 422 (1978).

53 At 337.

conspiracies to submit pre-arranged bids are *per se* violations of the Sherman Act. The courts have condemned the discussion and comparing of bids before they are submitted, systems of rotating bids,[54] agreements whereby parties would refrain from bidding,[55] and agreements to submit excessively high bids even where the bidding party had determined unilaterally not to take on the contract.[56] A relatively large proportion of the purely domestic anti-competitive arrangements prosecuted in the US as s 1 violations relate to bid-rigging, and there have also been some cases of international cartels which have involved bid-rigging in the US.

A similar approach is taken in relation to horizontally agreed output restrictions, in that '[b]ecause economics teaches that an agreement to limit output is tantamount to an agreement to fix price, courts also have applied the *per se* rule to agreements to limit production or set quotas'.[57] The law has been applied to agreements to discontinue production in a case related to plumbing suppliers who agreed to eliminate the production of a reduced-price range,[58] and in *Macaroni* an agreement by macaroni manufacturers to limit the durum wheat content of macaroni, thereby reducing the demand and price for durum wheat was condemned.[59]

Market Sharing and Customer Allocation

The courts treat market-sharing and customer-allocation agreements as if they were output restrictions, and they are *per se* illegal. Thus, for example, in *Blue Cross*[60] the court held that

> [t]he analogy between price-fixing and division of markets is compelling. It would be a strange interpretation of antitrust law that forbade competitors to

---

[54] See, for example, *United States v Portsmouth Paving Corporation* 694 F.2d 312 (4th Cir. 1982).

[55] See, for example, *United States v MMR Corporation* 909 F.2d 489 (5th Cir. 1990).

[56] See, for example, *United States v WF Brinkley & Son Construction Co* 783 F.2d 1157 (4th Cir. 1986).

[57] ABA, Antitrust Section, *Antitrust Law Developments (Sixth)* (2007), American Bar Association, note 30, at 86. See, for example, *United States v Andreas* 216 F.3d 645 (7th Cir. 2000) – one of the personal criminal prosecutions arising out of the ADM lysine cartel, discussed in Chapter 6, below.

[58] *United States v American Radiator & Standard Sanitary Corp* 433 F.2d 174 (3d Cir. 1970).

[59] *National Macaroni Manufacturers Association v FTC* 345 F.2d 421 (7th Cir. 1965).

[60] *Blue Cross & Blue Shield United v Marshfield Clinic* 65 F.3d 1406 (7th Cir, 1995).

> agree on what price to charge, thus eliminating price competition among them, but allowed them to divide markets, thus eliminating all competition among them.[61]

As early as 1899 the court had held that the allocation of markets necessarily restrained interstate commerce and invited condemnation.[62] In *Sealy*[63] and *Topco*[64] the Supreme Court took a robust approach where territorial restrictions were imposed in the context of joint-venture arrangements. In *Sealy*, two bedding manufacturers created a subsidiary joint venture which entered into a marketing arrangement with the parent companies under which each was licensed the right to sell products bearing the relevant trademark in specific territories. The Court held that this was 'unlawful under s 1 of the Sherman Act without the necessity for an inquiry in each particular case as to their business or economic justification, their impact in the marketplace, or their unreasonableness'.[65] In *Topco* a group of independent retail chains formed a cooperative association to engage in joint purchasing and the development of an own-label brand for its members. Members of the association were licensed the right to sell products bearing the Topco brand in specified territories. The district court had analysed the arrangement under the rule of reason, but the Supreme Court took the view that the case was one of *per se* illegality, and that it was equivalent to *Sealy*, holding that '[o]ne of the classic examples of a per se violation of s 1 is an agreement between competitors at the same level of the market structure to allocate territories in order to minimise competition'.[66] The Court also found to be illegal that part of the arrangement which prevented the retailers from selling the own-label goods to wholesalers, thus treating customer restrictions agreed horizontally as a *per se* violation. Parties do not have to be competitors in a particular geographic market, or in

---

61 At 1415.

62 *Addyston Pipe & Steel Co v United States* 175 US 211 (1899).

63 *United States v Sealy, Inc.* 388 US 350 (1967).

64 *United States v Topco Associates* 405 US 596 (1972). The Supreme Court has never overruled *Sealy* and *Topco*, but some lower courts have held that in light of *Broadcast Music, Inc. v CBS* 441 US 1 (1979), *NCAA v Board of Regents* 468 US 85 (1984), and *Northwest Wholesale Stationers v Pacific Stationery & Printing Co* 472 US 284 (1985) the principles enunciated in *Sealy* and *Topco* are no longer good law. In *Rothery Storage & Van Co v Atlas Van Lines* 792 F.2d 210 (DC Cir. 1986) the court argued that both cases dealt with ancillary restraints that were not naked, and suggested that more recent cases had indicated that both *Sealy* and *Topco* would now be discussed under the rule of reason. It is clear however that *naked* territorial and customer restrictions are *per se* unlawful.

65 At 357–58.

66 At 608.

respect of particular customers, for a market allocation agreement to be unlawful. Thus in *Palmer v BRG of Georgia Inc*[67] the Supreme Court held *per se* unlawful an agreement relating to the division of markets in which the parties did not at present compete: 'agreements are anti-competitive regardless of whether the parties split a market within which they both do business or whether they merely reserve one market for one and another for the other'.[68]

Where horizontal market and customer allocation arrangements are ancillary to another arrangement, such as a pro-competitive economic activity integration, they may be treated under the rule of reason.

THE EXPERIENCE OF ENFORCEMENT IN THE UNITED STATES

Early Case Law

The record of government success in early cases brought under s 1 of the Sherman Act was somewhat shaky. The first criminal case[69] brought under the Sherman Act was a failure for the Government, and demonstrates how far the position has changed in the last 120 years. *United States v Nelson et al*[70] was a case in which a number of dealers in lumber were indicted under s 1 for an alleged price-fixing conspiracy. A demurrer was sustained on the grounds that the defendants did not together control the market, and the court held that absent this market power, or the application of fraudulent methods (it did not appear to be the case that in 1892 the Court considered a price-fixing conspiracy to be by its very nature fraudulent), competition could be guaranteed to bring the prices down. The second criminal case brought under s 1, *US v Patterson et al*,[71] was also a failure for the government, with a case brought against a number of participants in the cash register business being dropped after part of it was quashed by the court, and after a settlement was reached with a number of competitors whose complaints had led to the instigation of the action. It is remarkable that

---

67 498 US 46 (1990) (*per curiam*).

68 At 49–50.

69 The very first case, *US v Jellico Mountain Coal and Coke Co et al* 43 Fed. 898 (1891), was a suit in equity.

70 52 Fed. 646 (1892). Although it is no longer the case, in the early period of the enforcement of the Sherman Act cases under s 2 were also brought on indictment. In this book only s 1 cases are dealt with.

71 55 Fed. 605 (1893).

the first case in which the Government was successful under s 1 is one in which a temporary injunction was granted to restrain the conduct of an organisation of trade unions.[72] The most significant early case was that of *US v Trans-Missouri Freight Association*[73] in which the Supreme Court held, on a case brought by way of a bill of equity, that s 1 applied to *every* restraint of trade. Justice Peckham, delivering the majority opinion, stated that:

> [a] contract may be in restraint of trade and still be valid at common law. Although valid, it is nevertheless a contract in restraint of trade, and would be so described either at common law or elsewhere. By the simple use of the term 'contract in restraint of trade,' all contracts of that nature, whether valid or otherwise, would be included . . . When, therefore, the body of an Act pronounces as illegal every contract or combination in restraint of trade . . . the plain and ordinary meaning of such language is not limited to that kind of contract alone which is in unreasonable restraint of trade.[74]

This somewhat changed the approach of the lower courts, and by the early 1900s, as was for example the case in *US v Chesapeake and Ohio Fuel Co*,[75] the Government began to have greater success in its cases, and was able, in *United States v Federal Salt Co*,[76] to secure a Grand Jury indictment, and a preliminary injunction, followed by a guilty plea and the imposition of a fine of $1000. The Court adopted an inflexible, 'literary', approach to the meaning of 'in restraint of trade' in *Trans-Missouri*, and it is perhaps not surprising that following this, challenged arrangements were more often found to be in breach of the law. This changed with the Supreme Court

[72] *United States v Workingmen's Amalgamated Council of New Orleans et al* 54 Fed. 994 (1893).

[73] 166 US 290 (1897).

[74] 166 US 308 at 328. See Peritz, RJR, note 11, at 29:

> [the Court] first formulated its Literalist interpretation of the Sherman Act in the *Trans-Missouri Freight Association* decision (1897), which reversed the federal district and circuit courts, both in their holdings and in their reasoning. These lower court judges were simply following the uniform practice of their peers, treating the statute as a congressional grant of jurisdiction to develop a federal common law. The doctrines of monopolisation and restraint of trade, were understood as requiring judges to determine the 'reasonableness' of trusts, cartels, and other restraints of trade.

[75] 105 Fed. 93 (1902). Although dealing with a different market, the situation in the case was similar to that of earlier cases, such as *Jellico Mountain Coal* (note 69) where the Government had been unsuccessful.

[76] (1902) and (1903), unreported (see Thorelli, HB, note 11, at 444).

judgment in *Standard Oil*,[77] which introduced the 'rule of reason' into the US antitrust lexicon (see above).

Heavy Electrical Equipment

Until the lysine (Archer Daniels Midland) and vitamins cases in the 1990s, both of which are discussed in Chapter 6, below, the most significant criminal case was that brought in relation to heavy electrical equipment in 1961 (sometimes termed the *General Electric* case, although there were 29 separate corporate defendants),[78] which 'focussed attention on American business practices as nothing else [had] in many years'.[79] Hay and Kelley suggest that the related cases 'seem to have done more for the enforcement of Section 1 than all of the cases prosecuted before them'.[80] At the time there was still sufficient doubt as to liability that GE's lawyers told the Executive Office that '[t]he trend of the law *appears to be* that a business corporation will be held criminally liable for the acts of an employee as

---

77 *Standard Oil Co v United States* 221 US 1 (1911).

78 See generally Walton, C, and Cleveland, F, *Corporations on Trial: The Electric Cases* (1964) Wadsworth Publishing; Heilbroner, RL, et al, *In the Name of Profit* (1972) Doubleday, and Geis, G, 'White Collar Crime: The Heavy Electrical Equipment Antitrust Cases of 1961', in Ermann, MD, and Lundman, RJ, *Corporate and Governmental Deviance: Problems of Organizational Behavior in Contemporary Society* (1978) Oxford University Press, at 59–79. See also Smith, RA, 'The Incredible Electrical Conspiracy' (1961) *Fortune*, April, at 132, and May, at 161; Watkins, MW, 'Electrical Equipment Antitrust Cases: Their Implications for Government and for Business' (1961) 29:1 *University of Chicago Law Review* 97; Neal, PC, and Goldberg, P, 'The Electrical Equipment Antitrust Cases: Novel Judicial Administration' (1964) 50 *ABA Journal* 621; 'Note' (1961–1962) 71 *Yale Law Journal* 280. The case was also discussed in some detail in a subsequent report by the Senate Committee on the Judiciary, Subcommittee on Antitrust and Monopoly (1961) 87th Cong. 2d Sess, 'Administered Prices'. It is curious, and perhaps symptomatic of the times, that at least one economist argued that in the relevant markets 'price competition [was] not appropriate' (Richardson, GB, 'The Pricing of Heavy Electrical Equipment: Competition or Agreement?' (1966) 28:2 *Bulletin of the Oxford University Institute of Economics & Statistics* 73 at 78.

79 Smith, RA, 'The Incredible Electrical Conspiracy' (1961) *Fortune*, May, 161 at 224. This was *not* the first case in which jail sentences had been handed down in respect of a s 1 violation. Although the practice of imposing fines only on those who entered pleas of *nolo contendere* had become so entrenched that some thought it to be a matter of law, only five months before the electrical cases a court had sentenced four company officers to terms in prison of 90 days each (*United States v McDonough Co* (1959) Trade Cas ¶69482, at 75887–88 (SD Ohio Oct 13, 1959)).

80 Hay, GA, and Kelley, D, 'An Empirical Survey of Price Fixing Conspiracies' (1974) *Journal of Law and Economics* 13 at 28.

long as the acts are reasonably related to the area of general responsibility entrusted to him'.[81] The defendants in that case were described as being 'middle-class men in Ivy League suits – typical business men in appearance, who would never be taken for lawbreakers'.[82] Geis quotes the lawyer for one of the defendants arguing that it was 'cold-blooded' on the part of the Government to seek a prison sentence, when his client was a 'fine man' who did not deserve to be put 'behind bars' with 'common criminals who have been convicted of embezzlement and other serious crimes'.[83] The grand juries involved in the investigation handed down 20 indictments, relating to 45 individuals and 29 corporations. The corporations pleaded guilty on most counts, and the majority of officials pleaded *nolo contendere*.[84] At sentencing, fines totalling $1 924 500 were set, with $137 000 falling on individuals.[85] Geis notes however that the impact of the jail terms imposed on seven defendants was more 'eye catching'.[86] Although these were widely reported at the time, and are generally believed to have signalled an important shift in enforcement activity,[87] it is, in light of the enforcement activity in the contemporary period, remarkable that the

---

81 Smith, RA, note 79, at 164 (emphasis added).

82 *New York Times*, Feb 7, 1961, quoted in Geis, G, note 78, at 59.

83 Geis, G, 'White Collar Crime', note 78, at 59.

84 GE's Executive Office had been advised that '[i]f a criminal case can be disposed of by a *nolo* plea, the prospective damage claimant is given no assistance in advancing a claim; it must be built from the ground up' (Smith, RA, note 79, at 165). Smith reported the following:

> . . . in the opinion of one veteran antitrust lawyer, everybody in the industry and 99 percent of the government thought the court would accept *nolos*. Indeed the Justice Department was so worried about the matter, and so anxious to forfend such a development, that for the first time in the history of the department an attorney general sent a presiding judge an affidavit urging rejection of *nolos*' (ibid).

85 Having first resisted claims, the corporations ended up paying in damages amounts considerably greater than the financial penalties. Geis, G, 'White Collar Crime', note 78, at 64, states that by mid-1964 General Electric had paid out $160m, and that at that point not all claims had yet been settled. Neal and Goldberg refer to 1880 private cases brought against the cartel participants by early 1964 (Neal, PC, and Goldberg, P, note 78).

86 Geis, G, 'White Collar Crime', note 78, at 62.

87 See Geis, G, 'Deterring Corporate Crime', in Ermann, MD, and Lundman, RJ, *Corporate and Governmental Deviance: Problems of Organizational Behavior in Contemporary Society* (1978) Oxford University Press, at 293: 'Government attorneys were convinced . . . that the 1961 antitrust prosecutions had been dramatically effective in breaking up price-fixing schemes by many other corporations'.

sentences imposed on seven defendants were only of 30 days each. Geis is eloquent on the treatment accorded to the convicted criminals:

> [t]he defendants sentenced to jail were handled essentially the same as other offenders with similar dispositions. They were handcuffed in pairs in the back seat of an automobile on their way to the Montgomery County Jail in Norristown, Pennsylvania, fingerprinted on entry, and dressed in the standard blue denim uniforms. During their stay, they were described as 'model prisoners,' and several were transferred to the prison farm. The remainder, working an eight-hour day for 30 cents, earned recognition from the warden as 'the most intelligent prisoners' he had had during the year on a project concerned with organizing prison records. None of the seven men had visitors during the Wednesday and Saturday periods reserved for visiting; all indicated a desire not to be seen by their families or friends.[88]

While the participants in the conspiracy had clearly gone to great lengths to ensure that they were not detected,[89] and had not anticipated detection, it was also clear that many were deeply aggrieved to be labelled 'criminal'. In the words of Geis:

> [a] not inconsiderable number of the defendants took the line that their behaviour, while technically criminal, had really served a worthwhile purpose by 'stabilizing prices' . . . This altruistic interpretation almost invariably was combined with an attempted distinction among illegal, criminal, and immoral acts, with the offender expressing the view that what he had done might have been designated by the statutes as criminal, but either he was unaware of such a designation or he thought it was unreasonable that acts with admirable consequences should be considered criminal. The testimony of a Westinghouse executive during hearings by the Senate Subcommittee on Antitrust and Monopoly clearly illustrates this point of view:
>
> *Committee Attorney*: Did you know that these meetings with competitors were illegal?
>
> *Witness:* Illegal? Yes, but not criminal. I didn't find that out until I read the indictment. . . . I assumed that criminal action meant damaging someone, and we did not do that. . . . I thought that we were more or less working on a survival basis in order to try to make enough to keep our plant and our employees.[90]

---

88 Geis, G, 'White Collar Crime', note 78, at 63.

89 See Geis, G, 'White Collar Crime', note 78, at 65:

> [a]nother went into some detail concerning the techniques of concealment: '. . . it was considered discreet not to be too obvious and to minimize telephone calls, to use plain envelopes if mailing material to each other, not to be seen together on travelling, and so forth . . . not to leave wastepaper, of which there was a lot, strewn around a room when leaving'.

90 Geis, G, 'White Collar Crime', note 78, at 67.

Of particular interest in the context of the debate surrounding the efficacy of imprisonment in relation to cartel conduct are the comments of a former GE vice-president who was questioned about his views of his conduct by the subcommittee. Quoting from Geis again: '[t]he taint of a jail sentence, he said, had the effect of making people "start looking at the moral values a little bit"'. He

> ultimately came to the point of saying that the consequences visited upon him represented the major reason for a re-evaluation of his actions. He would not behave in the same manner again because of what 'I have been through and what I have done to my family'.[91]

The Modern Cases

While it appeared that the Electrical Equipment cases had a significant influence in the decisions of firms in the US to increase compliance with antitrust law,[92] the impact of the case diminished over time, and although criminal enforcement continued, there were few such high-profile cases until the DOJ reinvigorated the area in the 1990s with the prosecutions in the lysine cartel involving in particular Archer Daniels Midland ('ADM'). This case is discussed in Chapter 6, below. The lysine prosecutions were followed by a substantial increase in criminal enforcement, and in particular of enforcement directed at international cartels, with fines paid by firms and by individuals increasing significantly, and with a dramatically increased recourse to incarceration. In respect of a significant proportion of enforcement cases brought against international cartels, the EU has also taken enforcement action, and in some cases enforcement efforts have spread around the world. There have been a small number of cases in which US enforcement efforts have impacted on UK participants: in one case the US has been successful in securing the extradition of a UK national who resisted US jurisdiction;[93] in *Marine Hose*, which is discussed

---

91 Geis, G, 'White Collar Crime', note 78, at 75.

92 See, for a discussion of compliance mechanisms at the time, Whiting, RA, 'Antitrust and the Corporate Executive' (1962) 48:1 *Virginia Law Review* 1.

93 Ian Norris was Chairman of the Carbon Division at Morgan Crucible Company plc ('MCC'). MCC was active in the market for various carbon products, including carbon brushes used in electrical motors. Along with a number of competitors MCC was involved in a price-fixing cartel in Europe. In the mid-1990s this cartel was expanded to bring the US within its sphere of operation, and it was alleged that Mr Norris played a vital role in the price-fixing arrangements. Norris was indicted by a federal grand jury sitting in the Eastern District of Pennsylvania on September 28, 2004. He was charged with conspiring to fix prices in respect of

extensively in Chapters 4 and 6, below, the prosecuting authorities reached a plea agreement with three UK executives; and in another case British Airways pleaded guilty to a s 1 violation and paid a penalty of $300m following its participation in a price-fixing arrangement with Virgin Atlantic

---

certain carbon products sold in the US in violation of s 1 of the Sherman Act. The US sought extradition from the UK, basing its application on the fact that the breach of s 1 of the Sherman Act was equivalent to the common law offence of conspiracy to defraud. This application was ultimately rejected by the UK courts on the grounds in part that the enactment of the Cartel Offence demonstrated that the UK common law did not have the same reach as section 1 of the Sherman Act (*R v Bow Street Metropolitan Magistrate, ex p Government of the United* States [2002] AC 21, on appeal *Norris v United States* [2008] UKHL 16). See, for example, Joshua, JM, 'Extradition: The DOJ's New Foreign Policy Weapon' (2005) June, *Competition Law Insight* 12; and see also Shaffer, GC, and Nesbitt, NH, 'Criminalizing Cartels: A Global Trend?' (2011) 12 *Sedona Conference Journal*; *Minnesota Legal Studies Research Paper No 11-26* (2011) University of Minnesota, School of Law). However, Mr Norris had also been charged with three additional counts by the grand jury:

> . . . in Count 2, with conspiring, in violation of 18 USC §371, to corruptly persuade and attempt to corruptly persuade other persons with intent to influence their testimony in an official proceeding, and to corruptly persuade and attempt to corruptly persuade other persons to alter, destroy, mutilate, or conceal documents with the intent to impair their availability for use in an official proceeding. . . . Counts 3 and 4 charged Norris with corruptly persuading and attempting to corruptly persuade other persons with intent to influence their testimony in an official proceeding in violation of 18 USC §1512(b)(1), and corruptly persuading other persons to alter, destroy, mutilate, or conceal documents with the intent to impair their availability for use in an official proceeding in violation of 18 USC §1512(b)(2)(B).

Mr Norris was extradited on the basis of Counts 2–4 on March 23, 2010 under the terms of the UK Order for Extradition Pursuant to Section 93(4) of the Extradition Act 2003 (September 22, 2008). Norris was convicted of conspiracy to obstruct justice (Count 2) on July 27, 2010 and was sentenced to 18 months' imprisonment, followed by three years' supervised release, and a $25 000 fine. Norris subsequently appealed. The case is illustrative of the efforts that cartel participants may go to in order to obstruct the detection of their activity, and to limit the evidence that may become available to investigators. See, for example, the brief for the US in *US v Ian P Norris*, Court of Appeals, 3rd Cir (February 11, 2011, No 10-4658):

> **Norris Initiates a 'Clean Up' of Morgan's Files**
> Norris also took steps to ensure that Morgan's incriminating documents would not be produced in the grand jury investigation. Shortly after the grand jury subpoena was issued, Norris asked Kroef if it was time to do another 'check' on Morgan's sales files. Morgan and its competitors had long been careful to store any documents related to their European cartel meetings offsite, but occasionally Morgan employees would make notes about prices they learned

(see Chapter 4, below); a British Airways executive subsequently served a jail term in the US.

The Department of Justice, Antitrust Division, continues to act vigorously against s 1 'hard core' breaches. In September 2011, for example, Furukawa Electric Co Ltd, a supplier of wire harnesses and related products for the car industry, pleaded guilty to price-fixing and bid-rigging charges. The company, whose anti-competitive conduct was investigated by the DOJ and the FBI, agreed to pay a fine of $200m, and three of its executives, non-US citizens, agreed to serve prison sentences ranging from one year and a day to 18 months. The DOJ stated in its press release of September 29, 2011, that the conspiracy had resulted in US manufacturers paying higher prices for the parts used in the manufacture of cars sold in the US, and that the action therefore harmed 'an important industry'.

At the same time it has been pointed out that more companies are prosecuted than individuals, suggesting strongly that not all culpable individuals are targeted for prosecution, notwithstanding that the DOJ has stated that prosecution of culpable individuals remains its policy.[94] It has been noted that the DOJ 'does not explain its decisions not to prosecute certain individuals' and that as a result it is not possible 'to be confident that prosecutorial selection does not involve a tendency to select "soft targets" or to avoid prosecuting individuals perceived as likely to engage in prolonged and expensive litigation'.[95]

INVESTIGATION

The factor which perhaps most clearly distinguishes the US and UK criminalisation of competition law is that in the US an action in respect of an unlawful anti-competitive arrangement will either be civil, or criminal.

---

from their competitors on copies of customer inquiries, which were then placed in the regular sales files. . . . Kroef called three other Morgan employees . . . and directed them to visit each of Morgan's European sales offices and review the sales files. 'Every time they found a copy of . . . a quotation to a customer, which had some . . . indication of cartel activities handwritten on them, they would take them out of the file, and throw them away, destroy them' [internal references omitted].

94 See DOJ, *Principles of Federal Prosecution of Business Organizations* (2008) 9 US Attorneys' Manual, at 28.200B.

95 Beaton-Wells, C, and Fisse, B, 'US Policy and Practice in Pursuing Individual Accountability for Cartel Conduct: A Preliminary Critique' (2011) 56 *Antitrust Bulletin* 277 at 287–88.

In no case will both avenues be pursued simultaneously by the public enforcement agency. In the UK this may not be the case, and both civil *and* criminal enforcement may be applied in respect of the same arrangement (as was intended to be the case in *British Airways*). Even in a system offering such a clear split, however, there can still be some work undertaken before the decision is made.

Preliminary Investigation

The DOJ may become aware of potential violations of the Sherman Act through three routes: on its own endeavours; by complaints; or by 'inside' information, obtained from whistle-blowers or leniency applicants.

A preliminary investigation into suspected unlawful competitive conduct may be conducted by the Division when: (1) there is sufficient evidence of a potential violation – as would likely be the case for example if a leniency application had been made; (2) the violation would affect a substantial amount of commerce in the United States; (3) there would not be unnecessary duplication with enforcement efforts conducted by others in the US, and (4) there are sufficient resources to do so. A fuller explanation is given in the *Division Manual* regarding the factors affecting the decision to open a preliminary investigation.[96] A request for the authority to conduct a preliminary investigation should be made, unless the initial evidence is so strong as to merit a move straight to a request for a grand jury proceeding. In the case of potential criminal violations:

---

[96] See Chapter III, Para B.1:

> [t]he first is whether the allegations or suspicions of a criminal violation are sufficiently credible or plausible to call for a criminal investigation. This is a matter of prosecutorial discretion and is based on the experience of the approving officials; legal authorities provide little firm guidance. The second question is whether the matter is significant. Determining which matters are significant is a flexible, matter-by-matter analysis that involves consideration of a number of factors, including the volume of the commerce affected; the breadth of the geographic area impacted (including whether the matter is international); the potential for expansion of the investigation or prosecution from a particular geographic area and industry to an investigation or prosecution in other areas or industries; the deterrent impact and visibility of the investigation or prosecution; the degree of culpability of the conspirators (for example, the duration of the conspiracy, the amount of overcharge, any acts of coercion or discipline of cheaters); and whether the scheme involved fraud on the federal government. . . . The third question – what resources will be required to investigate and prosecute the matter – is asked only for matters that are assessed as having lesser significance; the division is committed to prosecuting all matters of major significance.

> staff should address the background and source of the information presented, the alleged conduct, the significance of the matter, its proposed investigative approach, and past investigations. Staff also should discuss special considerations such as a statute of limitations problem, the presence of a governmental agency as a potential victim, the possible precedential or deterrent impact of the matter, or other legal or factual circumstances relevant to the decision-making process.[97]

At the early stage it may not in fact be clear whether the investigation is to be civil or criminal, and it is not until formal procedures are invoked that a decision must be made. While the categorisation of s 1 violations into the *per se* or rule of reason classes provides a relatively clear framework within which such an assessment can be made, it may not always be automatically obvious that a particular procedure will be used. The normal policy of the DOJ is to proceed by way of criminal investigation and prosecution when cases involve the *per se* infringements discussed above, in particular, price-fixing, bid-rigging, and market division. Civil enforcement is used in respect of cases which fall within the rule of reason rubric, and some conduct that, historically, might have fallen within the *per se* category, but which is now not considered to be at the very harmful end of the spectrum.[98] The Antitrust Division's *Staff Manual* further specifies that there are some cases in which conduct might appear to be *per se* but in respect of which a criminal investigation may not be appropriate. These are situations in which

> (1) the case law is unsettled or uncertain; (2) there are truly novel issues of law or fact presented; (3) confusion reasonably may have been caused by past prosecutorial decisions; or (4) there is clear evidence that the subjects of the investigation were not aware of, or did not appreciate, the consequences of their action.[99]

It is for the DOJ staff to make the decision in the preliminary stages of the investigation whether to proceed under a civil route (through the issuing

---

[97] *Division Manual*, III.B.2.

[98] Where cases are not prosecuted on the basis of criminal law the DOJ may instead proceed by way of a civil injunctive case under s 4A of the Clayton Act 1914 (as is the case, for example, in relation to cases brought under s 2 of the Sherman Act). In some instances a civil injunctive case may be filed alongside an indictment. In such cases the defendant is likely to seek to have the civil case stayed, which, in the words of the DOJ, 'preserves the more restrictive discovery rules of criminal prosecutions' (*GJM*, at VII-75).

[99] DOJ, *Antitrust Division Manual*, 4th edn, at III.B.5. (www.justice.gov/atr/public/divisionmanual).

of Civil Investigative Demands), or under a criminal route (by initiating a grand jury investigation). The *Staff Manual* states however that, in general:

> the nature of the suspected underlying conduct should determine the nature of the investigation. Thus, when the conduct at issue appears to be conduct that the Division generally prosecutes in a criminal case, the investigation should begin as a criminal investigation absent clear evidence that one of the complicating factors that might make the case inappropriate for criminal prosecution is present.

An investigation may involve liaison with other federal agencies, and in particular the cooperation of the Federal Bureau of Investigation ('FBI') may be sought. In the *Marine Hose* cartel investigation (discussed in Chapter 6, below) the cooperation was also sought of agencies of the Department of Defense, via the Inspector General's Office (thus leading to the involvement of the NCIS in the investigation).

Generally the DOJ anticipates that a preliminary investigation will run from 'a few weeks to a few months',[100] after which a final decision should be made either to proceed with a formal civil investigation, to close the investigation, or to open a criminal grand jury investigation.[101]

Grand Jury Proceedings[102]

The first formal stage of a criminal investigation is to convene a grand jury. As noted in the *Division Manual*, the decision to proceed to a grand jury investigation has legal consequences. In particular there are issues arising as to the extent to which evidence obtained via grand jury proceedings can be used in any subsequent criminal proceedings.[103] In order to request that the Division move forward with a grand jury proceeding, the staff involved in the preliminary investigation should prepare a memorandum for the Director of Criminal Enforcement setting out the

---

100 *Division Manual*, III.B.6.

101 In the case of the art-market auction cartel involving Sotheby's and Christie's, for example, the investigation had faltered, and was about to be closed, when Christie's filed an application for leniency, at which point matters moved swiftly to a grand jury investigation.

102 The rules relating to grand jury proceedings may vary from district to district within the US judicial system. I have attempted here to give a general overview which will be consistently accurate.

103 See *United States v Sells Engineering Inc*, 463 US 418 (1983), *United States v Baggott*, 463 US 476 (1983), and *United States v John Doe Inc I*, 481 US 102 (1987).

relevant position. It is noted in the *Division Manual* that although this memorandum may be based on information obtained as a result of a preliminary civil investigation, it will often be the case that 'information received from a complainant provides a sufficient basis for the request without conducting a preliminary investigation'. This will also be the case where an application for leniency has been made. A request for a grand jury investigation should:

- Identify the companies, individuals, industry, and commodity or service involved.
- Estimate the amount of commerce involved on an annual basis.
- Identify the geographic area affected and the judicial district in which the investigation will be conducted.[104]
- Describe the suspected criminal violations, including nonantitrust violations, and summarize the supporting evidence.
- Evaluate the significance of the possible violation from an antitrust enforcement standpoint.
- Explain any unusual issues or potential difficulties staff has identified.
- Identify the attorneys who will be assigned to the investigation.
- Explain the background of the investigation, including the source of the information.
- Explain the initial steps in staff's proposed investigative plan.
- State whether there have been any past criminal investigations by the Division of the product or service that is the subject of the grand jury request.[105]

Once a grand jury investigation is authorised, and a new grand jury empanelled, or the time of an existing grand jury utilised, the investigation can begin in earnest. The primary mechanism by which evidence is obtained by a grand jury is through the subpoena process, and perhaps through the execution of search warrants. Three kinds of subpoenas

---

[104] A grand jury investigation can only be conducted in a judicial district in which either the suspected violation has occurred, or where one of the participants resides or does business. A number of factors may affect the choice of district in which to proceed in the event that there is a choice: (1) the degree of nexus between the suspected violation and the district; (2) convenience for staff and witnesses; (3) the availability of grand jury time; (4) difficulties that may arise in particular districts in conducting grand jury investigations; and (5) the likely districts in which any eventual prosecution would be brought (see *Division Manual*, III.F.1).

[105] *Division Manual*, III.F.1.

may be issued: subpoenas *duces tecum*, which require the production of documentary materials, subpoenas *ad testificandum*, which require testimony to be given, and subpoenas for exemplars, which in antitrust cases most usually take the form of samples of handwriting for comparative purposes. Generally all forms of subpoena allow the recipient a generous amount of time to respond, but if considered necessary, such as if someone is considered to be a flight risk, or if it is suspected that evidence might either be destroyed or fabricated, 'forthwith' subpoenas may be issued, requiring attendance or the production of documentary materials within as little as one day. The courts are deferential in their treatment of subpoenas, and there is 'an explicit recognition that a presumption of regularity attaches to grand jury subpoenas'.[106]

The impact of the Fifth Amendment, which provides protection against self-incrimination, must not be overlooked when considering grand jury investigations. Corporate entities do not have Fifth Amendment rights, and therefore a holder of documents which are the property of a corporate entity cannot exercise the privilege as a means to refuse delivery in response to a grand jury subpoena.[107] The contents of documents which were voluntarily created, and which pre-date the commencement of the grand jury investigation are not subject to Fifth Amendment protections, but some rights against production may be provided in situations in which production by an individual might in and of itself confirm or provide evidence of participation in an unlawful act.[108]

Subpoenas will be served either by an FBI agent or an agent of another government department, but may also be voluntarily accepted by counsel acting on behalf of clients. Subpoenas will state a time for compliance, allowing sufficient time for the relevant documents to be identified and compiled. At the time that subpoenas are compiled it is unlikely that the staff will know precisely what material is available, and in what form it exists. It is likely, as the *Division Manual* recognises, that recipients'

---

106 See, for example, *United States v Under Seal (In re Grand Jury, John Doe No G.J.)* 478 F.3d 581, 585 (4th Cir 2007).

107 A Fifth Amendment protection does apply to any individual surrendering documents on behalf of a corporate entity, in that the Government cannot introduce as evidence against them the fact that they complied, on behalf of the corporation, with a subpoena request (see *Braswell v United States*, 487 US 99, 118 (1988)).

108 See *In re Grand Jury Subpoena Duces Tecum dated Oct 19, 1992*, 1 F.3d 87, 93 (2d Cir 1993). The *Division Manual* advises staff to 'consider whether the individual's act of producing the subpoenaed documents may have such testimonial significance, and whether alternative methods of proof are available' (at III.F.4.a.).

counsel may argue that the subpoena is 'overly burdensome', particularly where the material is stored on computer systems.[109] Although 'it is the policy and practice of the Antitrust Division to defend its subpoenas vigorously against motions to quash', the Division also recommends that staff consider requests for deferrals, and are encouraged, 'for example, to accept representative samples or defer production of specific types of documents'.[110] Where subpoenas are served on parties who are not directly involved in the suspected infringement, such as telephone companies and banks, the recipients will be told that the subpoena is part of a criminal process, and will be asked not to disclose the fact of their existence to the customer(s). Financial records may be obtained under the terms of the Right to Financial Privacy Act.[111]

Subpoenas *ad testificandum*, usually served by a US Marshall or an agent, or accepted voluntarily by counsel, will include a statement of rights available to the defence. These include: the Fifth Amendment right against self-incrimination; the fact that anything said may be used against the witness in a subsequent legal proceeding; and the right to step outside the room to consult with counsel if counsel has been retained. These rights are restated at the grand jury hearing itself. If the witness has received immunity, as would be the case where an application for leniency has been granted, the witness will be reminded that his or her testimony could still be used in any prosecution for perjury or making a false statement. Witnesses under subpoena are required to answer all questions put to them truthfully, unless there is a valid invocation of the Fifth Amendment.[112] The

---

109 The *Division Manual* states (at III.F.4.a) that:

[t]he Division's standard document subpoena requires companies to produce all electronically stored data in its possession that is responsive to the subpoena. The term 'document' is defined in the schedule to the subpoena to include all information stored on a company's computer systems. The subpoena also contains a lengthy instruction describing what steps the company must take to preserve all potentially responsive electronic data in its possession. That instruction describes what types of data must be preserved (for example, e-mails) and how that data should be preserved in various locations on the company's computer systems (for example, servers). Finally, the subpoena requires that all electronic data must be produced in an electronic format and that the company must contact staff to determine whether the company's proposed electronic format is compatible with the Division's equipment and resources. Production of electronic data in a paper format should never be accepted.

110 *Division Manual*, III.F.4.a.

111 12 USC §§3401-22.

112 See *Branzburg v Hayes* 408 US 665 (1972) at 688: the grand jury 'has a right to every man's evidence'.

Fifth Amendment cannot be invoked where the Government grants the witness immunity from prosecution.

Search warrants may be used as an alternative, or in addition, to subpoenas. For a search warrant to be issued there must be probable cause,[113] which may not exist during the early stages of an investigation (although a detailed leniency application may give sufficient cause). There are advantages to the use of search warrants if the requisite legal hurdle can be surmounted. These are noted in the *Division Manual*:

> [t]he use of search warrants as opposed to subpoenas *duces tecum* minimizes the opportunity for document destruction and concealment, prevents the failure to produce responsive documents either deliberately or through inadvertence, and often spurs a race for leniency.[114]

An application for search warrants must be made to a magistrate in the district where the property to be searched is located. Applications must set out in the application the factual basis for establishing probable cause, and include sufficient facts to establish both that the crime has been committed, and that evidence of this may be found at the premises to be searched. Once approved, search warrants are executed by agents, and staff attorneys may not be present. Individuals at the premises subject to search may be interviewed by the agents. Documents subject to legal professional privilege are protected both during the course of the execution of search warrants, and in the process of complying with subpoenas *duces tecum*. If a claim is made by counsel that documents subject to the privilege have been obtained, Division staff must take measures to ensure that the staff and case agent are not 'tainted' by reading them.

Baker argues that the grand jury process 'highly favours'[115] government prosecutors, and is one of the strengths of the US system. Witnesses before grand juries do not have access to legal representation at the time of giving testimony, and one result is that while the EU enforcement process relies very heavily on documentary evidence, US prosecutions place greater emphasis on witness testimony.

---

113 'Probable cause' applies to a probable cause for belief that a relevant crime has been committed, not that documents have been, or may be, destroyed.

114 At III.F.5.

115 Baker, DI, 'The Use of Criminal Law Remedies to Deter and Punish Cartels and Bid-Rigging' (2000–2001) 69 *George Washington Law Review* 693 at 699.

Criminal Suits

When a matter is before a grand jury investigation, the subjects of investigation may be categorised as either targets,[116] or subjects.[117] Targets may be notified during the grand jury process that they indeed fit into that category, and may be placed in the position where they expressly have to invoke the Fifth Amendment, rather than simply reading a statement and leaving the room. Where the Division staff are seriously contemplating that a criminal trial will be sought, defence counsel will be informed of that fact, although individual defendants will not be named as being likely eventual defendants. Counsel will be afforded the opportunity to meet with staff and to make representations regarding the recommendation to proceed to trial.

If a decision is made to bring a case forward, formal criminal charges must be made, either in the form of an 'indictment' or an 'information' (the legal effects of which are identical). These must, in the words of the Federal Rules of Criminal Procedure,[118] take the form of a 'plain, concise and definite written statement of the essential facts constituting the offence charged'.[119] Unless indictment is waived by the defendant,[120] any case under s 1 of the Sherman Act must be prosecuted by way of an indictment, as it is an offence punishable by a term of imprisonment in excess of one year. The essential legal requirement of an indictment is that it

---

[116] A target is defined as a person:

> as to whom the prosecutor or the grand jury has substantial evidence linking him/her[/it] to the commission of a crime and who, in the judgment of the prosecutor, is a putative defendant. An officer or employee of an organization which is a target is not automatically considered to be a target even if such officer's or employee's conduct contributed to the commission of the crime by the target organization. The same lack of automatic target status holds true for organizations which employ, or employed, an officer or employee who is a target (*United States Attorney's Manual*, 9-11.151).

[117] A subject is defined as 'a person whose conduct is within the scope of the grand jury's investigation (*United States Attorney's Manual*, 9-11.151).

[118] Para 7(c)(1). See also DOJ *GJM* (1991 edition), Chapter VII.

[119] The DOJ further notes that the indictment should be drafted so as 'to tell the Government's story in a simplified and persuasive manner, keeping in mind that the document itself will be seen and scrutinized by the trial judge, the jury, defence counsel, the press, the probation officer and the court of appeals' (*GJM* at VII-4).

[120] The fact that plea agreements may result in cases being brought by information rather than by indictment, and the preference of defendants in this respect, is discussed below.

must permit the defendant to identify clearly the matters of which they are accused, and permit them to determine whether double-jeopardy rights are being infringed. A standard format indictment, to be used in s 1 cases, is set out in the DOJ's *GJM* at VII-7–11. Paragraph 2 of the standard form of indictment sets out the specifics of the offence, and should contain 'the specific type(s) of *per se* offence(s) involved; the industry involved; and, in bid-rigging cases, the letting authority'. The last sentence of this paragraph 'should be substantially the same in all indictments': 'The combination and conspiracy, engaged in by the defendants and co-conspirators was an unreasonable restraint of interstate [and foreign] trade and commerce, in violation of section 1 of the Sherman Act (15 USC §1)'.

The choice of which defendants actually to prosecute is, as the Division recognises, one in respect of which 'prosecutorial discretion will most require careful consideration'.[121] The *Manual* makes reference to the *Principles of Federal Prosecution*, which state that

> the attorney for the Government should initiate or recommend federal prosecution if the attorney believes that the person's conduct constitutes a federal offence and that the admissible evidence will probably be sufficient to obtain and sustain a conviction. Thus, under the Principles, the standard is one of 'probable conviction'.

An important exception to this principle lies in the operation of the leniency programme, under which an express decision is made, subject to the terms of the programme being satisfied, *not* to prosecute a person who might otherwise fall within the above paragraph. 'Marginal' or 'fringe' participants in infringements will often not be prosecuted unless the evidence is strong.[122]

An issue that is not always easy to resolve is that of whether a defendant may be charged with more than one violation (and therefore be exposed to multiple punishments) in relation to a course of anti-competitive conduct. The position in essence is that if more than one unlawful conspiracy has taken place the defendant may be charged with more than one count.

---

[121] *GJM*, VII-39.

[122] Here the DOJ demonstrates a pragmatic and realistic approach to the dynamics of trial:

> [t]he lack of factual strength as to marginal defendants will often weaken the overall strength of the case against other defendants. In addition, it must be remembered that for every defendant added to an indictment, the trial judge will accord that many more jury selection strikes, each Government witness will face additional cross-examination, and the jury will hear that many more opening statements and closing arguments in favor of the defense. (*GJM*, at VII-40).

However, in the case of antitrust violations it may often be the case that there is rather a single conspiracy with multiple goals. In such a case the defendant may only be charged with one violation.[123] In cases using a 'totality of the circumstances' test to distinguish between single and multiple conspiracies, the following factors may be considered: (1) the number of alleged acts in common; (2) the overlap in personnel; (3) the time period; (4) the similarity in the methods of operation; (5) the locations in which the acts took place; (6) the extent to which the alleged conspiracies shared a common objective; and (7) the degree of interdependence needed for the overall operation to succeed.[124] In *United States v Consolidated Packaging Corp*[125] the Division prosecuted a bid-rigging arrangement in relation to folding carton manufacturers. The arrangement was a long-standing one, and involved at various times up to 70 defendants. The defendant argued that the Government had not proved that there was one single nationwide conspiracy, or that if it had done so, the Government had not proved that Consolidated had joined this conspiracy. The Court discussed single and multiple conspiracies in the following terms:

> [t]his illegitimate business practice appears to have flourished among so many of the business conspirators for so long that it could reasonably be considered the customary way of doing business. All the facts and circumstances fully justify the view that a custom-made conspiratorial understanding had been developed and fashioned in a size and style most suited to their particular

---

123 See *GJM*, at VII-46:

> [w]hether to charge the defendants' conduct as a single conspiracy or as multiple conspiracies may be difficult to evaluate, primarily because it is a mixed question of law and fact. In general, the final charging decision rests on an analysis of the facts; as the facts change, so may conclusions differ.

In a different, but relevant, context, the Supreme Court considered the approach to be taken in relation to a number of conspiracy counts brought against defendants charged with violations of tax law, holding that in the case where there was a single continuing agreement, each object of that agreement could not be prosecuted as a separate violation:

> the precise nature and extent of the conspiracy must be determined by reference to the agreement which embraces and defines its objects. Whether the object of a single agreement is to commit one or many crimes, it is in either case that agreement which constitutes the conspiracy which the statute punishes. The one agreement cannot be taken to be several agreements and hence several conspiracies because it envisages the violation of several statutes rather than one (*Braverman v United States* 317 US 49 (1942) at 54).

124 *GJM*, at VII-54.

125 575 F.2d 117 (7th Cir. 1978).

> needs. Whenever the needs of any conspirator might require it, the conspirator had only to plug into the system, get 'on the phone', and make the necessary arrangements. This system which developed and remained viable among them to be available for use by any conspirator was a persuasive aspect of the conspiracy. The many minor individual or particular conspiracies which the system fostered and spawned were evidence of the effectiveness of the general conspiracy. The conspiracy was in the nature of an industry utility, operated totally for the benefit of its shareholders, the carton producing conspirators, and to the detriment of its customs and the public.
>
> Because of the nature of this conspiracy, it could not reasonably be expected that any one conspirator would have full knowledge. Consolidated did not need full knowledge to participate in the benefits of the conspiracy and therefore proof that Consolidated had some knowledge that activities of the same type as practiced by them for the same mutual purposes must have been widespread in the industry. We believe it may reasonably be inferred from the evidence that the overall design, purpose and functioning of the conspiracy were within the reasonable contemplation of Consolidated when it engaged in the episodes. Consolidated endeavoured to abide by and assist in the enforcement of the rules of the conspiracy. By its behaviour, Consolidated demonstrated it knew enough about the conspiracy to use it to serve its own purposes when needed. There is more than suspicion; there was interested cooperation with a stake in the venture.

Although in these circumstances there was a highly complex number of individual links, and although each conspirator was only interested in its particular circumstances, the Court held that there was in place a single arrangement, which was strengthened and supported by each individual bid made within it. The Government is not obliged, however, only to charge to the maximum extent of the conspiracy – it can isolate out elements as forming the illegality, and charge different parties with being engaged in different elements, as long as each individual is charged only once.[126]

---

[126] The DOJ explains the principle in the following way in relation to bid-rigging:

> [t]he key issue in this area is whether the bid-rigging conspiracy is limited to individual rounds of bidding on each new contract. If individual negotiations concerning *quid pro quos* must be engaged in by the persons interested in each award to determine whether an agreement can be reached with respect to rigging that particular bid, and if the award will be bid competitively if those negotiations fail, then each separately negotiated agreement is best viewed as a separate conspiracy and not as part of some overreaching, on-going bid-rigging conspiracy' (*GJM*, at XII-58).

The position reached in the courts is not always consistent: *United States v Ashland-Warren Inc* 537 F. Supp. 433 (MD Tenn 1982) may be contrasted with *United States v Beachner Construction Co* 729 F.2d 1278 (10th Cir 1984).

Prior to the handing down of an indictment, potential individual defendants are likely to be informed that they are a target of the investigation, and the investigating attorneys are likely to inform counsel acting for corporations that action against their superiors is about to be recommended. This notice gives counsel for the defence an opportunity to discuss voluntary attendance before the grand jury, and an opportunity to present any arguments to the prosecution team. The DOJ attorneys are likely to agree to a meeting if one is requested. The DOJ states that:

> [t]he meeting is intended to provide counsel with a full and fair opportunity to address the substance of the evidence against his client as well as mitigating circumstances that should be considered in deciding whether to prosecute. For an individual, such mitigating circumstances include the individual's status in the company, personal and health problems, age and other circumstances that may lead the prosecutor to consider that indictment of the individual would not be in the public interest.[127]

These meetings may, in some cases, 'affect the final decision whether to prosecute'.[128] The Federal Rules of Criminal Procedure greatly limit the amount of information that the DOJ attorneys can give to the defence counsel, as grand jury investigations are guaranteed substantial secrecy. Every recommendation for an indictment must be reviewed and approved by the Assistant Attorney General. It is for the grand jury to vote a 'true bill', and to return the indictment to a federal magistrate in open court.[129] While there is no specified time within which arraignment must take place after indictment, defendants will typically voluntarily submit themselves to arrest at the arraignment, as this triggers the statutory requirement under which trial proceedings must begin within 70 days.

ENFORCEMENT AND PUNISHMENT

The statutory maximum penalty that may be imposed on a person convicted of a violation of s 1 of the Sherman Act combines both financial and custodial elements. In essence the maximum sentence is as follows:

---

[127] *GJM*, at VII-80.

[128] *GJM*, at VII-80.

[129] If the grand jury refuses to return an indictment (a 'no bill') the prosecutor may resubmit the evidence to a different grand jury. This requires the permission of the Assistant Attorney General, which is not ordinarily granted (*GJM*, at VII-92–93).

(a) a term of imprisonment of up to ten years;[130]
(b) in the case of a corporation a fine in an amount equal to the greatest of (1) $100m, (2) twice the gross pecuniary gain the conspirators derived from the crime, or (3) twice the gross pecuniary loss caused to the victims by the conspirators;[131] and in the case of an individual a fine not greater than $1 m; and
(c) a term of supervised release of three years following any term of imprisonment.[132]

Courts may also order defendants to pay restitution to the victims of the offence.[133] Sentencing guidelines, which are advisory but not mandatory,[134] are also applied in determining the amount of the financial penalty, if any, and the length of any jail term handed down. In practice the amount of fines paid by corporations may be much higher than those set out in the Sherman Act, which specify a maximum fine for a corporation of $100m. That this is possible rests on the fact that the DOJ relies on the Comprehensive Crime Control Act and the Criminal Fine Improvements Act to negotiate plea agreements (which are discussed below) which provide for fines above the Sherman Act statutory limits.

The Department of Justice website sets out figures in relation to criminal enforcement in the fiscal years 2000–2010,[135] which are given at Table 3.1.

As of March 22, 2011, there had been 82 instances of criminal fines of $10m or more being imposed on individual corporations, with the highest single penalty being the $500m imposed on F. Hoffmann-La Roche in 1999.[136] In 2007 British Airways plc paid the third highest penalty of $300m in respect of its involvement in price-fixing in the market for cargo and passenger air transportation. The focus of this book is not on the criminal fines imposed on corporations; in economic terms these have precisely the same impact as the civil penalties imposed in the EU and UK regimes by DG Competition and the OFT (although there may be

130 15 USC §1.

131 15 USC §1, 18 USC §3571(b) and (d). The latter provision was enacted in 1987 (see above).

132 18 USC §3559(a)(3) and 18 USC §3583(b)(2). In the event that there is a violation of any condition governing the supervised period following release, the defendant can be imprisoned for a further two years (18 USC §3583(e)(3).

133 18 USC §3663(a)(3).

134 See *United States v Booker* 543 US 220 (2005).

135 www.justice.gov/atr/public/criminal/264101.html.

136 For a discussion of the extent to which penalties have increased over time, see Stucke, ME, 'Morality and Antitrust' (2006) *Columbia Business Law Review* 443 at 460ff.

Table 3.1 Criminal enforcement (fines and jail)

	Total fines ($m)	Incarceration (total days)	Incarceration (average months)	% of Defendants sentenced to jail
1990s average	169	3313	8	37
2000	152	5584	10	38
2001	280	4800	15	46
2002	75	10501	18	53
2003	107	9341	21	50
2004	350	7334	12	71
2005	338	13 157	24	67
2006	473	5383	9	68
2007	630	31 391	31	87
2008	710	14 331	25	61
2009	1000	25 396	24	80
2010	555	26 046	30	78

an increased fear of reputational effects and public censure by virtue of the characterisation of the US penalties as 'criminal').[137] It is however worth noting that as of May 10, 2011, of the 85 instances of fines of $10m or more being imposed, only 13 relate to wholly owned companies of US origin. Of the ten highest penalties, with the lower being $160m and the highest $500m, all accrue to non-US firms.[138] In the air transportation

[137] Although it is almost certainly the case that the high penalties imposed under EU competition law amount, for the purposes of the ECHR, to criminal sanctions, they remain characterised by the EU legal system as civil penalties.

[138] These are, in order of magnitude: F Hoffmann-La Roche (1999) (vitamins) $500m, Switzerland; LG Display Co Ltd and LG Display American (2009) (LCD panels) $400m, Korea; Société Air France and Koninklijke Luchtvaart Maatschappij NV (2008) (air cargo transport) $350m, France and Netherlands; Korean Air Lines Co Ltd (2007) (air cargo transport) $300m, Korea; British Airways plc (2007) (air cargo and passenger transport) $300m, UK; Samsung Electronics Company Ltd and Samsung Semiconductor Inc (2006) (DRAM) $300m, Korea; BASF AG (1999) (vitamins) $225m, Germany; CHI MEI Optoelectronics Corporation (2010) (LCD panels) $220m, Taiwan; Hynix Semiconductor Inc (2005) (DRAM) $185m, Korea; and Infineon Technologies AG (2004) (DRAM) $160m, Germany. It is noteworthy that in respect of at least eight of these cases there are mature and well supported competition law regimes in place in the countries of origin. The fact that the DOJ has focussed on international cartels in its enforcement activity is clear. See, for example, Werden, GJ, Hammond, SD, and Barnett, BA, 'Recidivism Eliminated: Cartel Enforcement in

cartel alone, whose participants included, amongst others, Singapore Airlines, All Nippon Airways, and China Airlines, fines totalled in excess of $1.8 bn, the most ever imposed under a single antitrust investigation. Twenty-one companies and 19 individuals had been charged by the end of fiscal year 2010. As discussed in Chapter 2, even this level of financial penalty may be insufficient to secure optimal deterrence.

The evidence is also clear that incarceration for a substantial period is increasingly likely for those convicted of, or pleading guilty to, antitrust violations in the US. As Table 3.1 shows, in fiscal year 2010, defendants convicted of antitrust violations were sentenced in total to 26046 days, the second highest figure in history. In a recent case involving a concrete price-fixing and bid-rigging arrangement in Iowa, a defendant was sentenced to 48 months in prison, which, at the time of writing, ties the record for the longest single sentence in respect of a defendant found guilty of antitrust violations only.[139] The Division itself points out that it:

> has seen a steady increase in the percentage of defendants sentenced to prison. In the past two years [FY 2009, 2010], nearly 8 in 10 defendants went to prison. In the 1990s, only 37 percent of Division defendants went to prison. The percentage of Division defendants sentenced to jail in a single year reached a high of 87 percent in 2007, and remained high during FY 2010 at 78 percent. . . .
>
> Since May 1999, 49 foreign defendants have served, or are currently serving, sentences in US prisons for violating the Sherman Antitrust Act or obstructing a Federal antitrust investigation. The 'no-jail' sentencing recommendations

---

the United States since 1999' (2011) Georgetown Global Antitrust Enforcement Symposium, September 22, 2011 at 4:

> [i]n the 1990s international cartels became a central focus of the Antitrust Division. The Division had long viewed imprisonment of culpable individuals as critical to effective deterrence, but for most of the 1990s, the Division had to give up on the possibility of prison sentences for non-US citizens who participated in international cartels in order to secure admissions of guilt, cooperation, and submission to US jurisdiction. That practice came to an end with the prosecution of the vitamins cartels. Six non-US citizens were imprisoned within a year, with the first sentenced on July 23, 1999. From that date to the present, a total of 47 non-US citizens have been sentenced by US courts to prison terms for cartel activity, with nine receiving sentences of at least one year (internal footnotes omitted).

[139] See DOJ, 'Division Update Spring 2011' (www.justice.gov/atr/public/division-update/2011/criminal-program.html), see also below. In sentencing the court stated that: '[t]he defendants, although dressed in the attire of hard working businessmen, were nothing more than common thieves, and serial ones at that. Like a neighbourhood thief, they stole from friends, acquaintances, businesses, and local governments.'

that were once available to qualifying foreign nationals in the 1990s are no longer an option. Culpable foreign nationals, just like US co-conspirators, are expected to serve jail sentences in order to resolve their criminal culpability.[140]

Sentencing Guidelines

Sentencing guidelines applying to antitrust violations were introduced in 1987, following a long period in which there was clear reluctance of the courts, acting on a deterrence theory, to send to jail contrite executives of previous good standing who appeared to be unlikely to reoffend. The guidelines obliged courts to treat antitrust felonies as a serious offence, and made clear that imprisonment was to be considered as the appropriate punishment. A points system was set out, with a starting base indicating imprisonment, but with increases or reductions required in the face of other relevant factors.

Sentences can also be higher than that suggested by the sentencing guidelines. This was the case, for example, in *US v VandeBrake*.[141] Here the defendant pleaded guilty to three counts of a violation of s 1 of the Sherman Act, in that he, and a co-conspirator, Kent Robert Stewart, had fixed prices and rigged bids in relation to the sale of ready-mix concrete. VandeBrake was sentenced to a 48-month prison sentence, which was in excess of the sentencing guidelines' recommended range of 21 to 27 months. The court stated that such a lift in the sentence was possible when 'there exists an aggravating . . . circumstance of a kind, or to a degree, not adequately taken into consideration in the guidelines'. In the present case the court held that the violation was particularly serious on the grounds that: (1) ready-mix cement was an essential product; (2) a number of the relevant contracts were in the public sector; and (3) VandeBrake had created the cartel, the victims of which had no option, in the relevant geographic market, but to purchase their supplies from the cartel.

LENIENCY

The leniency programme in the US, which originally commenced operating in 1978 and which has been adapted since, has been influential in shaping the response of programmes adopted by other jurisdictions, and

---

[140] DOJ, 'Division Update Spring 2011' (www.justice.gov/atr/public/division-update/2011/criminal-program.html).

[141] Case Nos CR10-4025-MWB, CR10-4028-MWB, District Court, Northern District of Iowa, February 8, 2011.

is widely perceived as being effective. It applies only in respect of criminal violations of s 1 of the Sherman Act, and applies both to corporations and to individuals. There are therefore in operation in the US two leniency policies, one relating to corporate leniency (issued in August 1993), the other to individual leniency (issued in August 1994). The US scheme was compared favourably with the EU regime when the latter started operating on the grounds that, with minor exceptions, the US regime offered certainty to an applicant: if it was first to apply, did not initiate the illegal activity, and did not coerce others into the legal activity, leniency *would* be granted. Hammond, for example, argues that a 'key component in the success of the Division's cartel enforcement program, particularly the Corporate Leniency Program, is transparency and predictability'.[142]

It should be noted that both leniency programmes apply not merely to violations of s 1 of the Sherman Act, but may provide limited protection in relation to certain other criminal acts which may have been committed as part of that violation. This could extend, for instance, to mail or wire fraud arising out of communicating rigged bids, or bribery or failure to report transactions to the Internal Revenue Service.[143]

A key development in the DOJ's leniency policy in recent years has been the development of 'amnesty plus'. There has been a notable pattern of investigations discovering overlapping cartels. Thus, for example, if A (having made a leniency application), B, C and D are in a cartel operating in respect of X, which comes under investigation, it may be the case also that B, C, D and E are involved in a cartel in respect of Y, about which evidence is uncovered, or a leniency application made in the anticipation that evidence *might* be uncovered, during the investigation into the cartelisation of X. As the DOJ notes, a 'large percentage' of its investigations 'have been initiated as a result of evidence developed during an investigation of a completely separate conspiracy'.[144] In such a case if B, C, or D were to apply for leniency in respect of the Y cartel, not only would this be given, were the conditions set out below to be met, but also a recommendation would be made by the DOJ to the sentencing court in respect of X cartel

142 Hammond, SD, 'Measuring the Value of Second-In Cooperation in Corporate Plea Negotiations', 54th Annual ABA Section of Antitrust Law Spring Meeting, March 29, 2006 (www.justice.gov/atr/public/speeches/215514.htm).

143 The UK's 'no-action letters' are restricted solely to the operation of s 188 of the Enterprise Act 2002, and do not extend to ancillary criminal conduct, if it exists.

144 DOJ, 'Frequently asked questions regarding the Antitrust Division's leniency program and model leniency letters' (2008) (www.justice.gov/atr/public/criminal/239583.pdf).

that the applicant receive a discount in its penalty to reflect its cooperation in the uncovering of the newly identified cartel.[145]

The Antitrust Division will give only *one* corporate leniency in respect of any one conspiracy, and recognises the tension that may arise out of this policy. Any company wishing to apply for leniency is 'in a race with its co-conspirators and possibly its own employees who may also be preparing to apply for individual leniency'.[146] This 'race' can be started even after an investigation has begun. As noted above, the issuing of search warrants or subpoenas during the course of a grand jury investigation may trigger the race, and such applications will be accepted as long as the DOJ does not have, by that time, sufficient evidence to proceed to trial. The DOJ has confirmed rumours to the effect that there have been a number of occasions on which a company has failed to secure leniency because it has been beaten to the process by only a matter of hours. Given the dynamics of this race the DOJ has developed a 'marker system' under which a prospective applicant for leniency may hold their position in the queue for a 'finite

---

145 The DOJ states that '[t]he size of the Amnesty Plus discount depends on a number of factors, including: (1) the strength of the evidence provided by the cooperating company in the leniency product; (2) the potential significance of the violation reported in the leniency application, measured in such terms as the volume of commerce involved, the geographic scope, and the number of co-conspirator companies and individuals; and (3) the likelihood the Division would have uncovered the additional violation absent the self-reporting, *ie*, if there were little or no overlap in the corporate participants and/or the culpable executives involved in the original cartel under investigation and the Amnesty Plus matter, then the credit for the disclosure would be greater. Of these three factors, the first two are given most weight' (DOJ, note 144). For further explanation of the Amnesty Plus programme see also Hammond, SD, note 142.

146 DOJ, note 144. Hammond's characterisation of the dynamics involved is an engaging one:

> [h]ere is a remarkable statistic: roughly half of the Division's current international cartel investigations were initiated by evidence obtained as a result of an investigation of a completely separate market. Most of the corporate defendants in international cartel cases are multinational companies selling hundreds of different products. It will come as no surprise then to learn that the Division's experience is that if a company is fixing prices in one market, the chances are good that it is doing so in other markets as well. If an executive readily meets with competitors to allocate customers, then he or she has likely done it before in his or her career. And, if you go back further in time, you will likely find a mentor who taught the colluding executive the tricks of the trade. Armed with this experience, the Division has had great success engaging in a strategy of 'cartel profiling' techniques aimed at ferreting out violations that sprout 'cartel trees' where one investigation will eventually give root to prosecutions in a half-dozen or more different markets. (Hammond, SD, note 142)

period of time' while more details are sought to support a formal application. In order to book a place in the queue the DOJ requires the following of representing counsel, who must:

> (1) report that he or she has uncovered some information or evidence indicating that his or her client has engaged in a criminal antitrust violation; (2) disclose the general nature of the conduct discovered; (3) identify the industry, product, or service involved in terms that are specific enough to allow the Division to determine whether leniency is still available and to protect the marker for the client; and (4) identify the client.[147]

The standard of evidence required to obtain a marker is low, although the burden may be higher when the DOJ has already begun an investigation in the area concerned. It is thus noted that at the lowest level a mere conversation with an employee in which the counsel is told that she overheard a conversation relating to price-fixing by her employer may be sufficient. Typically a marker may remain valid for up to 30 days.

The corporate leniency policy exists in two parts: 'Type A leniency', and 'Type B leniency'. Type A leniency applies in situations where an investigation has not yet begun and where six conditions are met: (1) the applicant is the first to come forward and the DOJ has not received information about the activity from any other source; (2) the corporation took prompt action to terminate its involvement in the infringement as soon as it became aware of the illegality;[148] (3) the company 'reports the wrongdoing with candour and completeness and provides full, continuing and complete cooperation'; (4) the application and recognition of wrongdoing is truly that of the corporation, and not just of individual officers of it; (5) restitution to injured parties is made where possible; and (6) the applicant did not coerce any other party into the unlawful arrangement, and was 'clearly' neither the leader, nor the originator, of the unlawful activity. Type B leniency may be applicable where the DOJ already has commenced an investigation, but where no other party has applied for leniency, and where the DOJ does not have sufficient evidence against the applicant to sustain a conviction. The other conditions for Type B leniency are the same as for Type A, with the addition of a requirement that the DOJ not consider that granting leniency would be 'unfair to others, considering the

---

147 DOJ, note 144.

148 Some have questioned the extent to which, in for example a corporation in which the board of directors were all aware of the violation, a corporation could ever be said to have become aware of, or 'discovered' the violation other than at the point of its inception. The DOJ takes the view that in these circumstances the corporation may still qualify 'if the activity is terminated promptly after legal counsel is first informed of the activity' (DOJ, note 144).

nature of the activity, the confessing corporation's role in the activity, and when the corporation comes forward'.

Notwithstanding the requirement that the illegal activity be promptly terminated, there may be circumstances in which the DOJ asks a leniency applicant to continue to ostensibly participate in the cartel.[149] This might mean, for example, that the company would be asked to continue to participate in cartel meetings, which may be monitored (as was the case in the *Marine Hose* cartel investigation detailed in Chapter 6, below).

If a corporation qualifies for Type A leniency, all officers and employees of the company who admit criminal violations will also be granted leniency, without the need to take advantage of the individual leniency programme. However, the Division also maintains an individual leniency policy, which is short, and is as follows:

> **A Requirements for Leniency for Individuals**
> Leniency will be granted to an individual reporting illegal antitrust activity before an investigation has begun, if the following three conditions are met:
> 1. At the time the individual comes forward to report the illegal activity, the Division has not received information about the illegal activity being reported from any other source;
> 2. The individual reports the wrongdoing with candour and completeness and provides full, continuing and complete cooperation to the Division throughout the investigation; and
> 3. The individual did not coerce another party to participate in the illegal activity and clearly was not the leader in, or originator of, the activity.
>
> **B Applicability of the Policy**
> Any individual who does not qualify for leniency under Part A of this Policy will be considered for statutory or informal immunity from criminal prosecution. Such immunity decisions will be made by the Division on a case-by-case basis in the exercise of its prosecutorial discretion.
>
> If a corporation attempts to qualify for leniency under the Corporate Leniency Policy, any directors, officers or employees who come forward and confess with the corporation will be considered for leniency solely under the provisions of the Corporate Leniency Policy.
>
> **C Leniency Procedure**
> If the staff that receives the request for leniency believes the individual qualifies for and should be accorded leniency, it should forward a favourable recommendation to the Deputy Assistant Attorney General for Litigation, setting forth

---

[149] A similar position is maintained in the UK, where it may be required that an undertaking *continue* its involvement in the infringement, so as not to alert other participants to the fact that a leniency application may have been made, and an investigation launched (see Chapter 4, below).

> the reasons why leniency should be granted. The staff should not delay making such a recommendation until a fact memo recommending prosecution of others is prepared. The Deputy Assistant Attorney General for Litigation will review the request and forward it to the Assistant Attorney General for final decision. If the staff recommends against leniency, the individual and his or her counsel may wish to seek an appointment with the Deputy Assistant Attorney General for Litigation to make their views known. Individuals and their counsel are not entitled to such a meeting as a matter of right, but the opportunity will generally be afforded.

A model individual leniency letter is available on the DOJ website.

The DOJ places significant reliance on the efficacy of its leniency programme, and undertakes substantial efforts to ensure that it is transparent and public. It is, for example, noted in the *Division Manual* that staff may wish to draw attention to the programmes if appropriate when subpoenas *duces tecum* (discussed above) are being issued by a grand jury.

When a leniency application is made, and when it appears that the requirements are satisfied for the grant of leniency, the DOJ may issue first a conditional leniency letter. Only after all relevant obligations are satisfied will a final, non-conditional, letter be issued. Leniency applications are strictly confidential, and the fact that an applicant has been granted leniency will not be disclosed 'unless the applicant has previously made such a disclosure or the Division is authorized to make such a disclosure by the applicant or by court order'.[150] Neither will the fact of the grant of leniency be disclosed to any foreign government or authority, unless the applicant agrees to the disclosure. However, since litigation in the case of *Stolt-Nielsen*,[151] the DOJ releases on its website copies of all corporate leniency letters, with appropriate redactions. The DOJ intends to continue with this policy, but in 'order to mitigate concerns that the identity of specific leniency applicants or the information provided by the applicants could be determined, even with redactions [the DOJ] will release redacted leniency letters in large batches only'.[152]

Leniency in the US may, under the Antitrust Criminal Penalty Enhancement and Reform Act (ACPERA) 2004, also result in the successful applicant not being exposed to treble damages actions in the event that it is exposed to civil claims. A successful applicant still remains liable to damages as awarded by a jury, but these will not be trebled.

---

150 *Division Manual*, III.F.c.iv.

151 *Stolt-Nielsen SA v United States* 352 F Supp 2d 553 (ED Pa Jan 14, 2005); see also Harrison, G, and Bell, M, note 25, at 229ff.

152 Freedom of Information Act, DOJ, Redacted Leniency Letters (www.usdoj.gov/atr/foia/leniency_letters.htm).

PLEA AGREEMENTS

In addition to leniency applications, plea agreements also form an important plank in US enforcement activities, and may include within them recommendations for reductions in recommended sentences (both in terms of periods of incarceration and of the amount of financial penalties) subject to full cooperation with the authorities.[153] The Supreme Court has held that plea agreements are 'an essential component of the administration of justice'.[154] The range of imprisonment and fines possible following conviction in a criminal antitrust case are broad, and the DOJ has substantial scope in which to negotiate, while staying inside the Federal sentencing guidelines (see below). In some cases, particularly those where the defendant has offered 'substantial assistance to the authorities',[155] the Government may offer agreements which depart from the sentencing guidelines. It is the policy of the DOJ that 'absent unusual circumstances, criminal cases may be disposed of pursuant to plea agreements'.[156] In the

---

153 For a discussion of the economics of plea agreements see Gazal-Ayal, O, and Riza, L, 'Plea-bargaining and Prosecution' in Garoupa, N (ed), *Criminal Law and Economics* (2009) Edward Elgar at 145.

154 *Santobello v New York* 404 US 257, 260 (1971).

155 *Sentencing Guidelines*, Para 5K1.1; see also *GJM* at IX-62. The *Sentencing Guidelines* (November 2011 Revision) are in the following terms:

> **Substantial Assistance to Authorities (Policy Statement)**
> Upon motion of the government stating that the defendant has provided substantial assistance in the investigation or prosecution of another person who has committed an offense, the court may depart from the guidelines.
> (a) The appropriate reduction shall be determined by the court for reasons stated that may include, but are not limited to, consideration of the following:
> (1) the court's evaluation of the significance and usefulness of the defendant's assistance, taking into consideration the government's evaluation of the assistance rendered;
> (2) the truthfulness, completeness, and reliability of any information or testimony provided by the defendant;
> (3) the nature and extent of the defendant's assistance;
> (4) any injury suffered, or any danger or risk of injury to the defendant or his family resulting from his assistance;
> (5) the timeliness of the defendant's assistance.

156 DOJ, *GJM*, IX-1. The Federal Rules of Criminal Procedure authorise plea agreements at Rule 11(e)(1) which states in part that:

> [t]he attorney for the government and the attorney for the defendant or the defendant when acting *pro se* may engage in discussions with a view toward reaching an agreement that, upon the entering of a plea of guilty or *nolo contendere* to a charged offence or to a lesser or related offence, the attorney for the government will do any of the following:

case of DOJ actions under the Sherman Act the Department is unlikely to accept pleas of *nolo contendere*.[157]

The most frequent form of plea agreement in the context of antitrust prosecutions, and one which has been particularly effective where foreign parties are concerned, is the 'B' type agreement, under which the prosecuting attorney will agree to recommend a particular sentence or fine as the maximum, and the defendant remains free to argue for a lower sentence before the court. In the alternative, the defendant may agree not to oppose the recommendation, the agreement becoming, in effect, a joint sentencing recommendation. Any such recommendation does not bind the court, and the defendant will be alerted to the fact that a guilty plea cannot be withdrawn if the court chooses to disregard the sentence, and to impose one higher than that agreed between prosecution and defence. In the case of a 'C' agreement the Government and defendant may present their suggested sentence to the court, and give the court the opportunity to accept

---

> (A) move for dismissal of other charges; or
> (B) make a recommendation, or agree not to oppose the defendant's request, for a particular sentence, with the understanding that such recommendation or request shall not be binding upon the court; or
> (C) agree that a specific sentence is the appropriate disposition of the case.
> The court shall not participate in any such discussions.

While this rule states that the contemplated charge may be reduced to a lesser charge this is not possible in the case of actions brought under the Sherman Act, as there is no lesser offence. However, the Division *GJM* provides that 'a plea agreement could appropriately provide for the filing of a new charge, usually in an information, and the dismissal of the pending charge' (at IX-3). The Sentencing Reform Act 1984 provides that in respect of offences committed after, or continuing after, November 1, 1987, the Sentencing Guidelines published by the US Sentencing Commission apply.

157 The *GJM* discusses the link between *nolo contendere* pleas and plea agreements in the following terms (at IX-70):

> [s]ince it is Division policy to oppose the acceptance of *nolo contendere* pleas, except in unusual circumstances, a dilemma sometimes is created for the defendant who wishes to dispose of his criminal liability and is willing to agree to the sentence sought by the Government, but who is only willing to plead *nolo*. It should be made clear to the defendant that if he persists in refusing to plead guilty, he will not be able to enter into any type of plea agreement with the Division and, as a result, may be risking a more severe sentence. In certain rare situations, the Division may consider entering into negotiations with a defendant over an appropriate sentence after the defendant's *nolo* plea already has been accepted by the court. In that context, a true plea agreement is impossible, since the plea has already been accepted. If an agreement is reached, it becomes nothing more than a joint sentencing recommendation, which is not binding on the court.

it. If the court decides to reject the agreement the defendant is not bound to the guilty plea. The DOJ recognises that 'C' type agreements have the advantage of removing uncertainty for both parties, but that they are not popular with the courts as it removes judicial discretion. The DOJ will consider the following factors in determining whether or not to accept a plea agreement:

(1) the defendant's willingness to cooperate in the investigation or in the prosecution of others; this allows the DOJ to give recognition to defendants who are prepared to assist an investigation in return for a reduced penalty, but who have not met the conditions to benefit from the leniency programme;
(2) the defendant's history of criminal conduct;
(3) the nature and seriousness of the offence;
(4) the defendant's remorse or contrition, and his willingness to assume responsibility for his conduct;
(5) the desirability of a timely resolution of the case;
(6) the likelihood of obtaining a conviction at trial;
(7) the probable effect on witnesses. In this context the DOJ notes that although the prospect of violence or physical intimidation meted out to witnesses is 'remote' in the context of antitrust proceedings, the 'danger of economic retaliation of one form or another is very real';[158]
(8) the public interest in having the case tried rather than disposed of by a guilty plea;
(9) the expense of trial and appeals; and
(10) the need to avoid delay in relation to the disposing of other cases.[159]

Given that in the context of antitrust proceedings the fact that private plaintiffs are often waiting in the wings may impact on the plea agreement process, a factor recognised by the DOJ in the *GJM*.[160] The content of any discussions and negotiations leading to plea agreements are

---

158 *GJM*, at IX-8.

159 In respect of this condition the DOJ has stated at IX-8 of the *GJM* that:

> In an ongoing antitrust grand jury investigation, this standard, or a variant of it, may be the most important factor to consider in favour of a plea agreement, because a plea may lead to the speedy resolution of other cases, including the filing of some which might never be made if the case is tried, particularly if the defendant should be acquitted, or if the statute of limitations runs out on other possible cases in the meantime.

160 At IX-11.

protected from disclosure in any subsequent civil actions, save in very limited circumstances.[161] Plea agreements cannot limit subsequent civil liability.[162]

In many antitrust cases the defendant may be facing more than one charge. The question as to what to charge in a plea agreement is akin to that in other criminal prosecutions, and the *GJM* cites the *Principles of Federal Prosecution*:

> [t]he charge or charges to which a defendant pleads guilty should bear a reasonable relation to the defendant's criminal conduct, both in nature and in scope. . . . In regard to the seriousness of the offence, the guilty plea should assure that the public record of conviction provides an adequate indication of the defendant's conduct. In many cases this will probably require that the defendant plead guilty to the most serious offence charged. . . .
>
> The requirement that a defendant plead guilty to a charge that bears a reasonable relationship to the nature and extent of his criminal conduct is not inflexible. There may be situations involving cooperating defendants in which [special] considerations . . . take precedence. . . .
>
> The attorney for the Government should also bear in mind the legal requirement that there be a factual basis for the charge or charges to which a guilty plea is entered. . . . it is essential that the charge or charges selected as the subject of a plea agreement be such as could be prosecuted independently of the plea.[163]

---

161 Rule 11(e)(6) of the Federal Rules of Criminal Procedure provides that:

> Except as otherwise provided in this paragraph, evidence of the following is not, in any civil or criminal proceeding, admissible against the defendant who made the plea or was a participant in the plea discussions:
> (a) a plea of guilty which was later withdrawn;
> (b) a plea of *nolo contendere*;
> (c) any statement made in the course of plea discussions with an attorney for the government which do not result in a plea of guilty or which result in a plea of guilty later withdrawn.
> However, such a statement is admissible (i) in any proceeding wherein another statement made in the course of the same plea or plea discussion has been introduced and the statement ought in fairness be considered contemporaneously with it, or (ii) in a criminal proceeding for perjury or false statement if the statement was made by the defendant under oath, on the record, and in the presence of counsel.

162 A typical plea agreement in an antitrust context might therefore require the inclusion of a term similar to the following:

> . . . the defendant understands that it (he/she) may be subject to civil and equitable claims, demands or causes of action by the United States and others, and that this plea agreement in no way affects these claims, demands or causes of action (*GJM*, IX-49).

163 Cited in the *GJM* at IX-16–18.

There may be significant benefits for defendants who enter into plea agreements. In most instances a defendant will receive a downward reduction to the offence level. Where a defendant cooperates in providing information that strengthens a case against others, the Government may agree not to use any self-incriminating information provided against the defendant when determining the defendant's guideline penalty range. The simple fact of agreeing to plead guilty may lead to the Government agreeing to seek a penalty that lies at the bottom of the applicable range. In the *GJM* the DOJ also implies that it may be more flexible in some other aspects under plea agreements. Thus, for example, it is suggested that it might be prepared to provide that the payment of a fine be staggered over a period of time.[164] Agreements may also, importantly, specify that any time served in prison is to be served in a *specific* prison, and allow some flexibility in the date on which the defendant is to report to prison.[165] Plea agreements entered into with corporations may limit the exposure to criminal prosecution of any corporate officers not yet subject to prosecution, and may provide that evidence given by corporate officials, particularly those who are less culpable of participation in the unlawful conduct, will not be used to form the basis of any subsequent prosecution against them. The fact that plea agreements may lead to lower enforcement burdens for the Government is, as indicated above, a significant rationale for their acceptance. The simplified court procedures are also likely to be attractive to defendants. Only two court hearings are normally required where plea agreements are accepted. At the first hearing the defendant will indicate his intention to plead guilty, and the terms of the agreement will be laid before the court. All the terms of the agreement must be set out in open court, unless there is a good reason as to why an *in camera* proceeding should be held.[166] In the case of type B agreements the court will normally accept the terms at the first hearing. The court will then order a pre-sentence investigation and report, unless it believes that it already has in front of it all the information necessary to allow the proper exercise

---

164 *GJM*, at IX-28. In this event interest will be charged on the unpaid balance unless this requirement too is expressly waived.

165 Thus, for example, at IX-40 of the *GJM* a draft 'B' agreement reads, in respect to sentencing provisions, that:

> [t]he United States further agrees that it will not oppose any reasonable request of the defendant for imprisonment in a specific federal prison camp, for example, (*identify specific federal prison camp*), and a reasonable request regarding his ability to report directly to such institution as may be designated, or the date on which he must report to begin service of his sentence.

166 Rule 11(e)(2) of the Federal Rules of Criminal Procedure.

of sentencing discretion. The final stage of this truncated process is the holding of a sentencing hearing.[167]

In the context of US criminal procedure it is important that plea agreements may be entered into both before and after indictment by a Grand Jury. The Department stresses the fact that there are significant advantages, both to the Government and to defendants of entering into an agreement before indictment. In such cases actions proceed by way of a 'criminal information'. This substantially reduces the workload of the Government in building the case, while retaining the role of the Grand Jury. In the case of defendants it is particularly interesting that individuals appear to have strong preference for pleading guilty to an information rather than to an indictment. Given that there is, in fact, no legal difference between the effect of the two, the DOJ concludes that 'the reason for the preference may be largely emotional, ie, an indictment simply sounds more serious than an information'.[168] This may tell us something about the extent to which business executives seek to avoid labels which may significantly impact on their future prospects, reputation and status.

While plea agreements form a vital part of the administration of criminal justice in the US, the agreement itself is treated as being a contractual bargain, and 'is subject to contract law standards'.[169] As the Division states in the *GJM*, however, the courts view the issue of compliance with the agreement on the part of the Government as one of the right of the fairness accorded to the defendant. A failure on the part of the Government to adhere to the terms of a plea agreement may, for example, result in permitting a defendant to withdraw a guilty plea,[170] or in the court ordering the imposition of a specific sentence where other remedies are not available or impractical.[171]

The *Marine Hose* cartel is discussed in some detail in Chapters 4 and 6, below. In that case a number of UK executives, subsequently convicted of breaching the Cartel Offence in the UK, pleaded guilty in the United States of infringing s 1 of the Sherman Act. The case of Mr Peter Whittle

---

[167] The procedure is a little different, but not in fundamental effect, in relation to type A and C agreements.

[168] *GJM*, at IX-24.

[169] *United States v Krasn* 614 F.2d 1229, 1233 (9th Cir 1980). See also *Cooper v United States* 594 F.2d 12, 15–16 (4th Cir 1979): 'a constant factor is that when a plea rests in any significant degree on a promise or agreement of the prosecutor so that it can be said to be part of the inducement or consideration, such promise must be fulfilled'.

[170] *United States v Hammerman* 528 F.2d 326 (4th Cir 1975).

[171] *Correale v United States* 479 F.2d 944 (1st Cir 1973).

provides an interesting example of some of the terms which may be found in a plea agreement. In particular the agreement reveals the extent to which a defendant not eligible for full leniency under the Department's leniency programme may be encouraged to cooperate with an investigation in return for a reduced sentence. A motion was made for significant reductions conditional upon the defendant's ongoing full cooperation. The terms of this are specified in the Plea Agreement:[172]

> The ongoing, full and truthful cooperation of the defendant shall include, but not be limited to:
>
> (a) producing in the United States and at other mutually agreed-upon locations all non-privileged documents, including claimed personal documents, and other materials, wherever located, in the possession, custody, or control of the defendant, requested by attorneys and agents of the United States;
> (b) making himself available for interviews in the United States and at other mutually agreed-upon locations, not at the expense of the United States, upon the request of attorneys and agents of the United States;
> (c) responding fully and truthfully to all inquiries of the United States in connection with any Federal proceeding, without falsely implicating any person or intentionally withholding any information, subject to the penalties of making false statements and obstruction of justice;
> (d) otherwise voluntarily providing the United States with any non-privileged material or information, not requested in (a)–(c) of this paragraph, that he may have that is related to any Federal proceeding;
> (e) when called upon to do so by the United States in connection with any Federal proceeding, testifying in grand jury, trial and other judicial proceedings in the United States, fully, truthfully, and under oath, subject to the penalties of perjury, making false statements or declarations in grand jury or court proceedings, contempt, and obstruction of justice; and
> (f) consenting to any request by the United States while the defendant is in custody in the United Kingdom that the defendant be temporarily transferred in custody to the United States for interviews and testimony in connection with any Federal proceeding.

There has been limited research into the effect of the plea agreement process on antitrust enforcement. There may be reasons, based on arguments relating to 'fairness' or 'justice', to be concerned about their use; a defendant faced with a possible, albeit unlikely, sentence of ten years in jail may find the prospect of a certain sentence of two years irresistible, even where he or she may (privately) protest innocence. The fact that plea

---

[172] Case H-07-487-03, *US v Peter Whittle,* District Court, Southern District of Texas, entered on March 12, 2007, at Para 21 (internal references to legislative citations omitted).

agreements are so readily used in the US, and are not available in the UK (see Chapter 4), represents a major difference between the two systems.

THE SUCCESS OF THE US POLICY

As stated at the start of Chapter 1 of this book, there is widespread agreement that the US policy of criminalising cartel behaviour is successful. It is, as indicated in Chapter 2, hard to obtain firm statistical evidence which supports this view. A critic of the policy could argue that each case uncovered and prosecuted represents a failure of a policy of deterrence rather than a success. Nevertheless, the strong evidence flowing from enforcement practice, and in particular from the vigorous application of the US leniency policy (the success of which is indivisible from the threat of criminal sanctions in the event of detection absent a leniency application), is supported by robust analysis. The levels of recidivism in cartelists has been referred to in Chapter 2, with particular attention paid to the findings of Connor.[173] A remarkable figure emerges when the US experience since 1999 is examined. July 23, 1999 marks the date on which the first non-US national was sentenced to imprisonment following a s1 violation. Werden et al report that having reviewed the US data (with respect to both home-grown *and* international cartel cases brought in the US after that date)

> we found not even a single instance of cartel recidivism within the United States. No company and no individual convicted in the US of a cartel offence after July 23, 1999 subsequently joined a cartel prosecuted in the United States. Moreover, no company and no individual granted conditional leniency after July 23, 1999 subsequently joined a cartel prosecuted in the United States.[174]

This robust empirical evidence is supported more generally by the authors:

> [w]e have not investigated cartel recidivism outside of the United States, but we have observed how the presence and absence of individual accountability, with the threat of a prison sentence, has influenced international cartels. On numerous occasions, the Antitrust Division has interviewed members of international cartels who provided first-hand accounts of their participation in cartels that spanned the globe but stopped at the US border because the participants feared

---

[173] Connor, JM, 'Recidivism Revealed: Private International Cartels 1990–2009' (2010) 6:2 *Competition Policy International* 101.

[174] Werden, GJ, Hammond, SD, and Barnett, BA, 'Recidivism Eliminated: Cartel Enforcement in the United States since 1999' (2011) Georgetown Global Antitrust Enforcement Symposium, September 22, 2011 at 6.

> going to jail. The eyewitness testimony is compelling evidence that enforcement in the United States is deterring cartel activity. . . . All available evidence indicates that US cartel enforcement in the United States is at least achieving the specific deterrence of convicted offenders.[175]

It is part of the argument made in Chapter 4, below, that the only successful prosecution under the Cartel Offence in the UK at the time of writing was based on the work of the DOJ and the plea agreement under which the UK defendants agreed, *with the US authorities*, to plead guilty in the UK to a breach of UK domestic law.

---

[175] Ibid, at 8. It would appear that the hopes of Joel Klein, expressed in remarks following the bringing of the vitamins cases in the US may have been fulfilled:

> [w]ith the imposition of the fines and prison sentence in these cases, we are hopeful that multinational companies who currently engage in cartel activity or who are faced with the opportunity to do so in the future will assess their risks differently and will think twice before ripping off America's consumers and businesses (DOJ, 'Statement of Assistant Attorney General Joel I Klein', May 20, 1999).

One of the interesting aspects of the story told in *The Informant* (Eichenwald, K, *The Informant: A True Story* (2000) Broadway) relates to the efforts of Mark Whitacre to persuade members of the cartel to attend a meeting in the US, and only the compromise of Hawaii, and the promise of good golf courses, secured attendance at a meeting on US soil. See also O'Kane, M, 'Does Prison Work for Cartelists? The View from Behind Bars: An Interview of Bryan Allison by Michael O'Kane' (2011) 56 *Antitrust Bulletin* 483 at 487:

> . . . then having come back home and talked to one or two others who were involved in the cartel prior to me, they said 'What on earth are you doing meeting in the United States, we never had meetings there'.

4. Criminalisation in the UK: the Cartel Offence

INTRODUCTION

In an express attempt to increase deterrence,[1] the Cartel Offence ('the Offence') was introduced into the law of the UK with the enactment of the Enterprise Act 2002, which received Royal Assent on November 7, 2002.[2] Whether the Offence should be considered as being part of the UK law of competition – although clearly it is – is itself, given the relationship between UK and the superior EU law of competition, problematic (as will be discussed below). This chapter discusses the introduction of the Offence, its terms, its relationship with EU competition law, the operation of the Offence to date, and the impetus for reform that found expression in the 2011 Consultation Document.[3] At the time work began on this book, in March 2011, the OFT's website[4] indicated that three investigations into breaches of the Cartel Offence were ongoing: an investigation into commercial vehicle manufacturers; an investigation into the automotive sector; and an investigation into the agricultural sector. In the case of the first two investigations the OFT stated only that work was at an early stage, whereas in relation to a suspected cartel in the agricultural sector

---

1 See, for example, the Undersecretary of State during the passage of the Bill: 'there is an important relationship between an offence on the statute book and a deterrent. The current measures do not have that deterrent effect, as they do not deal with individuals' (*Hansard*, House of Commons, Standing Committee B, Enterprise Bill, Fifth Sitting, April 23, 2002, col 169). It is implicit here that the Government did not believe that penalties directed *solely* at companies would be sufficient to deter all cartel activity.

2 For a review of the Offence shortly after it was introduced, see MacCulloch, A, 'The Cartel Offence and the Criminalisation of United Kingdom Competition Law' (2003) *Journal of Business Law* 616; for a more considered overview by the same author see MacCulloch, A, 'The Cartel Offence: Is Honesty the Best Policy?', in Rodger, BJ (ed), *Ten Years of Competition Law Reform* (2010) Dundee University Press.

3 Department for Business, Innovation and Skills, *A Competition Regime for Growth: A Consultation on Options for Reform* (March 2011).

4 www.oft.gov.uk/OFTwork/competition-act-and-cartels.

the OFT had executed a search warrant 'at a business address in the West Midlands'. Two cases had been concluded, both of which are discussed in detail throughout this chapter. By November 2011 the OFT had closed its investigations in relation to the automotive and agricultural sectors without launching prosecutions; and by January 2012 the OFT's website indicated that there were *no* open Cartel Offence investigations.

THE OFFENCE

The Offence, as originally enacted, is set out in ss 188–202 of the Enterprise Act 2002 ('EA 02'). Section 188 created the Offence, s 189 provided further gloss on this, ss 190–91 set out the penalties applying on conviction and measures relating to extradition. The remaining sections of this part of the EA 02 related to the criminal investigations that would be carried out by the OFT. The latter provisions are linked into, and amended, the Criminal Justice and Police Act 2002, and the Regulation of Investigatory Powers Act 2000. *Inter alia*, these provisions allow the OFT to authorise intrusive surveillance. It is not at the time of writing clear whether these powers have in fact been used in investigations conducted to date; these powers were almost certainly not used in either of the two cases in which prosecutions have been launched at the time of writing. To focus the argument and evidence in this book solely on the substance of the Offence would be too limiting. One of the most unusual characteristics of the UK regime – and as I shall argue this is a fundamental flaw – is the relationship of the Offence to the civil law of competition in the UK. It is impossible to discuss the efficacy of the Offence without a consideration of the relationship between civil and criminal enforcement, and in particular without discussing whether the OFT is the appropriate investigative organisation.[5] Procedural, and to an extent structural, matters will therefore be considered below.

The first thing that a competition lawyer will be struck by when reading the statutory provisions, particularly if she is not from a common law jurisdiction, is the precision and formalism of the language

---

[5] See Gorecki, PK, and McFadden, D, 'Criminal Cartels in Ireland: The Heating Oil Case' (2006) *European Competition Law Review* 631: 'cartels are typically treated as civil breaches . . . criminal activity should be dealt with by the police, not by lawyers and economists that typically populate a competition agency'. The Department of Justice would perhaps argue otherwise. Gorecki and McFadden note (at 631, n 7) that: 'the person responsible for cartel enforcement in Ireland until 2002 argued in 2003 – after he had left the Competition Authority – that the police should deal with criminal cartel cases'.

used.[6] This is at some distance from the approach taken in the TFEU,[7] or in the UK's equivalent Competition Act 1998, and is nothing like the language used in s 1 of the Sherman Act.[8] Given its central importance, s 188 is reproduced here in its entirety, as is s 189:

Section 188 Cartel Offence

(1) An individual is guilty of an offence if he dishonestly agrees with one or more other persons to make or implement, or to cause to be made or implemented, arrangements of the following kind in relation to at least two undertakings (A and B).

(2) The arrangements must be ones which, if operating as the parties to the agreement intend, would –

- (a) directly or indirectly fix a price for the supply by A in the United Kingdom (otherwise than to B) of a product or service',
- (b) limit or prevent supply by A in the United Kingdom of a product or service,
- (c) limit or prevent production by A in the United Kingdom of a product,
- (d) divide between A and B the supply in the United Kingdom of a product or service to a customer or customers,
- (e) divide between A and B customers for the supply in the United Kingdom of a product or service, or
- (f) be bid-rigging arrangements.

---

6 This language has been criticised. See Peretz, G, and Lewis, J, 'Go Directly to Jail: Losing Badly in "Monopoly"' (2003) *New Law Journal* 99, who argue that the result is an Offence which is 'absurdly complex, taking two pages and 14 subsections of dense text to sort out'.

7 Writing shortly after the enactment of the Enterprise Act, Joshua explained the rejection of a rubric based on art 101 TFEU, an option which

> was soon discarded, the government accepting that finding a breach of either Article [101] or Chapter I [of the Competition Act 1998] could require a lay jury with no competition expertise to consider potentially complex economic arguments, unless there had been a prior determination by another body (which itself raises enormous problems in common law criminal jurisprudence). The fundamental argument mitigating against such a device, quite apart from the political sensitivities attached to putting individuals in jail for frustrating a not universally popular 'Euro-agenda', is that the administrative prohibitions of Article [101] and Chapter I are so widely drawn and interpreted that they catch virtually any kind of anti-competitive conduct, including ordinary commercial agreements, not just cartel behaviour. Article [101] was never designed as a matrix for a criminal offence' (Joshua, JM, 'The UK's New Cartel Offence and Its Implications for EC Competition Law: A Tangled Web' (2003) *European Law Review* 620 at 622, internal footnotes omitted).

8 Harding and Joshua noted that '[i]n forging the constituent elements of the new "cartel offence", there was surprisingly little in the way of workable precedent' (Harding, C, and Joshua, J, 'Breaking Up the Hard Core: the Prospects for the Proposed Cartel Offence' (2002) *Criminal Law Review* 933 at 934).

(3) Unless subsection (2)(d), (e) or (f) applies, the arrangements must also be ones which, if operating as the parties to the agreement intend, would –
  (a) directly or indirectly fix a price for the supply by B in the United Kingdom (otherwise than to A) of a product or service,
  (b) limit or prevent supply by B in the United Kingdom of a product or service, or
  (c) limit or prevent production by B in the United Kingdom of a product.

(4) In subsections (2)(a) to (d) and (3), references to supply or production are to supply or production in the appropriate circumstances (for which see section 189).

(5) 'Bid-rigging arrangements' are arrangements under which, in response to a request for bids for the supply of a product or service in the United Kingdom, or for the production of a product in the United Kingdom –
  (a) A but not B may make a bid, or
  (b) A and B may each make a bid but, in one case or both, only a bid arrived at in accordance with the arrangements.

(6) But arrangements are not bid-rigging arrangements if, under them, the person requesting bids would be informed of them at or before the time when a bid is made.

(7) 'Undertaking' has the same meaning as in Part 1 of the 1998 Act.

Section 189 Cartel Offence: supplementary

(1) For section 188(2)(a), the appropriate circumstances are that A's supply of the product or service would be at a level in the supply chain at which the product or service would at the same time be supplied by B in the United Kingdom.

(2) For section 188(2)(b), the appropriate circumstances are that A's supply of the product or service would be at a level in the supply chain –
  (a) at which the product or service would at the same time be supplied by B in the United Kingdom, or
  (b) at which supply by B in the United Kingdom of the product or service would be limited or prevented by the arrangements.

(3) For section 188(2)(c), the appropriate circumstances are that A's production of the product would be at a level in the production chain –
  (a) at which the product would at the same time be produced by B in the United Kingdom, or
  (b) at which production by B in the United Kingdom of the product would be limited or prevented by the arrangements.

(4) For section 188(2)(d), the appropriate circumstances are that A's supply of the product or service would be at the same level in the supply chain as B's.

(5) For section 188(3)(a), the appropriate circumstances are that B's supply of the product or service would be at a level in the supply chain –
  (a) at which the product or service would at the same time be supplied by A in the United Kingdom, or
  (b) at which supply by A in the United Kingdom of the product or service would be limited or prevented by the arrangements.

(6) For section 188(3)(b), the appropriate circumstances are that B's supply of the product or service would be at a level in the supply chain –
  (a) at which the product or service would at the same time be supplied by A in the United Kingdom, or
  (b) at which supply by A in the United Kingdom of the product or service would be limited or prevented by the arrangements.

(7) For section 188(3)(c), the appropriate circumstances are that B's production of the product would be at a level in the production chain –
  (a) at which the product would at the same time be produced by A in the United Kingdom, or
  (b) at which production by A in the United Kingdom of the product would be limited or prevented by the arrangements.

Restating the specifics of legislation in non-specific language is fraught with danger, but, in essence, the two sections quoted above make it unlawful for an individual to make any of the specified 'arrangements' dishonestly with another individual (as discussed below the dishonesty need not be mutual; it is sufficient that the defendant acted dishonestly), where the result is, or is intended to be, a horizontal price-fixing, an output-reducing, a market-sharing, or a bid-rigging arrangement. Although the language is not that found in arts 101 and 102 of the TFEU, or in the Competition Act 1998, it will be noted that there is a reference to 'undertakings', and that this term is expressly given, in s 188(7), the meaning it has under the Competition Act 1998, and therefore the meaning it has in relation to the application of EU competition law. It may also matter, but it appears not yet to have inspired much debate, that although the term 'arrangement' is used throughout the definition of the Offence, an overriding requirement is that an individual 'dishonestly *agrees*' with another to make one of the relevant arrangements. Given that the 2011 Consultation Document raises concern regarding the relationship of the Offence to the terms of Regulation 1/2003 specifically, and, as discussed below, that the question is one of whether the law is, or is not, one which provides 'sanctions [which] are the means whereby competition rules applying to undertakings are enforced', some of the wording here may be problematic. This specific issue is discussed below.

This drafting flowed from recommendations in the Penrose Report[9] and the White Paper.[10] In the latter the need for clarity was stressed: '[t]o

[9] Office of Fair Trading, *The Proposed Criminalisation of Cartels in the UK – a Report Prepared for the Office of Fair Trading by Sir Anthony Hammond QC and Roy Penrose OBE QPM* (OFT 365, November 2001) [2002] UKCLR 97.

[10] Department of Trade and Industry, *Productivity and Enterprise: A World Class Competition Regime* Cm 2533 (July 2001).

be effective, it is critical that the offence is defined in a way which is both clear and easy for business and the courts to understand. It *must also be actively applied* so that its deterrent effect is genuinely felt.'[11]

It was always likely to be the case that the Offence would apply only to what is normally characterised as 'hard-core' anti-competitive conduct,[12] in relation to which economic harm may be presumed to flow, or be intended to flow, from the very nature of the practice. To frame the Offence this way obviates the ability of parties to argue in their defence that the arrangements would in some way be pro-competitive. Thus one of the sources relied on by the Government in bringing the Offence forward was a recommendation of the Organisation for Economic Co-operation and Development ('the OECD') published in 1998. Here the following may be found:

> CONVERGENCE AND EFFECTIVENESS OF LAWS PROHIBITING HARD CORE CARTELS
> 1. Member countries should ensure that their competition laws effectively halt and deter hard core cartels. In particular, their laws should provide for:
>   (a) effective sanctions, of a kind and at a level adequate to deter firms and individuals from participating in such cartels; and
>   (b) enforcement procedures and institutions with powers adequate to detect and remedy hard core cartels, including powers to obtain documents and information and to impose penalties for non-compliance.[13]

The OECD recommendation, it should be noted, does not privilege any particular *method* of combating such cartels, arguing only that there should be effective means of so doing.

In the Penrose Report it was argued, at Para 1.12, that the Offence should extend only to horizontal conduct:

---

[11] At Para 7.33. We may query the clarity with which the Offence is framed as eventually written, and it is clear that the Offence has not been 'actively applied'.

[12] Although the term 'hard-core cartel' is widely used in the analysis and discussion of cartel conduct, it should be borne in mind that the term has no specific legal meaning. In the OECD Recommendation, referenced below, a 'hard-core cartel' was defined as:

> an anti-competitive agreement, anti-competitive concerted practice, or anti-competitive arrangement by competitors to fix prices, make rigged bids (collusive tenders), establish output restrictions or quotas, or share or divide markets by allocating customers, suppliers, territories, or lines of commerce . . . (at Para A.2(a)).

[13] OECD, *Recommendation of the Council Concerning Effective Action Against Hard Core Cartels*, March 25, 1998 [C/M(98)7/PROV].

> [w]e understand the view of those who are experts in the field of competition law is that the criminal offence should only be applicable to horizontal agreements between individuals representing 'competing' undertakings operating at the same level of the supply-chain for the purposes of the agreement in question. It should not apply to vertical agreements, many of which are considered to have pro-competitive or other beneficial effects . . .

This was followed in the White Paper, where the following appeared:

> 7.19 The new criminal offence will cover hard-core cartels only – widely recognised as the most serious forms of competition breach. The most common form of hard-core cartel involves illegal price-fixing – where a number of firms agree what price should be charged for a particular product. In most cases, this will be above what the competitive market price would be.[14]
>
> 7.20 However, cartels can also involve conduct which achieves the same economic result by different means. This includes agreeing not to compete for each other's customers – which leaves each firm free to set higher prices (market-sharing). Or firms could agree to reduce levels of output – which also increases the price that they can charge.
>
> 7.21 In some cases, firms will agree to inflate the price charged in a tender-bidding process, and enter bids which ensure that one company in the cartel will win, but on better terms than would otherwise be the case (collusive tendering). The OFT believes that public sector contracts are particularly vulnerable to these practices . . .
>
> 7.22 In all these cases, the effect is the same – prices rise and consumers pay more than they should. The Government intends that the new criminal offence will cover each of these different types of cartel.

In the event, while the Government sought clarity in the Offence, the language employed is *not* a model of clarity (Joshua described the Offence as consisting of an 'over-complicated factual catalogue'[15]), although on the basis of the limited evidence gained through enforcement efforts at the time of writing, it is not possible to lay the blame for failures at this element of the statutory language.

'Dishonesty'

The Offence requires that the agreement made be entered into 'dishonestly' on the part of the defendant. From the introduction of the Offence

---

[14] Note, however, that instances may also arise of coordinated pricing conduct designed to exclude competitors by lowering prices so as to replicate predatory pricing.

[15] Joshua, JM, note 7, at 627.

this formula has been subject to robust and effective criticism. The adoption of the dishonesty test, and whether to maintain it, has been at the heart of discussion following the collapse of the *British Airways* case, and the subsequent publication of the consultation on reform of the Offence (discussed below). There are those who defend the application of the rubric, and who argue, persuasively, that the problem lies not in the language of the Offence, but is in fact more fundamental, flowing both from the institutional structure of enforcement in the UK, and from the relationship between the civil and criminal law.

The adoption of the dishonesty rubric was criticised early on by Harding and Joshua, who argued that the term had been employed so as to 'bridge a perceived weakness in the objective definition of the prohibited conduct'.[16]

---

[16] Harding, C, and Joshua, J, note 8, at 939. Elsewhere Joshua was more critical of the inclusion of the dishonesty rubric, arguing, *inter alia,* that:

> [i]t may be that the drafters had an uneasy awareness that their definition of the *actus reus* was so confusing and elusive that 'dishonesty' might give the jury something meaty they could get to grips with. If the factual elements of the offence had been defined with sufficient clarity, there would be no need to muddy the waters with what is on any view a troublesome and contentious area of the criminal law (Joshua, JM, note 7, at 625).

MacCulloch did not reject the use of the dishonesty test, but did point to possible difficulties:

> [w]hile the average jury member will be fully aware of dishonesty within theft and the moral view of ordinary people, it is questionable whether they have adequate experience of the morality of company directors while negotiating arrangements between multinational companies. It is therefore imperative for a prosecution to be successful that the prosecution team can adequately explain the nature of the cartel and the impact that the cartel would have . . . on the market, in a manner which indicates to a lay jury that the behaviour of the individuals concerned was of a nature that they should have known that the ordinary person would consider . . . dishonest' (MacCulloch, A, 'The Cartel Offence and the Criminalisation of United Kingdom Competition Law', 616 at 622, internal footnote omitted).

Parkinson criticised the test on different grounds, pointing to a potential incompatibility with the European Convention on Human Rights, article 7 (Parkinson, S, 'The Cartel Offence under the Enterprise Act 2002' [2004] *Company Lawyer* 187 at 188):

> [i]t is a general principle underlying the [ECHR] that legal provisions which interfere with legal rights must be adequately accessible and formulated with sufficient precision to enable the citizen to regulate his conduct. This means in effect that offences must be clearly described by law: it should be possible to determine from the description of the offence what act or omission is subject to criminal liability. The individual must be able to know from studying the

Writing after the collapse of the British Airways case, Joshua argued that, rather than making the operation of the offence *easier*, as had been hoped, the dishonesty test invited the very defence – that the activity in question was not reprehensible – that its proponents wished to avoid.[17] At Para 6.6 of the 2011 Consultation Document it was suggested that the dishonesty test had become part of the problem:

> [o]ne of the reasons that has been suggested for the small number of cases is that the definition of the offence, and particularly the need to prove dishonesty on the part of defendants, may artificially limit the scope of cases that can be brought and make those cases disproportionately difficult to prove.

The reasons given in the Consultation Document for the inclusion of the dishonesty rubric are not entirely convincing (perhaps this is understandable in a Document whose purpose is to propose changes to the test). The Consultation Document sets out three reasons for the adoption of the dishonesty requirement:

> 6.8 . . . First, to ensure that the offence did not apply to agreements that would be lawful under the civil antitrust prohibitions. . . . Including 'dishonesty' was a way to ensure that the offence only applies to harmful agreements that are unlikely to have countervailing benefits.
>
> 6.9 Second, it was included to reduce the likelihood that conviction would depend on judgments taken on detailed economic evidence. . . .
>
> 6.10 Third, the 'dishonesty' element was intended to provide juries with a test that they would recognise and to signal the seriousness of the offence and correspondingly weighty penalties – so as to enable the offence to have maximum deterrent effect.

> wording of the relevant provision, if necessary with the assistance of the court's interpretation of it, what acts or what omissions will make him criminally liable. The reason for this is that he should be able to foresee, within limits which are reasonable, the consequences which any particular action he takes might entail.
>
> The problem with offences which are based on dishonesty alone is that this degree of precision is not possible.

The argument made by Parkinson, which is a little fanciful, does not appear to have been raised in either of the cases prosecuted to date. For a discussion of the proposal to incorporate dishonesty as part of the relevant test in Australia see Fisse, B, 'The Cartel Offence: Dishonesty?' (2007) 35 *Australian Business Law Review* 235.

[17] Joshua, JM, 'Shooting the Messenger: Does the UK Criminal Cartel Offense Have a Future?' (2010) *theantitrustsource*, August (www.antitrustsource.com), at 5.

The test with which juries might be familiar (although the Consultation Document perhaps assumes that jury service is a regular feature of all of our lives) is the common law test established in the case of *R v Ghosh*,[18] which is an accepted part of English and Welsh, but not of Scottish, law. The facts of the case are not relevant here, but the so-called *Ghosh* direction is. This is in the following terms:

> [i]n determining whether the prosecution has proved that the defendant was acting dishonestly, a jury must first of all decide whether according to the ordinary standards of reasonable and honest people what was done was dishonest. If it was not dishonest by those standards, that is the end of the matter and the prosecution fails.
>
> If it was dishonest by those standards, then the jury must consider whether the defendant himself must have realised that what he was doing was by those standards dishonest. In most cases, where the actions are obviously dishonest by ordinary standards, there will be no doubt about it. It will be obvious that the defendant himself knew that he was acting dishonestly. It is dishonest for a defendant to act in a way which he knows ordinary people consider to be dishonest, even if he asserts or genuinely believes that he is morally justified in acting as he did.[19]

Only one question relating to the operation of the dishonesty test has been expressly dealt with in the case law arising under the Cartel Offence at the time of writing. This arose in a preliminary appeal in the *British Airways* case. In *R v George, Burns, Burnett and Crawley*[20] the defendants, employees and former employees of British Airways, were charged on the basis that they had 'dishonestly agreed' with each other and with certain employees of Virgin Atlantic Airways ('VAA') to fix prices. The issue in this, the second of two preliminary appeals, was that of whether the requirement of dishonesty in s 188 was fulfilled if only the defendants were shown to be dishonest, or whether the prosecution was required to show that *all* parties to the alleged agreement had been dishonest. The trial judge had held that 'the subject of the verb [dishonestly] is "an individual"'. The Court of Appeal agreed, holding that this conclusion was 'self-evident'.[21] The Consultation Document of 2011 however suggested further that 'the pre-trial rulings in the *British Airways/Virgin* criminal case suggest that evidence of effects, including economic evidence, would be relevant to the issue of dishonesty'.[22] It was suggested in particular that 'defendants might

18 [1982] QB 1053 [1982] 2 All ER 689.
19 [1982] 2 All ER 689 at 696.
20 [2010] EWCA Crim 1148.
21 At Para [8].
22 At Para 6.13.

contend that they were not dishonest because an arrangement had or was believed to have had no detrimental effect on consumers'.[23] An interesting argument is made in Para 6.15:

> . . . proving dishonesty in cartel cases may be particularly difficult because cases may not always involve an individual who is clearly motivated by personal gain. Arguably, in the context of cartels, dishonesty would be better considered as a factor in determining whether to prosecute a case in the first place or in determining the severity of the penalty on conviction rather than being an element in the offence itself.

The distinction between the gain of the company entering the cartel, and the gain of the individual(s) actually making any such agreement or putting it into effect has been discussed in Chapter 2, and apparently remains pertinent.[24]

In *Norris*,[25] Auld LJ quoted with approval the work of Lever and Pike, appearing to give judicial support to the dishonesty rubric:

> [t]here should be little if any difficulty in proving dishonesty where the cartel agreement involved the taking of active steps to mislead counterparties into a belief that the parties to the agreement were engaged in normal competition with each other . . . in many situations today, third parties who deal with undertakings that are in fact parties to cartel agreements will proceed on the assumption that they are dealing with undertakings that are lawfully engaged in normal competition with each other: and the cartelists will know that this is so, and will in effect act in a dishonest and therefore criminal manner if the existence of the cartel is kept secret.

In fact, establishing dishonesty to the *Ghosh* standard may be difficult in the context of the Cartel Offence (but then maybe a high hurdle should be set for a prosecutor determined to see that an individual is deprived of his or her liberty). That the *Ghosh* direction may be generally problematic, and has had a 'somewhat chequered history',[26] is evidenced in the fact that, in some cases, it will not be issued where it may be 'likely to confuse'

---

23 At Para 6.13.

24 In a different context, as is discussed below, this has clearly had an impact on the approach taken to penalties in the one case resulting in conviction in the UK to date.

25 *Norris v Government of the United States of America and Others* [2007] EWHC 71 (Admin) (see Chapter 3, above), quoting from Lever, J, and Pike, J, 'Cartel Agreements, Criminal Conspiracy and the Statutory "Cartel Offence": Part 1' (2005) *European Competition Law Review* 90 at 95.

26 MacCulloch, A, 'Honesty, Morality and the Cartel Offence' (2007) *European Competition Law Review* 355 at 356.

the jury.[27] This is the case for example in some theft and fraud trials. The point has been well made by Joshua that the test 'requires the jury to have a view on acceptable moral standards', and that (as discussed in Chapter 2), 'as surveys show, there is no community consensus that price fixing equals turpitude'.[28] In *R v IB* further complications were raised as it became evident that the issue of dishonesty, or rather the lack of it, would be a central argument for the defence. There was little evidence brought forward that suggested that the leniency applicant, Virgin, had recognised at the time that *its* acts in participating in the price-fixing were dishonest, although the leniency application itself required that this admission be made. The very fact that an applicant is required to admit personal dishonesty to secure comfort from the risk of prosecution may, it has been suggested, serve to deter leniency applications.

A number of commentators have argued that the dishonesty test is an inappropriate one to bring to bear on the Cartel Offence, and that it should be removed, as was suggested in the Consultation Document,[29] and accepted in the response. There has been a limited defence of the inclusion of the dishonesty requirement, the most persuasive of which is made by Bailin,[30] who argues that the attack on the requirement 'appears to be centred on the need to restore the credibility of the OFT following the collapse of the BA/Virgin trial'.[31] While accepting that the failure in the BA case did cause the OFT to suffer severe reputational damage, Bailin argues that 'it did not undermine the viability of the offence itself'.[32]

The OFT itself, in its response to the Consultation exercise, unsurprisingly argued in favour of the withdrawal of the requirement, stating that the damage caused to consumers by cartels does 'not depend on the dishonesty with which they were made'.[33] The OFT is able to draw on its

---

27 See *R v Price* (1989) 90 Cr App R 409 (CA). See also The Law Commission, *Legislating the Criminal Code: Fraud and Deception* (1999) Consultation Paper No 1555, which identifies a number of problems arising from the *Ghosh* test.

28 Joshua, JM, 'Shooting the Messenger', note 17 above.

29 See, for example, Parkinson, S, 'The Cartel Offence under the Enterprise Act 2002' (2004) *Company Lawyer* 187; Stephan, A, 'How Dishonesty Killed the Cartel Offence' (2011) *Criminal Law Review* 446; Joshua, JM, note 28; Wardhaugh, B, 'Closing the Deterrence Gap: Individual Liability, the Cartel Offence and the BIS Consultation' (2011) *Competition Law Journal* 175.

30 Bailin, A, 'Doing Away with Dishonesty' (2011) *Competition Law Journal* 169.

31 At 171.

32 At 171.

33 OFT, *A Competition Regime for Growth: A Consultation on Options for*

limited experience to date to advance a number of possible justifications that would seek to demonstrate that an arrangement falling with s 188 of the Enterprise Act was not in fact dishonest. These include: (1) that the purpose of the cartel was to protect jobs; (2) that the individual did not directly benefit financially from the arrangements; (3) that while the defendant was aware that the arrangement was unlawful under competition law the defendant did not consider it to be dishonest. At Paras 5.5–5.6 of its response the OFT argued that:

> there is no certainty as to how a jury would approach any of these matters when assessing dishonesty, particularly in relation to conduct which many jury members may not consider inherently dishonest . . .
>
> The OFT believes that such uncertainty is inherently undesirable, both for business and employees seeking advice in this area, as well as for those under investigation or facing prosecution. It also makes it more difficult and resource-intensive to investigate and prosecute the offence, as even those who may be ready to admit their involvement in cartel conduct will have an incentive to contest the case in the hope that a jury will be persuaded that they were not acting dishonestly. This in turn impacts on the number of cases that can realistically be investigated and prosecuted and the level of deterrence that can be achieved.[34]

Reform. The OFT's Response to the Government's Consultation (OFT 1335, June 2011) at 5.4.

[34] Ibid. See also Para 5.8:

> [a]s regards the other objectives which informed the inclusion of dishonesty as an element of the offence, the OFT considers that it should be possible to achieve these either equally or more effectively by other means, without the uncertainty and resulting difficulties created by the dishonesty requirement . . . Specifically:
>
> - It seems to the OFT that it should be possible to frame the offence in other ways, that do not rely on dishonesty as an element of the definition of the offence, of ensuring that agreements that would be lawful under the civil antitrust prohibitions are excluded from the offence.
> - Retaining dishonesty as an element of the offence would also not appear to be essential for ensuring that the OFT remains able to prosecute individuals for their participation in cartels that are the subject of civil enforcement action by the European Commission. The OFT agrees with the consultation document, however, that this may be more difficult to achieve if the dishonesty requirement were to be removed without making other changes to the offence.
> - As regards the objective of excluding the need for juries to consider the economic effects of an agreement, it appears likely that trial courts will in fact be asked to admit expert economic evidence of effects as being potentially relevant to establishing dishonesty. As well as being contrary to the intention of Parliament at the time the EA02 was debated, the OFT believes that this is likely to present considerable difficulties in jury trials. Rather, the OFT believes that consideration of the effects, or likely effects, of cartel behaviour is better addressed by the prosecutor in determining

This is an audacious argument to bring forward, and may be, as Bailin suggests, 'unprecedented'.[35] The OFT would have the dishonesty requirement removed because it makes it difficult to prove that a person is guilty of a criminal offence and to deprive him of his liberty on conviction. A robust response might be to suggest that the OFT, having been made to look ridiculous and not fit for purpose in the light of the collapse of the BA case, was seeking simply to move the goalposts, rather than learning to play the game better. Bailin is persuasive:

> [t]o reason that *potential* arguments relating to dishonesty make the offence so uncertain that dishonesty should be removed altogether from the offence is surprising, to say the least. It is *meant to be* difficult to prove dishonesty: that is precisely why it is an element in the criminal offence.[36]

The OFT was clearly not persuaded by these arguments and stated that to rely 'on a normative concept, such as dishonesty, to define the criminal cartel offence inevitably introduces some uncertainty'.[37] It has been noted elsewhere that there is a link between the language of 'dishonesty' and morality.[38] The Law Commission has recognised as much, stating that 'dishonesty' 'necessitates a moral as well as a factual enquiry'.[39] It may be that in urging the removal of the constraint of 'dishonesty' the OFT was responding in part to a recognition that the public have not been persuaded yet of the moral wrongs associated with cartelisation (see Chapter 2, above).

As discussed below there is the need, given the framework of enforcement adopted in the UK, to retain the clear water between the civil enforcement system of arts 101 and 102 TFEU and the Chapter I and II Prohibitions and the criminal enforcement of the Cartel Offence, and whilst that separation is tendentious, it was facilitated by the inclusion of the dishonesty rubric.[40] As I will argue later, the greater failing in the system is the attempt to run a system of individual criminal prosecution

---

which cases merit prosecution, and in the event of a conviction, by the sentencing court in considering the seriousness of the offence and mitigation (internal footnotes omitted).

35 Bailin, A, note 30, at 173.

36 Ibid at 173.

37 OFT, note 33, at 5.5.

38 See, for example, MacCulloch, A, note 26, at 359.

39 The Law Commission, *Fraud: Report on a Reference under Section 3(1)(e) of the Law Commissions Act 1965* (2002) Law Com 276 at 5.1.

40 Bailin, for example, states that this is 'a simple and principled way to achieve that separation' (note 30, at 173).

alongside the civil enforcement system: in effect, operating different trains, on different tracks, with the same engine driver.[41]

THE RELATIONSHIP BETWEEN UK AND EU COMPETITION LAW

If the Cartel Offence falls within Recital (8) of Regulation 1/2003 (see below), it can be applied outside the framework of obligations and restrictions imposed on national competition authorities by that Regulation. If, on the other hand, the Offence is considered to be part of the more general body of competition law under which the rules of competition law are applied to undertakings, any enforcement would have to proceed within the framework of Regulation 1/2003 (which does not preclude the imposition of criminal law sanctions[42]). The fact that the latter situation *may* be the case cannot be ignored, if for no other reason than that attempts to avoid this outcome have shaped the wording of the Offence. It is more likely that the stand-alone nature of the Offence *is* compatible with EU

---

[41] That this could be a significant problem was recognised by MacCulloch in 2003:

> [u]nder the reformed scheme of antitrust enforcement in the EC the OFT will take on the primary enforcement role for arts [101 and 102 TFEU] in the United Kingdom alongside its responsibilities under the Competition and Enterprise Acts. If [civil] investigations are delayed because of criminal investigations relating to the Cartel Offence it is therefore possible that the effectiveness of a Europe wide approach to cartels may be hampered. Or alternatively, will the importance of [civil] matters mean that the OFT decide (*sic*) not to risk instigating criminal investigations which have a limited chance of success? It is possible that the existence of the Cartel Offence will complicate the co-ordinating relationship, envisaged within the network of Competition Authorities . . . between the OFT and the European Commission as both institutions have divergent priorities (MacCulloch, A, note 16, 616 at 623).

[42] Article 5 of Regulation 1/2003, provides in part that the 'competition authorities of the Member States shall have the power to apply articles [101] and [102] of the Treaty in individual cases. For this purpose, acting on their own initiative or on a complaint, they may take . . . decisions . . . imposing fines, periodic penalty payments or any other penalty provided for in their national law'. As noted by Wils:

> Member States can thus in their national law provide for administrative or civil fines for violations of Articles [101] or [102 TFEU], or criminal fines, or fines on individuals, of an administrative, civil or criminal nature, or imprisonment, or indeed 'any other penalty' (Wils, WPJ, 'Is Criminalization of EU Competition Law the Answer?' (2005) 28:2 *World Competition* 117 at 129).

competition law, in that it falls within the exclusion of the last sentence of Recital (8) of Regulation 1/2003 (see below).[43] It may also be the case that the question can only be answered on a case-by-case basis; if, for example, the defence were to argue in a particular case that the arrangement in question fell within the terms of art 101(3) TFEU a criminal court could find itself in the position of ruling on the direct effect of that provision. A more difficult question raised by the operation and enforcement of the Offence is that of the dual nature of the UK regime, with civil cases against undertakings being brought alongside criminal cases against employees of those undertakings. This is a challenge that is not faced, as explained in the previous chapter, by the Antitrust Division of the US Department of Justice (nor indeed in Ireland). The consequences are a greatly muddied playing field, where the relationships between the actors – the enforcement agency, the undertakings, and employees – become much more complicated.[44] This has consequences for the timing of proceedings, for rights available to the defence, and particularly for leniency programmes, which, as discussed in Chapter 2, have become of fundamental importance in the international action against cartelisation.

The relationship between UK and EU competition law is governed by

---

[43] See however, Wils, who must be taken seriously:

> [t]he UK authorities' view that Regulation No 1/2003 would not apply to the criminal cartel offence apparently also relies upon the very last sentence of recital 8 of Regulation No 1/2003 . . . this sentence in my view merely specifies, with regard to national laws which impose criminal sanctions on natural persons, what already follows from Article 3(3) of Regulation No 1/2003, namely that Article 3(1) and (2) of this Regulation do not preclude the application of provisions of national law that predominantly pursue an objective different from that pursued by articles [101] and [102 TFEU]. Article 3(1) and (2) of the Regulation would however appear to apply to all national laws that do not predominantly pursue an objective different from that pursued by articles [101] and [102 TFEU], irrespective of the question whether those laws impose criminal sanctions on natural persons. I have difficulty seeing how one could consider that the UK cartel offence predominantly pursues an objective different from that pursued by article [101 TFEU]. Indeed, it is perfectly clear from the history of the Enterprise Act 2002 that the cartel offence was introduced in UK law because it was considered that the existing fines on companies were insufficient to deter hard-core cartels prohibited [by existing law] and that imprisonment was the most effective additional deterrent. The cartel offence in the United Kingdom should thus in my view be considered *a means whereby competition rules applying to undertakings are enforced* (Wils, WPJ, note 42, at 132–33, emphasis added, internal footnotes omitted).

[44] This is not a novel conclusion. Thus Joshua noted that criminal enforcement 'does not fit easily into the European template' (Joshua, JM, note 7, at 629).

EU constitutional law generally, by EU competition law specifically, and is also embedded expressly within the Competition Act 1998, which was itself introduced in order to very substantially align domestic competition law, at least as regards the law of anti-competitive agreements and the law of abuse of dominant position, with that of the then European Community. The Cartel Offence was brought forward at a time when the EC Commission was engaged in the process of bringing forward its modernisation package for EC competition law, of which Regulation 1/2003 became the cornerstone. The wisdom of the UK making its move before the final shape of the EU regime became clear was questioned at the time. In the debates relating to the passage of the Enterprise Act, and in Committee, the Government was repeatedly pressed on the relationship between the proposed Offence and art 101 TFEU. Miss Melanie Johnson, then Undersecretary of State for Trade and Industry, resorted to a formulaic answer:

> [t]he criminal offence is separate from and compatible with the EC civil regime. The UK criminal offence targets individuals; the EC civil regime covers broader competition breaches committed by undertakings. Some Hon. Members suggested that we should await the outcome of the EC modernisation proposals before we introduce the criminal offence for cartels. However, we do not know when those proposals will be brought into force and there is no reason to delay the introduction of the offence in the meantime.[45]

One of the ways in which the UK Offence was to be distinguished from the EU civil law was by its focus on the requirement of 'dishonesty', discussed above.[46]

Recital (8) Regulation 1/2003 is key. Often in the context of discussion of the Offence this is quoted only in part, but it is necessary here to reproduce this recital in its entirety:

---

[45] *Hansard*, HC, Standing Committee B, Enterprise Bill, Fifth Sitting, Tuesday April 23, 2002, col 167. See also, at col 170:

> [o]n the interplay with the EC regime, under the exemptions from article [101] of the Treaty, there is no Community law requirement for an exact correspondence between EU competition law and the criminal offence. However, as far as possible, we should seek to ensure that the two operate consistently in practice. That will be achieved on the one hand by prosecutorial discretion – for example, the OFT and SFO will not prosecute where genuine possibility of compatibility with Community law on the agreement exists – and importantly, on the other hand by the need to prove dishonesty.

[46] And see, for example, MacCulloch, A, note 2, at 620 who describes this as a 'key distinction'.

> (8) In order to ensure the effective enforcement of the Community competition rules and the proper functioning of the cooperation mechanisms contained in this Regulation, it is necessary to oblige competition authorities and courts of the Member States to also apply articles [101] and [102] of the Treaty where they apply national competition law to agreements and practices which may affect trade between Member States. In order to create a level playing field for agreements, decisions by associations of undertakings and concerted practices within the internal market, it is also necessary to determine pursuant to article [103(2)(e)] of the Treaty the relationship between national laws and Community competition law. To that effect it is necessary to provide that the application of national competition laws to agreements, decisions or concerted practices within the meaning of article [101(1)] of the Treaty may not lead to the prohibition of such agreements, decisions and concerted practices if they are not also prohibited under Community competition law. The notions of agreements, decisions and concerted practices are autonomous concepts of Community competition law covering the coordination of behaviour of undertakings on the market as interpreted by the Community Courts. Member States should not under this Regulation be precluded from adopting and applying on their territory stricter national competition laws which prohibit or impose sanctions on unilateral conduct engaged in by undertakings. These stricter national laws may include provisions which prohibit or impose sanctions on abusive behaviour toward economically dependent undertakings. *Furthermore, this Regulation does not apply to national laws which impose criminal sanctions on natural persons except to the extent that such sanctions are the means whereby competition rules applying to undertakings are enforced* (emphasis added).

As previously noted, the Regulation was drafted at a time when the UK was contemplating introduction of the Offence, and when certain other Member States maintained criminal law in relation to some competition areas (see Chapter 5, below). There was a general assumption to the effect that the terms of Recital (8) specifically allowed accommodation of the Offence. With hindsight, and with more careful thought, such assumptions can be shown to have been hasty. In essence, if the Cartel Offence was to be deemed to be a law under which 'competition rules applying to undertakings are enforced' its operation would be constrained by the requirements of EU competition law. As the experience in Ireland, discussed in Chapter 5 below, demonstrates, it is not impossible to marry the enforcement of arts 101 and even 102 TFEU, and their national equivalents, into a criminal law framework. The Irish constitution requires this, and the Irish experience, where there is a single enforcement mechanism, has been in some respects a more positive one than has been the UK experience, although it is clear that there remain difficulties with this approach.

There is much to support the view that the Offence is, in fact, however framed, a means whereby 'competition rules applying to undertakings are enforced'. There is express recognition in the preparatory documents that the aim of the Offence was to cover 'different kinds of cartel';[47] there is reference in s 188 itself to the need to establish that the 'agreement' in question relates to arrangements 'between at least two *undertakings*', and 'undertakings' is given precisely the same meaning that it has in relation to the CA98, and therefore that it has in relation to the competition law of the TFEU. In the *Explanatory Notes* published by the DTI to accompany the Act it was stated at Para 406 that the actions prohibited 'are a sub-set of the practices for which undertakings may be pursued under the civil provisions of [the Competition Act 1998].' Indeed, at a more fundamental level, if it is *not* the purpose of the Offence to be part of the armoury in the fight against unlawful cartels, and therefore of anti-competitive arrangements between undertakings, what is its purpose? Even when, as in *R v IB*,[48] the Court found that the Offence *was* compatible with Regulation 1/2003, Hughes LJ still commented that the objective of the Offence was to 'provide a stronger deterrent' to 'anti-competitive practices'.[49] It may be, notwithstanding the apparently clear signal sent by recital (8) of Regulation 1/2003, that any such offence, however framed, must be applied in a manner consistent with the Regulation.

In *R v IB*[50] an interim appeal challenged the legal basis on which the Crown Court had jurisdiction to hear the case. It was argued for the defendants that the subject matter of the charge lay properly within the terms of art 101 TFEU, that the Offence was in fact a 'national competition law', and that the combined effect of arts 3.5 and 35 of Regulation 1/2003 was that '*only* a designated national competition authority has the power to impose a fine or other penalty, but that the Crown Court is not a designated competition authority'.[51] The Court referred to recital (8), and Hughes LJ stated that:

> [i]t may or may not have been thought in some circles that this sentence demonstrates that a national law such as s 188 is outside the scope of the Modernisation Regulation. Taken by itself, however, its meaning seems to us to be obscure. It begs the question whether s 188, which is transparently a new law designed to strengthen local prevention of anti-competitive behaviour, is a means of enforcing competition rules applying to undertakings, or an ancillary law which bolsters the effectiveness of competition rules but is not concerned

---

47 See the White Paper, note 10, at Para 7.22.

48 [2009] EWCA Crim 2575 [2010] UKCLR 1.

49 At Para [22]. It is also perhaps worth noting that the long title of the Enterprise Act refers in part to the creation of an offence 'for those entering into certain anti-competitive agreements'.

50 [2009] EWCA Crim 2575 [2010] UKCLR 1.

51 At Para [19(iii)].

> with directly enforcing them against undertakings. In order to answer that question it is necessary to read the Modernisation Regulation as a whole.[52]

Taken as a whole, the Court held that Regulation 1/2003 was clearly directed at issues relating to the enforcement of arts 101 and 102 TFEU, and was aimed at ensuring that the same standards were applied across member states in relation to agreements and infringements falling under these articles. The Court held that such considerations did not arise in relation to a prosecution under s 188. While the question of dishonesty was fundamental to the Offence as first defined, this was not something, the Court held, which went to the enforcement of art 101 TFEU. Although there was a risk of inconsistency arising between prosecution under s 188 and questions as to the validity of an agreement under art 101 TFEU, this was considered to be merely a 'residual risk'.[53] Finally the Court held that even if it was wrong in holding that s 188 was *not* a 'national competition law' in the sense that the term was used in Regulation 1/2003, it would nevertheless be the case that the effect of the Regulation was not to make the enforcement of a part of national competition law 'the *exclusive* province of the designated national competition authority'.[54]

In the Consultation Document of 2011 the Government argued that it was necessary further to differentiate the Offence from the 'civil antitrust prohibitions'.[55] It is interesting then that at the same time it sought to remove the requirement of 'dishonesty' from the Offence. Although the case of *R v Goldshield Group Plc and others*[56] is subject to reporting restrictions, an early published version indicated that the view of the then House of Lords was that a prosecution in relation to the common law offence of conspiracy to defraud would be compatible with Regulation 1/2003 on the grounds that it was the dishonesty, and not the price-fixing, that applied in that case, which was the target of the law.

That the introduction of the Cartel Offence may complicate matters relating to the exchange of information within the ECN is discussed below,

---

52 At Para [30].

53 At Para [36].

54 At Para [38].

55 See, for example, Para 6.18:

> [i]t is important not to lose sight of the need for any alternative to sufficiently differentiate the cartel offence from the civil antitrust prohibitions that it can be prosecuted in parallel with enforcement action taken under them. Only if this is possible can the offence continue to target the most serious and damaging international cartels . . .'

56 [2008] UKHL 17.

but there is another potential procedural issue. It is unlikely that the OFT could persuade either the EU Commission, or another ECN considering bringing an action on the basis of art 101 TFEU or a national equivalent, to delay that action if the OFT was minded to target an individual in the UK with a cartel offence prosecution. That this might be the case was recognised by Peretz and Lewis in 2003.[57] It might be possible for the OFT to mount a prosecution in the UK while civil action was proceeding contemporaneously in another jurisdiction, but this further complicates what is already a complicated decision. It is notable that in the case of the marine hose cartel, the only successful prosecution to date in the UK, the EC Commission did take an infringement decision, so these problems, if they exist, can clearly be circumvented.

INVESTIGATION

The OFT was given responsibility at the time of the introduction of the Offence for investigating and prosecuting breaches, working alongside the Serious Fraud Office ('SFO') (which has not yet played a significant role in the cases investigated). It was always evident that to dovetail the criminal aspects of investigation and enforcement under the auspices of a single authority would be complex. In May 2002 Margaret Bloom, then Director of Competition Enforcement at the OFT, stated that:

> [a]t an early stage an assessment will be made of whether a cartel is likely to be sufficiently serious to justify criminal enforcement. All those cases where criminal enforcement is a possibility will be pursued to criminal standards of evidence gathering from the start. In the early stages of each case, the criminal investigation against the individuals will proceed in parallel with the civil one against the undertakings, under their appropriate powers of investigation. The civil case may well be able to go as far as the Rule 14 notice and the written and oral representations as all of this is confidential. But the final civil decision will need to await the conclusion of the criminal trial in order to avoid any risk of prejudicing the outcome of the trial. The considerable benefit of increased deterrence is well worth the delay in issuing these decisions.[58]

---

[57] Peretz, G, and Lewis, J, note 6.

[58] 'Key Challenges in Public Enforcement', speech to the BIICL, May 17, 2002. Writing in 2003 MacCulloch stated that:

> [i]t seems likely that in a situation where the OFT receives information which suggests an investigation may lead to a viable prosecution it must initiate an investigation which is in accordance with the criminal standard of proof and therefore delay any Chapter I investigation. This will obviously have a major

The powers of investigation given to the OFT under the EA 02 are strong, and link in further to powers in the Criminal Justice and Police Act 2001, the Police Act 1997, and the Regulation of Investigatory Powers Act 2000 ('RIPA'). Section 32 *et seq* of the latter provides for the authorisation of intrusive surveillance, and amendments effected to RIPA by the EA 02 confer these powers on the OFT. The powers conferred on the OFT by virtue of ss 193–99 are subject to the scope of s 192. This is in the following terms:

> (1) The OFT may conduct an investigation if there are reasonable grounds for suspecting that an offence under section 188 has been committed.
> (2) The powers of the OFT under ss 193 and 194 are exercisable, but only for the purposes of an investigation under subsection (1), in any case where it appears to the OFT that there is good reason to exercise them for the purpose of investigating the affairs, or any aspect of the affairs, of any person . . .

Given that the OFT also acts as the UK's National Competition Agency ('NCA') for the purposes of the application of EU competition law, and also has primary responsibility for the public enforcement of the two prohibitions set out in the CA98, the introduction of the Offence raised a number of issues relating to the dual (civil/criminal) nature of the UK's regime. This is acknowledged at a number of places in the Enterprise Act, which introduces protections into the CA98 designed to ensure that evidence obtained in civil proceedings, in which the rights of the defence may not be as rigorously protected as is the case in relation to criminal proceedings, is not used in criminal proceedings. Section 198 of the Enterprise Act for example, amends the 1998 Act, inserting a new s 30A, which is intended to protect against self-incrimination in respect of oral statements compelled under the powers available under the CA98.[59] It has been suggested

---

impact on the OFT's decision making as the primary body investigating cartels in the United Kingdom (MacCulloch, A, note 16, at 626).

[59] Section 30A is in the following terms:

> A statement made by a person in response to a requirement imposed by virtue of any of sections 26 to 28 may not be used in evidence against him on a prosecution for an offence under section 188 of the Enterprise Act unless, in the proceedings –
> (a) in giving evidence, he makes a statement inconsistent with it, and
> (b) evidence relating to it is adduced, or a question relating to it is asked, by him or on his behalf.

A clear statement as to the purpose of this provision is set out in the Explanatory Notes published by the then DTI which state the following at Para 429:

that the hurdle of s 192(1) itself may be met in the event that the OFT, acting in its role as the UK's NCA, is alerted to the existence of a cartel operating within the UK by virtue of information shared amongst the ECN or disseminated through the EU Commission. The OFT however, relying on Regulation 1/2003, art 28, and paras 37–42 of the *Commission Notice on co-operation within the Network of Competition Authorities*,[60] has stated that it would not be able to use any information obtained from the EU Commission or from other NCAs through the circulation of information relating to leniency applications as 'a basis for starting its own criminal investigation'.[61] The OFT recognises that this is not a precise reflection of the statutory language, and that there is a 'lacuna' in the law, but takes the view that it would 'be contrary to the spirit' of the Network Notice to act in this way.[62]

While it was envisaged that investigations may have to proceed with the full panoply of covert tactics, this has not been the case to date. The marine hose cartel investigation was carried out using such tactics, but in the United States, and in the case of British Airways, the alleged cartel was one to which only two undertakings were party, and where a leniency application had been made. Thus, although the OFT has substantial investigative powers,[63] and has published guidance in relation to these, they have not yet been fully employed.

> [t]he Chairman of the OFT . . . will continue to have the powers . . . to require the provision of information by an individual on behalf of an undertaking under Part I, Chapter III of CA 1998 as part of a civil investigation. This section amends CA 1998 to provide a safeguard with regard to the use of any such information obtained under CA 1998 by compulsion, for the purposes of the criminal offence under section 188. This is intended to provide protection against self-incrimination.

60 (2004) OJ C101/3.

61 *Applications for Leniency and No-action in Cartel Cases. OFT's Detailed Guidance on the Principles and Process: A Consultation on OFT Guidance* (OFT 803con, October 2011), draft guidance, Para 8.11.

62 Ibid, Para 8.11. It is interesting that Wils takes a different view, arguing that it would be quite legitimate for the UK to initiate an investigation after having received information to the effect that a violation existed from another member of the ECN (Wils, WPJ, note 42, at 153).

63 See, for example, *Powers for Investigating Criminal Cartels* (January 2004), *Covert Surveillance in Cartel Investigations: Code of Practice* (OFT 738, August 2004) and *Covert Human Intelligence Sources in Cartel Investigations: Code of Practice* (OFT 739, August 2004).

Territoriality

The UK maintains, in the wording of s 193(3), its long-standing hostility to the effects doctrine. Adopting similar language to that used in the Competition Act 1998 in relation to territorial scope, s 193(3) provides that:

> [n]o proceedings may be brought for an offence under section 188 in respect of an agreement outside the United Kingdom, unless it has been implemented in whole or in part in the United Kingdom.

The term 'implemented' is drawn from EU case law in which a form of jurisdiction somewhat more limited than that which applies under the effects doctrine is recognised.[64]

Section 199(3) also has the effect of slightly modifying the terms of the Offence when applied to agreements outside the UK. In the case of agreements entered into in the UK s 188 applies where the arrangements '*would*' give rise to one of the specified circumstances. In the case of agreements entered into outside the UK the use of the term 'implemented' requires that the agreement actually take effect in the UK.

It is clear therefore that the terms of the Offence may apply to foreign companies and to foreign executives who 'implement' their cartel in the UK. The Explanatory Notes published to accompany the Bill suggested that this requirement could be met where, for example, an e-mail was sent to a recipient in the UK. [65] As has been discussed in the previous chapter, the US practice is to pursue foreign executives engaged in s 1 violations aggressively, and in fact many of those indicted voluntarily surrender themselves to US jurisdiction. Whether the UK authorities would be able to secure similar surrenders remains to be seen, as does the extent to which extradition would in practice be sought – the law has not yet been applied to non-UK nationals. The range of countries from which extradition could be sought is relatively small, as the requirement of dual criminality is met in only a limited number of jurisdictions. While the EU Arrest Warrant greatly simplifies extradition procedures, it does so only in respect of a closed list of offences, which while drawn broadly, does not appear to encompass cartelisation. It has been widely assumed that the introduction

---

[64] First put forward in the case of *Wood pulp* (*Ahlström (A.) Oy v Commission* cases C89/85 etc [1988] 4 CMLR 407.

[65] Thus Para 412, suggested that this might be the case where there was '[a]n instruction to others to implement the agreement, delivered into the UK by telephone or electronic mail'.

of the Offence does ensure that dual criminality applies as between the UK and the US.[66] The House of Lords has held that dual criminality did not exist prior to the enactment of the Cartel Offence.[67]

---

[66] See, for example, Joshua: '[t]he criminalisation of cartel conduct in the United Kingdom will mean that extradition to the United States of price fixers in "global" cartels will henceforth be possible under the "dual criminality" rules' (Joshua, JM, note 7, at 636).

[67] See *Norris v United States* [2008] UKHL 16, where the Court held that there was not an equivalence between the common law offence of conspiracy to defraud and a violation of s 1 of the Sherman Act. In reaching this conclusion the Court relied in part on the enactment of the Cartel Offence, which was presumed to be equivalent for the purposes of dual criminality, and stated that price-fixing was not in itself dishonest unless it was accompanied by 'aggravating features such as fraud, misrepresentation, violence, intimidation or inducement of a breach of contract' (at [17]). Any statements as to the meaning of dishonesty in the context of the Cartel Offence were *obiter* and it is not clear whether the description of the constituents of the dishonesty requirement in relation to the Offence will be followed. See also Morgan, EJ, 'Criminal Cartel Sanctions under the UK Enterprise Act: An Assessment' (2010) 17:1 *International Journal of the Economics of Business* 67 at 76:

> [t]he *Norris* judgement and subsequent collapse of the costly six year investigation ('Operation Holbein') into the drugs case, a further blow to the SFO's battered morale, is likely to have dulled the SFO's appetite for taking further criminal prosecutions under common law. . . . As legal commentators have observed . . . it will be difficult to base a charge of dishonesty on the secrecy of price fixing in the absence of other aggravating factors after the *Norris* judgement unless secret price fixing of itself is to be regarded as dishonest as a result of the Enterprise Act. This remains to be seen but it is important to note that the legal context has changed with the criminalisation of individual cartel behaviour and so the judgements in these earlier cases may be less relevant to future cases than has sometimes been suggested.

Norris was subsequently extradited on different grounds (see Chapter 3, above). See Whelan, P, 'Resisting the Long Arm of Criminal Antitrust Laws: *Norris v The United States*' (2009) 72:2 *Modern Law Review* 272; and Lester, M, 'Prosecuting Cartels for Conspiracy to Defraud' (2008) *Competition Law Journal* 134. In relation to conspiracy to defraud and its link to cartelisation, see also the approach taken by the House of Lords in *R v Goldshield Group plc and others* (2008) UKHL 17. The OFT clearly considers that it remains a possibility that cartel conduct may give rise to prosecutions on the basis that fraud has been committed. In *Applications for Leniency and No-action in Cartel Cases. OFT's Detailed Guidance on the Principles and Process: A Consultation on OFT Guidance* (OFT 803con, October 2011), at Para 7.30, the OFT thus states that:

> . . . applicants must accept that the OFT could refer cases of potential serious or complex fraud, in the form of cartel behaviour, to the SFO and the expectation should be that such referrals will be on the basis of a full disclosure of all material in the OFT's possession that relates to the cartel.

TRIAL AND PUNISHMENT

Prosecutions brought forward under s 188 may be brought by either the SFO, or the OFT.[68] Private prosecutions may *only* be brought with the permission of the OFT. In Scotland the power to prosecute rests with the Lord Advocate.

The penalties that may be levied following a successful prosecution are set out at s 190(1) of the Enterprise Act 2002. A person guilty is liable:

(a) on conviction on indictment, to imprisonment for a term not exceeding five years, or to a fine, or both;
(b) on summary conviction, to imprisonment for a term not exceeding six months or to a fine not exceeding the statutory maximum, or to both.

Only one case to date in the UK has resulted in custodial sentences being imposed, and, as noted above, this case is an unusual one. The case is *R v Whittle*[69] in which the three defendants, Peter Whittle, Bryan Allison and David Brammar, each entered guilty pleas. At trial the sentences handed down were of three years' duration for Mr Whittle and Mr Allison, and two-and-a-half years for Mr Brammar. On appeal, on the matter of the sentence terms only, these were reduced to two-and-a-half years, two years, and 20 months respectively. The response of the Court on appeal is important, and although the OFT indicated satisfaction with the result, the Court's response undermines the efficacy of the Offence as a deterrent. The circumstances surrounding this case, which also led to prosecutions in the US, and to an infringement decision taken by the EU Commission, are discussed much more thoroughly in Chapter 6, below, but it needs to be noted here that the defendants had entered into a plea agreement in the US, under the terms of which sentences were agreed with the US authorities, with any sentence in the UK being deducted from that time. This arrangement in itself, which had the effect that although the appellants were arguing for reduced sentences they also argued that the sentences should not fall *below* a certain level, was questioned by the Court of Appeal at Para [28] of its judgment:

> [i]t follows that this court has not had the benefit of the kind of argument from counsel to which it is accustomed; we emphasise that this is through no fault of theirs. They were acting upon their instructions and their instructions were imposed upon them by the terms of the plea agreements. We have our doubts as

---

68 Enterprise Act 2002, s 190(2).
69 [2008] EWCA Crim 2560 [2009] UKCLR 247.

> to the propriety of a US prosecutor seeking to inhibit the way in which counsel represent their clients in a UK court, but having heard no argument on the subject we shall express no concluded view.[70]

The Court then turned to the pleas of mitigation entered on behalf of the appellants at trial. It started from the position that:

> each was of good character, each admitted his involvement readily, each has offered to assist the authorities further . . ., each has pleaded guilty at the first opportunity, each has lost a livelihood and there will be significant financial consequences for him and his family.[71]

The Court assumed from this that the trial judge 'must have taken the starting point as at or near the statutory maximum'.[72] The Court also noted that although the profits engendered by the cartel probably amounted to some £2.5m, these 'did not, of course, go directly into the pockets of any of the applicants'.[73] The Court reduced the sentences imposed at trial, and indicated that, had it been asked to do so, it 'may well have been persuaded to reduce the sentences further'.[74]

The fact that the Court was clearly not persuaded that participation in the marine hose cartel by the appellants merited a penalty towards the upper end of the available spectrum should be a matter of some concern, and may undermine the deterrent effect of the Offence. In the specific context of cartelisation one may question the value of references to good

---

[70] In practice, plea bargaining is a common feature of criminal antitrust prosecutions in the United States, and is used in many of the cases involving foreign defendants. In particular a plea bargain may secure a conviction and a term in jail in situations where extradition would be problematic. Given the emphasis placed on international cooperation by antitrust authorities, and the fact that many cartels spill across national boundaries, it is likely that arrangements such as those made in the *Marine Hose* case will continue to be entered into, although the agreement was unprecedented at the time. While it may be unpalatable for a UK court to find defence arguments constrained by accommodations towards other legal systems, this is probably something that lies outside the control of the UK courts.

[71] At Para [29].

[72] At Para [30].

[73] At Para [21]. The question of whether cartelists may benefit directly from the cartels that they participate in is discussed in part in Chapter 2, above. See also Braithwaite, J: '[i]ndividuals acting on behalf of a corporation, in contrast, are not benefiting personally, and therefore are *more* deterrable. Hence in such instances the utilitarian analysis recommends the punishment of the individual rather than the corporation' ('Challenging Just Deserts: Punishing White-Collar Criminals' (1982) 73:2 *Journal of Criminal Law and Criminology* 723 at 727).

[74] At Para [31].

character,[75] and to cooperation with the authorities. In the present case the cartel had been in existence for a minimum of eight years,[76] and required constant supervision and maintenance. The participants clearly understood the illegal nature of their activity and took efforts to avoid detection. Cooperation and guilty pleas flowed from the legitimate threat of sanction coupled with possibly incontrovertible evidence obtained by covert surveillance. Viewed from within the general law of competition the breach of art 101 TFEU was one by object, and, as the EU Commission noted, the infringements perpetrated by the cartel were 'by their very nature among the most harmful restrictions of competition'.[77] It is unlikely that those

---

[75] It has been noted by Stephan that '[m]any of these individuals may otherwise be considered "decent" members of their community'. Stephan also draws attention to the character references presented in mitigation following Mr Lambe's guilty plea in the Irish Heating Oil case (see Stephan, A, 'Survey of Public Attitudes to Price-Fixing and Cartel Enforcement in Britain' (2008) *Competition Law Review* 133. The difficulties involved in handing out high sentences to white collar criminals were pointed out at least as long ago as 1963 by Geis (Geis, G, 'Deterring Corporate Crime', in Ermann, MD, and Lundman, RJ, *Corporate and Governmental Deviance: Problems of Organizational Behavior in Contemporary Society* (1978) Oxford University Press, at 283–84):

> [w]hite-collar criminals also benefit from two prevalent, although contradictory, community beliefs. On the one hand, neighbours of the corporate criminal often regard him as upright and steadfast; indeed, they will probably see him as solid and substantial a citizen as they themselves are. Witness, for example, the following item in the hometown newspaper of one of the convicted price fixers in the 1961 heavy electrical equipment antitrust case:
>
> > 'A number of telegrams from Shenango Valley residents are being sent to a federal judge in Philadelphia, protesting his sentence of Westinghouse executive John H Chiles Jr to a 30-day prison term. . . .
> > The Vestry of St John's Episcopal Church, Sharon, adopted a resolution voicing confidence in Chiles, who is a member of the church . . .
> > Residents who have sent telegrams point out that Chiles was an outstanding citizen in church, civic and community affairs and believe that the sentence is unfair.'

[76] The EU Commission found that the cartel lasted from at least 1986, although its membership changed over time. The cartel may have existed as early as the 1970s (EU Commission Decision, *Marine Hoses*, COMP/39406, January 28, 2009, para 116).

[77] Ibid, para 439. In his original sentencing remarks Judge Rivlin QC stated that there were

> four main aggravating features of this case. First, this was a very carefully planned and executed criminal fraud. Second, this crime was carried on by all of you for a prolonged period . . . Third, the sums of money involved in this case were substantial . . . Fourth, the great mischief of the offence is not just

accused of the Cartel Offence, who are most likely to be senior executives, will come to Court with substantial evidence of prior bad character, and it is possible that, benefiting from good legal advice, such defendants may be keen to cooperate with the authorities.

Disclosure

The European Convention on Human Rights ('ECHR') safeguards, *inter alia*, the right to a 'fair' trial. In the UK there are many recognitions of this right embedded in criminal procedure. In England and Wales, the Criminal Procedure and Investigations Act 1996, s23, required the creation of a code of practice, paragraph 3.5 of which states in part, in a revised version, that 'the investigator should pursue all reasonable lines of enquiry, whether these point toward or away from the suspects'.[78] In an aspect of significant relevance in the case of *R v George, Crawley and Others*, this principle has been further clarified in relation to the duty of disclosure. Paras 51–52 of the *Attorney General's Guidelines on Disclosure*[79] are as follows:

> . . . where the investigator . . . believes that a third party . . . has material . . . reasonably capable of undermining the prosecution case or of assisting the case for the accused, the prosecutor should take what steps they regard as appropriate . . . to obtain the material.
>
> If . . . the third party declines or refuses to allow access to it, the matter should not be left [and the prosecutor] should apply for a witness summons causing a representative of the third party to produce the material to the courts.

As discussed in Chapter 2, one of the key features of the prosecution of individuals under the Cartel Offence is that the interests of the employing undertakings and the individuals may differ, and that the number of legal personalities involved in the competition law arena have been multiplied. Although the case of *R v George, Crawley and Others* was brought against individuals, it was apparent that material held by the undertakings Virgin Atlantic and British Airways (and perhaps by *other* competition/antitrust law agencies) could be relevant to the defence of the accused. The defence was supplied with a copy of the draft statement of objections which

---

the amount of money involved, but the damaging effect that it is bound to have upon the confidence with which the business community is entitled to have in the whole process of contract bidding.

[78] The Criminal Procedure and Investigations Act 1996 (Code of Practice) Order 2005 (SI 2005/985).

[79] April 2005.

the OFT had prepared in relation to the civil case under the Chapter I Prohibition of the CA98, and the interplay between the civil and criminal processes became of central importance.[80] This would have been a substantial document, containing much detail and reference to sources, some of which would have been submitted by the leniency applicant, and some of which would have been obtained under compulsory powers. Owen J was asked to rule on the disclosure of material, and in particular on the disclosure of material that would have been subject to legal professional privilege. The judge noted that the OFT's leniency programme required applicants to 'maintain continuous and complete co-operation throughout the OFT's investigation and any subsequent proceedings', and that the OFT's guidance stated that the OFT may, in certain circumstances, 'expect an undertaking . . . to waive any applicable privilege to the extent that the OFT is advised that it is necessary'.[81]

The material sought by the defendants included that relating to the three VAA executives who had been granted immunity from prosecution, and who were slated to be key prosecution witnesses. Legal

---

[80] It has been argued that the trial judge, Owen J, 'conducted the case throughout with a high degree of sensitivity to the tensions caused by the interaction between civil and criminal processes' (Purnell, N, Bellamy, C, Kar, N, Piccinin, D and Sahathevan, P, 'Criminal Cartel Enforcement – More Turbulence Ahead? The Implications of the BA/Virgin Case' (2010) *Competition Law Journal* 313 at 319).

[81] See *Leniency and No-action. OFT Guidance on the Handling of Applications* (December 2008), Para 8.29:

> [i]t is accepted that the undertaking may contend that legal professional privilege will attach to notes [of internal investigations and witness interviews]. However, there may be circumstances where the OFT is advised by Counsel that disclosure to the OFT and to others is necessary to enable a case to proceed and in those circumstances the OFT will expect an undertaking or individual to waive any applicable privilege to the extent that the OFT is advised that it is necessary. The OFT will not require the disclosure to it of such notes as a matter of course – it simply asks that notes are taken by the undertaking or its advisers and duly preserved pending any possible issues which might subsequently arise.

The OFT's 2011 consultation in relation to leniency and no-action letters suggested an expansion of the guidance relating to the waiver of privilege (see below).

In the United States the *Principles of Federal Prosecution of Business Organizations* revised by the DOJ in August 2008 state that, at least in relation to plea agreements, credit for cooperation will not depend on the defendant having waived attorney client privilege or work product protection. There are only two exceptions to this principle: communications made in furtherance of a crime or fraud, or communications allegedly supporting an asserted advice-of-counsel defence.

professional privilege had been claimed in respect of that material. The fact that the material sought by the defence was relevant to the defence was acknowledged at Para 21 of Owen's judgment:[82]

> [s]o far as the first category is concerned, the defence seek disclosure not only of all previous accounts of the relevant events given by the three VAA witnesses, but any record of the context in which such accounts were given, i.e. the questions put to or comments made to them in the course of giving their accounts. It is submitted on behalf of Mr George that in the light of the disclosure that has now been given, it can be seen that each of them give accounts that develop significantly and change over time. Moreover none of the witnesses, either in their first or subsequent more detailed accounts suggested that they were guilty of the cartel offence, yet subsequently admitted their guilt when required to do so by the OFT. [Counsel for Mr George] also relies upon the fact that the statements made by them to lawyers acting for VAA are inconsistent with the statements served by the OFT. She submits that it is therefore reasonable to infer that the witnesses were put under pressure either to give statements and/or to tailor their evidence to safeguard their own position and/or to protect the perceived interests of VAA. It is submitted that the material in relation to which disclosure is now sought is likely to support the proposition that such witnesses were subject to inducement or pressure, and that that could have the most serious effect upon their reliability or credibility. I accept that it is possible that such material could have that effect, and I have no doubt that if in the possession of the OFT, it would be disclosable.

At Paras 11–12 the judge held that:

> [w]here there are reasonable grounds to suspect that a third party has material or information that might be disclosable if in the possession of the OFT, the OFT is under a duty to take reasonable steps to obtain it.
>
> Material or information will be disclosable by the OFT if relevant to an issue or issues that may arise at trial, and might reasonably be considered capable of undermining the prosecution case or assisting the case for the defence.

At Paras 31–32 the judge addressed the specific question of material covered by legal professional privilege:

> [f]urthermore the argument that the OFT would not have succeeded in obtaining the relevant material, had the airlines sought to protect the privilege that they claimed by the application to the court, appears to me to miss the point. The question is whether, as the case has evolved, it would be reasonable for the OFT now to press for disclosure of the material, notwithstanding the claim to [legal professional privilege], on the basis that both airlines and VAA witnesses are under the duty to give continuous and complete co-operation as a condition

---

[82] *R v George, Crawley and Others* (unreported) December 7, 2009.

> of leniency/immunity, and failing a satisfactory response, to have invoked its power to revoke the leniency agreements and no-action letters.
>
> In my judgment the OFT ought reasonably to take such steps. I arrive at that conclusion for a number of reasons. First I have borne in mind the overriding obligation of the OFT as the prosecuting authority to deal fairly with the defence. Secondly I take account of the duty on the airlines and VAA witnesses to give continuous and complete co-operation, and of the fact that the airlines are required to grant the OFT access to all relevant documentary material as a condition of the leniency agreements. Thirdly I take account of the nature of the material sought, and of the fact that it may shed light upon an issue likely to be of considerable importance at trial, namely whether the VAA witnesses were subject to pressure or inducement with regard to the changes in their account of the events in question. Fourthly I bear in mind that waiver would not result in any unlimited loss of the applicable privilege since any waiver would be for the purposes only of the criminal trial. If a request for waiver is made, it may be that the airlines, and more importantly the VAA witnesses, will respond favourably, bearing in mind that if they do not do so, they will face the risk that immunity/leniency will be withdrawn.[83]

Even more interesting is the approach taken to material held by the US Department of Justice:

> I am not satisfied that the OFT has taken all reasonable steps to obtain the DOJ material . . . a request has been made . . . but the DOJ has declined to release it. In my judgment the OFT . . . ought further to press the DOJ by means of a formal letter of request, and if that does not yield results, to consider making use of the powers contained in the Crime (International Co-operation) Act 2003.[84]

The significance of this argument cannot be understated. If the position taken by Owen J is correct, the effects of the judgment may be very significant. Leniency programmes are widely believed to be of essential importance in the detection, and therefore deterrence, of cartel activity (see further Chapter 2, above). Applicants are urged to come forward with the guarantee of as much confidentiality as can reasonably be maintained. They may be required to subject themselves to repeated interviews by the relevant competition authority, and may be prepared to disclose

---

[83] It must be emphasised that this is a single judgment given at first instance and not tested on appeal. The position adopted by Owen J was discussed in the case of *R v Daniels and Others* [2010] EWCA Crim 2740, in a different context. Here the Court held that there were 'points of distinction between the cases', and that 'the reasoning in *R v George* cannot necessarily be transposed to the present context' (Para 63, per Richards LJ). The Court therefore did not discuss whether the argument made by Owen J was correct.

[84] At Para 38.

information that would otherwise be withheld on the grounds that this information will not form part of the case used against the targets of any subsequent investigation, and does not therefore have to be disclosed to those targets. An additional consideration is the concern that such information might, without leniency secrecy being safeguarded, become available to private claimants in subsequent civil litigation. This is particularly important in the US where the availability of treble-damages actions, class actions, and the recovery of a reasonable attorney fee from the unsuccessful defendant, gives rise to a much greater level of private litigation than is the case in the EU. Where leniency applicants may be required to disclose material in respect of which legal professional privilege would otherwise be claimed, as may – unusually – be the case in respect of the OFT process, these concerns become not unreasonably heightened.

In the US the courts have on a number of occasions considered arguments in relation to the disclosure of evidence obtained by foreign competition authorities, and the EU Commission in particular has resisted such disclosures,[85] although sometimes with only partial success. Thus, for example, in *Re Rubber Chemicals* the Commission resisted the disclosure of material relating to a leniency application made by Flexsys. Following the Commission infringement decision, which contained significant details about the unlawful activity, Flexsys was sued by a Korean company in the US. The Court performed a balancing test set out by the Supreme Court in the case of *Aérospatiale*[86] which, in discussing the principle of comity required that, *inter alia*, a court considering a request for discovery ask 'how much would complying with the request undermine foreign-sovereign interests?'. In *Re Rubber Chemicals* the court held that 'a foreign entity has taken a clear position and articulated reasons why it believes that production of the requested documents would harm its interests'.[87] The Court therefore, on balance, held that discovery would not be granted. In a later case, the District Court for the Eastern District of New York denied a motion to compel the discovery of documents held by the EU Commission, and argued in so doing that:

---

[85] See, for example, *In re Payment Card Interchange Fee and Merchant Discount Antitrust Litigation*, US District Court, Eastern District of New York, August 27, 2010; *In re: Rubber Chemicals Antitrust Litigation*, 486 F. Supp. 2d 1078 (ND Cal. 2007); *In re: Vitamin Antitrust Legislation*, US District Court, District of Columbia, January 23, 2002.

[86] *Société Nationale Industrielle Aérospatiale v US Dist Court for the S District of Iowa*, 482 US 522, 107 S. Ct 2542 (1987).

[87] *In re: Rubber Chemicals Antitrust Litigation*, 486 F. Supp. 2d 1078 (ND Cal. 2007) at 1084.

> [t]he confidentiality the Commission promises is particularly important in engaging voluntary cooperation by third parties. . . . Moreover, the confidentiality of the investigative and adjudicative process is also important to encourage candour by the targets of the investigation. That the proceedings are secret encourages free and open participation by the parties under investigation, which in turn serves the Commission's interest in detecting and punishing violations of its laws. The Commission's interests would be significantly undermined if its confidentiality rules were disregarded by American courts in this case and others like it.[88]

The Commission has made similar arguments in the context of civil proceedings in England, in relation to an application for disclosure dealt with in the case of *National Grid*.[89] In this case the claimant sought damages following an art 101 TFEU infringement decision. Defendants resisted applications to disclose information relating to materials relating to, or in support of, leniency applications. On April 12, 2010, the solicitors for the claimant wrote to the Director-General for Competition at DG Competition to ask whether the Commission would have any objection to the disclosures sought. After a significant delay the DG replied, stating in part that:

> . . . the Commission is requiring a high level of protection of information that has been specifically prepared by the parties for voluntary submission to the Commission within the framework of its leniency program set out in the Commission Leniency Notice. Such information is of vital importance to the Commission's ability to accomplish the tasks entrusted to it. . . This position only applies to information specifically prepared for voluntary submission to the Commission under the leniency program (including documents prepared by leniency Applicants in the context of the continuous cooperation with the Commission). The Commission, however, does not object to the disclosure of other information, such as pre-existing information and documents in the possession of the parties that were used in the preparation of any such submission.[90]

The Commission declined to expand on this statement, pointing to the fact that the matter was pending before the English Court. Roth J made

---

88 *In re Payment Card Interchange Fee and Merchant Discount Antitrust Litigation*, US District Court, Eastern District of New York, August 27, 2010 at 29–30. In other cases the US courts have been prepared to compel discovery in relation to documents voluntarily submitted to the European Commission where the interests of justice in the US have outweighed the concerns of the EU (see, for example, *In re Vitamins Antitrust Litigation*, US District Court, District of Columbia, December 18, 2002).

89 *National Grid Electricity Transmission plc v ABB Ltd and others* [2011] EWHC 171 (Ch). See also *National Grid Electricity Transmission plc v ABB Ltd and others* [2012] EWHC 869 (Ch).

90 Quoted in *National Grid*, at Para [16].

reference to the then recent *Pfleiderer* judgment (discussed below), when considering whether to order the disclosure of information from one of the defendants of documents that might have included leniency material. The Judge adjourned the proceedings and invited the Commission to make submissions to the Court in writing.[91]

Under the system of civil enforcement set up by Regulation 1/2003 the OFT may exchange information with other members of the European Competition Network, and with the EU Commission, including in certain cases information that has flowed through leniency applications. While it may not be possible for a UK court to require disclosure of evidence held by the EU Commission or by other NCAs, it may well be the case that it could require, in the event that the defence argued that such disclosure was necessary to protect the rights of a defendant, the disclosure of any such evidence held by the OFT. This would be a matter of grave concern to the EU Commission and to other NCAs, and could put at risk the ability of the OFT to prosecute the Cartel Offence and, at the same time, simultaneously to perform its civil functions adequately.[92] That this might be the case was recognised by the ECJ sitting in Grand Chamber in the case of *Pfleiderer*.[93]

In this case the ECJ dealt with a reference from a court in Bonn in which the claimant had sought full access to a file held by the Bundeskartellamt in relation to a cartel proceeding under which the Bundeskartellamt had imposed fines on three cartel participants. Pfleiderer was a significant consumer of the products affected by the cartel. The file requested included material obtained under the German leniency programme, with Pfleiderer seeking access to this in order to prepare an action for civil damages. After

---

91 Article 15 of Regulation 1/2003 permits the Commission to make representations to national courts in relevant cases. The *Pfleiderer* judgment and its consequences are discussed extensively in *National Grid Electricity Transmission plc v ABB Ltd and others* [2012] EWHC 869 (Ch) at paras [20]ff.

92 Thus, for example, Para 49 of the European Competition Network Model Leniency Programme is in the following terms:

> [t]he ECN Model Programme also stipulates that no access will be granted to any records of any oral statements before the statement of objections has been issued. In addition, given the differences in the rules concerning access to file and/or public access to documents in the various jurisdictions, the ECN Model Programme stipulates that the exchange of records of oral statements between Competition Authorities is limited to cases where the protections afforded to such records by the receiving Competition Authority are equivalent to those afforded by the transmitting Competition Authority.

93 Case C-360/09 *Pfleiderer AG v Bundeskartellamt* [2011] 5 CMLR 219.

two requests for information the Bundeskartellamt restricted access to the file to a printed version from which certain information covered by point 22 of the Bundeskartellamt's leniency programme had been removed. The court at first instance in Germany ordered disclosure, but stayed the effect of the order until a preliminary reference to the ECJ had been disposed of. The question asked was the following:

> [a]re the provisions of Community competition law . . . to be interpreted as meaning that parties adversely affected by a cartel may not, for the purpose of bringing civil-law claims, be given access to leniency applications or to information and documents voluntarily submitted in that connection by applicants for leniency which the national competition authority of a member state has received, pursuant to a national leniency programme, within the framework of proceedings for the imposition of fines which are (also) intended to enforce [article 101 TFEU]?[94]

The ECJ discussed whether such an application should be granted by examining the framework for the enforcement of competition policy in the European Union laid down in Regulation 1/2003, art 12 of which provides in part that:

> 1. For the purpose of applying articles [101 and 102 TFEU] the Commission and the competition authorities of the Member States shall have the power to provide one another with, and use in evidence, any matter of fact or of law, including confidential information.
>
> 2. Information exchanged shall only be used in evidence for the purpose of applying [arts 101 or 102 TFEU] and in respect of the subject-matter for which it was collected by the transmitting authority. However, where national competition law is applied in the same case and in parallel to Community competition law and does not lead to a different outcome, information exchanged under this Article may also be used for the application of national competition law.

Article 35(1) of Regulation 1/2003 provides that the member states are to enforce competition law 'in such a way that the provisions of this regulation are effectively complied with'. In the context of the German case, the German Code of Criminal Procedure made provision for the obtaining of evidence, in certain circumstances, from 'the authorities'.[95] The Court

---

[94] Ibid, Para [18].

[95] See German Code of Criminal Procedure (*Strafprozessordnung*), Para 406(e):

> (1) On behalf of an aggrieved person, a lawyer may inspect the documents which have been submitted to a court, or, if a public prosecution were commenced,

pointed to the existence of the EU Commission notices on leniency[96] and on cooperation within the framework of the ECN,[97] as well as the model leniency programme developed by the ECN, but held that

> even if the guidelines set out by the Commission may have some effect on the practice of the national competition authorities, it is, in the absence of binding regulation under European Union law on the subject, for Member States to establish and apply national rules on the right of access, by persons adversely affected by a cartel, to documents relating to leniency procedures.[98]

Nevertheless, the Court held, the discretion open to the member states must be exercised 'in accordance with European Union law',[99] and could not be permitted to 'render the implementation of European Union law impossible or excessively difficult ... and, specifically, in the area of competition law, they must ensure that the rules which they establish or apply do not jeopardise the effective application of [art 101 TFEU]'.[100] The Court recognised the efficacy of leniency programmes, and accepted that their value could be threatened 'if documents relating to a leniency

---

would have been submitted, and may inspect evidence held by the authorities, in so far as the aggrieved person holds a legitimate interest. ...

(2) Inspection of the files shall be refused if overriding interests worthy of protection, either of the accused or of other persons, constitute an obstacle thereto. Access may be refused if the purpose of the investigation appears to be compromised as a result or if it would give rise to a significant delay in the proceedings ...

(3) Upon application, and unless precluded by compelling reasons, the lawyer may be permitted to take the files, but not the evidence, to his offices or place of residence. Such a decision cannot be challenged.

(4) The decision on whether to permit inspection of the files shall be made by the public prosecuting authority in preparatory proceedings and after final determination of the proceedings and, in other circumstances, by the presiding judge of the court seised of the case. The court with jurisdiction ... may be requested to reverse such a decision of the public prosecuting authority under the preceding sentence. ... Reasons for those decisions shall not be stated, where attainment of the investigation's objective might be jeopardised by their disclosure.

(5) Under the conditions in subparagraph (1), the aggrieved person may be given information and copies of the files... (quoted in *Pfleiderer* at Para [7]).

96 (2006) OJ C298/17.
97 (2004) OJ C101/43.
98 At Para [23].
99 At Para [24].
100 At Para [24].

procedure were disclosed to persons wishing to bring an action for damages.'[101] As the Court put it:

> [t]he view can reasonably be taken that a person involved in an infringement of competition law, faced with the possibility of such disclosure, would be deterred from taking the opportunity offered by such leniency programmes, particularly when, pursuant to Articles 11 and 12 of Regulation No 1/2003, the Commission and the national competition authorities might exchange information which that person has voluntarily provided.[102]

At the same time however the Court recognised the existence of the right to claim damages in respect of loss caused by conduct falling within art 101 TFEU, and noted that such actions had the possibility of significantly enhancing the potency of EU competition law. While calling on national courts to undertake a balancing exercise where faced with an application such as that made by Pfleiderer, the Court answered the question in the following terms:

> . . . the answer to the question referred is that the provisions of European Union law on cartels, and in particular Regulation 1/2003, must be interpreted as not precluding a person who has been adversely affected by an infringement of European Union competition law and is seeking to obtain damages from being granted access to documents relating to a leniency procedure involving the perpetrator of that infringement. It is, however, for the courts and tribunals of the Member States, on the basis of their national law, to determine the conditions under which such access must be permitted or refused by weighing the interests protected by European Union law.[103]

It appears to be the case therefore that a recourse to European Union legal principles may not provide a way out of the cul-de-sac introduced by Owen J. If it is reasonable for a national court to balance the right to damages against the threat that such actions pose to leniency programmes when determining whether to grant access to materials submitted under those programmes to competition authorities, the balance must swing even further against the authorities and leniency applicants when one side

---

101 At Para [26].

102 At Para [27].

103 At Para [32]. Note that in *Henkel and Henkel France v Commission*, case T-607/11, the General Court may return to some of these issues. Here the applicant sought the transfer of 15 documents held by DG Competition in relation to the consumer detergents cartel (case COMP/39.579) to the French Autorité de Concurrence. The Commission refused to release the documents, and it is this decision that is being challenged (see (2012) OJ C25/64).

of the scales contains a threat to personal liberty. If Owen J's conclusion stands, and we will not know the answer to this until such time as there is an appeal on this point, one solution would be to separate out the prosecution of the cartel offence from the authority applying a leniency programme in the context of civil enforcement. Only where no material submitted as part of a leniency application would be available to found the basis of a criminal prosecution might access to such material be protected; even in this case there would remain the possibility that the material might be relevant to the defence. An alternative would be for an express statutory amendment in the UK to protect absolutely information submitted to a leniency programme from disclosure. Any such move would lay the system open to manipulation (an applicant might be able to protect *all* evidence held by it by submitting it), and to human rights' challenges.

The treatment of the duty of disclosure by Owen J may be of limited significance were it to apply *solely* to use of evidence in criminal prosecutions. It has, however, been pointed out that

> [o]nce material has been disclosed in criminal proceedings it is difficult to see why the same material should not be subject to discovery claims in subsequent third party proceedings, despite the confidentiality restrictions placed on the OFT by Part 9 of the Enterprise Act 2002.[104]

Given the significant growth in private litigation in the European Union, and the availability of treble damages in the US, there can be little doubt that parties considering applying for leniency would, at the margin, be persuaded not to were they to believe that any material disclosed would become available to complainants in subsequent civil litigation.[105]

LENIENCY

The role of leniency generally, and the discussions of this in relevant literature, have been considered in Chapter 2, above. The position that applies in the United States was discussed in the previous chapter. The situation

---

104 Purnell, N, et al, note 80 at 322.

105 Ibid: '. . . it is clear that this possibility makes whistleblowing by cartel participants a less attractive and more complex decision to take than it was prior to the introduction of the criminal cartel enforcement regime'. Care should be taken in reporting, and relying on, anecdotal evidence, but I have heard professional advisers stating that they would counsel *against* leniency applications to the OFT until such time as the position in relation to continuing obligations and disclosure becomes clarified.

in the United Kingdom is somewhat more complex in practice than it is in the US, in that procedures in the UK may proceed along the parallel tracks of civil *and* criminal enforcement, if not simultaneously, at least in close relationship (some of the relevant issues have been discussed above). The OFT may, in appropriate circumstances, grant both civil leniency, and issue 'no-action' letters in respect of individual criminal prosecutions. The position is more complex in Scotland, and the OFT has entered into a memorandum of understanding with the Crown Office relating to leniency in that jurisdiction.[106] In being given the power to offer leniency, the OFT was placed in the position of being the first prosecutorial body in the UK to be given the statutory power to offer immunity from prosecution in this way.

The starting point for the OFT is that it 'wishes to encourage individuals to come forward with information relating to any cartel activities in which they are involved'.[107] Provision for 'no-action letters' is made in s 194 of the Enterprise Act:

> [w]here, for the purpose of the investigation or prosecution of offences under section 188, the OFT gives a person written notice under this subsection, no proceedings for an offence under section 188 that falls within a description specified in the notice may be brought against that person in England and Wales or Northern Ireland except in circumstances specified in the notice.

It became clear after the collapse of the *British Airways* case that the OFT's guidance relating to no-action letters might have to be revised (this would be the case also were the substantive terms of the Offence to be altered). A consultation document to this effect was published in October 2011.[108]

The OFT's first guidance in relation to no-action letters was published in 2003,[109] and was subsequently replaced in 2008.[110] The original guidance, and its subsequent restatement, was not detailed, but did set out the

---

106 *Memorandum of Understanding between the Office of Fair Trading (OFT) and the National Casework Division (NCD), Crown Office, Scotland* (OFT 546, June 2009). This has been extended to operate until June 2012.

107 Office of Fair Trading, *The Cartel Offence: Guidance on the Issue of No-action Letters for Individuals* (OFT 513, April 2003), Para 1.2, internal reference omitted.

108 Office of Fair Trading, *Applications for Leniency and No-action in Cartel Cases. OFT's Detailed Guidance on the Principles and Process: A Consultation on OFT Guidance* (OFT 803con, October 2011). The consultation period expired on January 26, 2012.

109 OFT, note 107.

110 *Leniency and No-Action: OFT's Guidance Note on the Handling of Applications* (OFT 803, December 2008).

conditions to be met for a no-action letter to be issued. These are that the individual must: 'admit participation in the criminal offence'; provide the OFT with all relevant information; 'maintain continuous and complete cooperation throughout the investigation and until the conclusion of any criminal proceedings arising as a result of the investigation'; not have coerced another party into the cartel; and refrain from participation in the cartel post-application, unless encouraged to continue to participate by the OFT. It is further the case that a no-action letter may not be issued where 'the OFT believes that it already has, or is in the course of gathering, sufficient information to bring a successful prosecution to an individual'.[111] The link between criminal and civil leniency is made clear at Para 3.5 of the original guidance.[112] There is no reference in the guidance to confidentiality surrounding no-action letters, but it may be assumed that in some cases the fact that one is issued will not become public knowledge at an early stage of the proceedings. This will particularly be the case if there is an ongoing investigation in which the OFT wishes the recipient to maintain links with the cartel, so as not to alert other members to the fact that an investigation might be underway. Initial approaches seeking a no-action letter may be made by lawyers representing the parties on an anonymous basis. This would allow, for example, a party to determine whether the conditions, and in particular those of Para 3.4, are met.

A no-action letter may be revoked where the recipient ceases to satisfy the conditions of Para 3.3 of the guidance, or where he or she 'has knowingly or recklessly provided information that is false or misleading in a material particular'.[113] Following the collapse of the *British Airways* case, in which no-action letters were issued to certain staff employed by VAA, and where the undertaking benefited from an offer of leniency under the civil regime, it was suggested by the OFT that the latter status would be re-examined in order to ascertain whether VAA was in breach of the civil leniency requirements of full disclosure and ongoing cooperation.

One of the key issues to have emerged from the *British Airways* case is a

---

111 OFT, note 107, Para 3.4.

112 This states, *inter alia*, that an approach may be made

> on behalf of named employees, directors, ex-employees or ex-directors, by an undertaking (or by a lawyer representing such undertaking) seeking leniency from the OFT in accordance with the OFT's *Guidance as to the Appropriate Amount of a Penalty* . . . or in conjunction with an application for leniency from the European Commission in accordance with the Commission Notice on immunity from fines or reduction of fines in cartel cases . . .

113 Para 3.12.

refined understanding of the relationship between civil and criminal leniency applications, and in particular of the level of confidentiality accorded to information disclosed under them (see above). It would appear, for example, that information disclosed under a civil leniency application may be requested as a right of the defence if it leads to a criminal trial. This might not always be the case in relation to the imposition of a civil penalty. Where an application for a no-action letter is made, the OFT will interview the applicant, on the understanding that no information they provide in the interview will be used against them in a subsequent criminal proceeding unless a no-action letter is granted and then revoked, or if one is not issued, the individual 'has knowingly or recklessly provided information that is false or misleading in a material particular'.[114]

It is certain that had the British Airways trial proceeded, the defence would have probed the operation of the leniency programme,[115] and it is likely, for example, that the defence would have argued that the admission of 'dishonesty' made by the Virgin officials was made only to secure leniency for their employers.

In practice, before a leniency application is made, or during an iterative process, it is likely that the applicant undertaking would have had a significant internal investigation conducted, often supervised by external independent professional legal advisers. A complex interplay exists in this process between individuals, who may have to be incentivised to cooperate with internal procedures, and the undertaking. Given that the applicant undertaking anticipates a 'reward' for its participation in the leniency programme, it may well be possible for relevant employees and officers of the undertaking to in turn secure benefits.[116] Purnell provides a practitioner's perspective on this process:

---

[114] Para 3.7.

[115] The trial transcript makes clear that the defence would have moved for dismissal on the grounds that the 'whole investigation had been skewed by the leniency regime' (transcript, April 29, 2010) at 48.

[116] It was reported, for example, that one of the key participants in the Sotheby's/Christie's fine art auction cartel, Christopher Davidge, received a very substantial severance package from Christie's in return for his cooperation in the course of the legal proceedings (see, for example, Mason, C, *The Art of the Steal: Inside the Sotheby's-Christie's Auction House Scandal* (2004) Putnam, at 241–44; and Rossiter, N, *Sotheby's and Christie's: A Crime amongst Gentlemen* (2002) BBC (Documentary)). Purnell notes that this dynamic 'was illustrated in the BA case where Mr Stephen Ridgway remained the CEO of Virgin Atlantic despite having admitted to the OFT his dishonest involvement in the cartel' (Purnell, N, et al, note 80, at 323).

> [b]y the time relevant witnesses are exposed to OFT investigators, considerable legal input will have been given. The overall circumstances of the cartel activity, the impact on the applicant company, the degree of complicity of the witnesses, the extent to which the infringement is continuing and any possibility that an employee might be a coercer or the directing mind of the cartel arrangement are among the issues likely to have been extensively examined.[117]

It is unlikely that all relevant facts are disclosed in a first internal interview, and lawyers involved in the process expect to interview key personnel on a number of occasions. This is particularly the case where, as required by the OFT, the applicant seeking the benefit of a personal no-action letter must admit his criminality. This may not be an easy step for a professional employee, perhaps believing himself to be working under the direction of others, to admit. In the case of criminal actions the success or failure of a prosecution may depend on an extremely precise presentation of relevant facts.[118] It appears clear, following the collapse of the British Airways prosecution, that the OFT has found the process of managing the leniency/no-action letter interface difficult, and the evidence is strong that the civil/criminal enforcement split is making a difficult job even harder.[119] Suggestions that the OFT may itself seek to interview leniency applicants at an early stage, instead of relying on the undertaking's internal investiga-

---

117 Purnell, N, et al, note 80, at 322. The OFT has stated that:

> . . . the establishment in the UK of a criminal cartel regime has made it particularly important for internal investigations prior to an approach for leniency to be conducted with care and precision and to be limited to that which is necessary. The OFT only requires that undertakings act reasonably, reducing the risks as best they can having regard to all relevant considerations. (OFT, note 108, Para 3.8)

The OFT provides explicit guidance relating to internal investigations prior to the making of a leniency application at Annexe C of the draft revised guidance.

118 This was made clear in the *British Airways* case, when, as noted above, 'the "final straw" [leading to the collapse of the case] concerned an email exchange which altered, by a mere few hours' difference, the significance of a piece of evidence relied upon by the OFT prosecutors as a principal pointer towards the guilt of the accused men' (Purnell, N, et al, note 80, at 323).

119 See Purnell, N, et al, note 80 at 325:

> the case is a harbinger of a likely change of attitude toward civil leniency applicants. Leniency applicants, already subject to onerous obligations of ongoing co-operation for the life of both the civil and criminal investigatory and court processes, should expect more rigorous demands from the authorities in relation to both prosaic matters: document disclosure, retrieval efforts, IT functionality and a fundamentally more critical eye to and forensic scrutiny of their evidence and any inconsistencies or other weaknesses within it.

tions and the advice of expert counsel, have been met with concern in the practitioner community. The iterative process referred to above is time consuming and detailed, and it is not clear that the OFT has either the resources or the expertise to engage in this effectively.

The OFT consultation exercise launched in 2011, and the proposed amendments to the guidance in respect of leniency and no-action letters, proposed a number of changes to the conditions for leniency and to the guidance, which may have arisen in part from the failures in *British Airways*. In particular the OFT included '[e]xplicit references . . . to the need for applicants to provide exculpatory material and to . . . minimise the risk of applicants overstating the nature of the reported activity and/or supporting evidence'.[120] In relation to the question of the waiver of legal privilege, which was so important in *British Airways*, the OFT stated that waiver would not be required in civil cases, but

> that we cannot exclude that possibility in criminal cases. This is most likely to arise in the context of witness account material that is protected by legal professional privilege. As a blanket requirement, waiver of privilege in all witness account material may not always be necessary. The OFT will seek advice from counsel, and the guidance of the court where necessary, on the need to obtain privileged material before requesting waivers, and to do so only at a late stage in the OFT's investigation when the OFT considers that it has sufficient evidence to charge individuals with a cartel offence. The OFT does not consider that it would be appropriate, in the context of criminal proceedings, to exclude the possibility of such waivers being requested. . . .[121]

The OFT is not prepared, in its guidance, to specify with precision what material may be privileged, stating only that '[t]his will need to be assessed on the facts and circumstances of each case'.[122]

The revised guidance put forward in October 2011 offers expanded treatment of the disclosure of information given to the OFT in leniency applications. Paragraphs 7.11–7.13 deal with the disclosure of leniency material in the course of criminal prosecutions. There is here recognition of the effect of the Criminal Procedure and Investigations Act 1996, as amended, and the relevant Codes of Practice. The OFT states that material subject to disclosure would 'inevitably' include any material

---

[120] OFT, note 108, Para 5.8(b).

[121] Ibid, Para 5.9(c). Note that this suggests that the OFT may go quite some way through an investigation using its civil powers before determining that a criminal prosecution under the Cartel Offence may be an appropriate enforcement route. See also paras 3.13–3.22 of the draft revised guidance.

[122] Ibid, Para 3.15.

provided by the leniency applicant, including transcripts of interviews, 'where such statements are capable of having an impact on issues arising in the criminal case'.[123] The fact that no-action letters have been issued may be disclosed, but the OFT has stated that it would seek to protect the identities of those to whom they have been issued by way of applications for public interest immunity. The OFT takes the view that material disclosed in the course of criminal proceedings to defendants has not been disclosed to the public, and therefore does not fall within the terms of the Enterprise Act 2002, Part 9[124] as being material which is no longer protected from further disclosure.

At Part 8 of the revised guidance the OFT deals with a number of other issues related to criminal prosecutions. First, it states that undertakings should not be deterred from applying to DG Competition for leniency on the basis of a fear that officials may be exposed to individual prosecution in the UK. The OFT states that '*most* undertakings that qualify for immunity under the Commission Leniency Notice will also be able to gain "blanket" criminal immunity in the UK for current and former employees and directors'.[125] There does remain the possibility, albeit in the view of the OFT a remote one, that individual prosecutions could be launched even where the undertaking with which the relevant individual is associated. This could arise where, for example, there is a pre-existing criminal investigation under way in the UK, or where there is an attempt to 'game the system'.[126] Given the lack of criminal enforcement to date, and the need to prioritise its work, it would be extremely unlikely that the OFT would act against an individual whose employer benefited from leniency at the EU level. Were, however, such an action to proceed, it is possible that this could be challenged on the grounds that it would undermine leniency applications in the future, and would not be consistent with the UK's duty of sincere cooperation with EU requirements.

Plea Bargaining

While leniency applicants may benefit from full immunity from prosecution, subject to their compliance with the terms and conditions of the leniency programme, plea bargaining offers a more flexible approach to be taken with respect to participants in a cartel who do not benefit from

---

123 Ibid, Para 7.11.
124 See s 241(2).
125 Draft guidance, Para 8.2, emphasis added.
126 Draft guidance, Para 8.6.

leniency. The extent to which plea agreements are relied on in the context of US enforcement has been discussed in the previous chapter, and there would be benefits in adopting such a system in the UK, which 'could be seen as the criminal counterpart of civil settlements, which are gaining momentum in the UK'.[127] Thus it has been argued that plea bargaining has advantages that go beyond those offered by leniency programmes:

> [p]lea bargaining might be seen to imply a specific form of deterrence in further destabilising cartels (ie increasing the probability of punishment and the risk that a co-cartelist will reveal further information to the authorities, even after the basic facts have come to light and a no-action letter is not available). . . . [Plea bargaining] would also avoid or reduce the risk of a failed prosecution, which undermines the credibility of the prosecuting authorities.[128]

There are indications that the UK criminal law system is moving towards an acceptance of more flexible approaches to prosecution and sentence than has been the case in the past, although the courts continue to be reluctant to embrace the practice. Thus, for example, in *R v Goodyear*[129] the Court of Appeal noted that a judge was not to be seen as 'conducting nor involving himself in any plea bargaining'.[130] However, the Serious Organised Crime and Police Act 2005 made some provision for reductions in sentences to be offered in return for assistance in the course of prosecution. Facially, it would appear to be inconsistent to permit full leniency to be given, largely on a first-past-the-post system, but not for those enforced with prosecuting cartels to be able to make binding agreements with those prosecuted. However, in the BIS response to the 2011 consultation exercise, the Government rejected moves to introduce a plea-agreement system into the UK enforcement mechanism, the adoption of which 'would have wider ramifications across the criminal justice system, and . . . would need to be considered carefully'.[131]

---

[127] Lawrence, J, et al, 'Hardcore Bargains: What Could Plea Bargaining Offer in UK Criminal Cartel Cases?' (2008) *Competition Law Journal* 17 at 18.

[128] Ibid, at 23–24. Scott Hammond has argued that the DOJ's 'experience of using negotiated plea agreements in cartel cases has very few, if any, detractors, however. Doing so benefits the government, cooperating defendants, the judicial system, the victims, and the public at large by encouraging early cooperation and acceptance of responsibility by cartel members through the promise of a transparent, proportional, expedited, certain and final plea disposition' (Hammond, SD, 'The U.S. Model of Negotiated Plea Agreements: A Good Deal with Benefits for All' (2006) OECD Competition Committee, Working Party 3, at 3).

[129] [2005] EWCA Crim 888.

[130] At para [67].

[131] *Growth, Competition and the Competition Regime: Government Response to Consultation*, March 2012 at Para 7.40.

CASE LAW AND PRACTICE TO DATE

As noted at the outset of this chapter, and indeed at the outset of this book, at the time of writing only two cases have been prosecuted in the UK under the Cartel Offence. The first of these, *R v Whittle* (*Marine Hose*) has been referred to above in relation to the sentencing of the three defendants. It is also discussed much more extensively in Chapter 6, below. That leaves *R v Burns (British Airways)* as the other case, which as we have seen collapsed in May 2010. Some aspects of this case have been discussed as relevant to content above, but it is appropriate to turn more fully to the history and consequences of that case, as its ramifications have been significant.[132]

R v Burns and others (British Airways)

Perhaps better known as the *British Airways* case, *R v Burns* was to be the most ambitious prosecution to date under the Cartel Offence, and its collapse was, undoubtedly, an embarrassment for the OFT,[133] which has publicly acknowledged as much.[134] It was, at the least, an interesting decision to make this the first major prosecution. The alleged price-fixing (the subject also of a civil proceeding) was engaged in by two parties only, the case 'outlined to the jury by the prosecution did not involve much more than bilateral telephone calls between the alleged conspirators',[135] and did not appear to contain within its facts a clear demonstration of the

---

132 See Purnell, N, et al, note 80. In an article replete with effective criticism the authors argue, at 325, that:

> . . . from an institutional perspective, the *BA* case drives home the concerns raised by [the Penrose Report] about the OFT as prosecutor and in particular 'the tendency for the prosecutors . . . to become isolated from general developments in criminal law and practice'. In failing to discharge its obligations of disclosure in the criminal prosecution, and . . . its general deference to resistance from Virgin's counsel to disclose witness interviews and other materials, the OFT committed an error unlikely to be seen from a seasoned criminal prosecutor.

133 It has been stated that the collapse was 'a humiliating public failure for the OFT' (Joshua, JM, 'DOA: Can the UK Cartel Offence Be Resuscitated?', in Beaton-Wells, C, and Ezrachi, A (eds), *Criminalising Cartels: Critical Studies of an International Regulatory Movement* (2011) Hart Publishing at 129).

134 OFT, *Project Condor Board Review*, OFT 2010. The OFT recognised that this had resulted in 'adverse reputational impacts for the OFT and the competition regime and significant costs for the taxpayer'.

135 Joshua, JM, 'Shooting the Messenger', note 17, at 7.

most egregious forms of dishonesty that the OFT had originally indicated would drive prosecutions. It has been noted by others that at the same time as the OFT was bringing this case forward it was also in the process of closing a civil case relating to bid-rigging in the construction industry when there had been earlier indications that the full weight of the cartel offence would be brought to bear on these arrangements.[136] Stephan has suggested that one reason for the OFT's pursuit of this case lay in the criticism that was levied against the OFT following the *Marine Hose* prosecutions – in particular that the market in marine hose was of such marginal interest that the case attracted little publicity.[137] The situation would have been very different were the OFT to be successful in a prosecution relating to passenger airline flights.

In March 2006 the OFT was contacted by Herbert Smith, acting on behalf of VAA. This contact culminated in a successful leniency application by VAA, and the issuing of no-action letters to certain individuals. The OFT began two investigations, one into possible infringements of the CA98, and a criminal investigation, codenamed 'Project Condor'. At the time of writing, the civil investigation has not yet been concluded. In August 2008 four men, current and former employees of British Airways, were charged.[138] The Particulars of Offence in this case were as follows:

> Martin George, Andrew Crawley, Alan Burnett and Iain Burns, between July 1, 2004 and April 20, 2006 dishonestly agreed with each other and with [three VAA employees] to make or implement arrangements relating to at least two undertakings, namely British Airways and [VAA], which directly or indirectly fixed the price for the supply by British Airways and [VAA] in the United Kingdom of passenger air transport services.

Following the resolution of a number of preliminary legal challenges,[139] the trial began on April 26, 2010, but on May 10, 2010 was abandoned

136 See Joshua, JM, 'the failure of the OFT to bring any criminal prosecutions against individuals for bid rigging practices in the construction industry – a sector marked as a priority target for enforcement action – raises serious questions as to the criteria for "case selection"' (Joshua, JM, note 133, at 141).

137 Stephan, A, note 29; and '"The Battle for Hearts and Minds": The Role of the Media in Treating Cartels as Criminal', in Beaton-Wells, C, and Ezrachi, A (eds), *Criminalising Cartels.*

138 The US authorities had earlier secured the conviction of Keith Packer, of British Airways, in relation to the price-fixing of air cargo fuel surcharges (see DOJ Press Release, September 30, 2008)

139 Some of this procedure is discussed below, but the issue of the compatibility of the prosecution with the requirements of EU competition law has already been considered above (see discussion of *R v IB* [2009] EWCA Crim 2575).

when new electronic evidence held by VAA came to light.[140] This had previously been believed to be irretrievable due to the corruption of the computer files.[141] Joshua explains matters slightly differently:

> [a]fter a series of embarrassing disclosure failures, and charges that the OFT had excessively deferred to Virgin's lawyers in the conduct of the prosecution, the judge was led to express doubts as to whether the four defendants could ever receive a fair trial. The OFT had little alternative but to offer no evidence.[142]

The jury was directed to hand down not guilty verdicts, and the OFT was subject to severe criticism. Stephan has argued that 'it soon became clear that the [case] had been a poor choice for the purposes of demonstrating dishonesty'.[143]

---

140 'OFT withdraws criminal proceedings against current and former BA executives', OFT Press Release 47/10, May 10, 2010. The relevant paragraph of the press release is in the following terms.

> The events leading to today's decision date back to the early stages of the OFT's investigation which started in 2006 and was the OFT's first major criminal investigation to be launched on the basis of an application for immunity. In the early stages of the investigation electronic material was provided to the OFT by Virgin Atlantic pursuant to its obligation as a leniency applicant to provide the OFT with continuous and complete cooperation. The omission from this material of a significant number of emails only came to light after the start of the trial. Had the omission been uncovered earlier, the OFT believes that there is every prospect that the trial would have been able to proceed.

141 The OFT described this as a 'large volume' of material, and, given that neither the OFT nor the defence had had time to review this material, 'accepted that it would potentially be unfair to continue the trial' (OFT, *Project Condor Board Review* (2010), Annex, 9). It is believed that the new evidence consisted of some 70000 emails! It has been reported in a number of sources that one of the emails purported to show that the surcharges that the OFT alleged arose from the unlawful activity were already in place *before* the conversation in which it was alleged that the arrangement had been made (see, for example, Purnell, N, et al, note 80).

142 Joshua, JM, note 133, at 128.

143 Stephan, A, note 29, at 452. *Inter alia* Stephan draws attention to the fact that the allegations were 'vigorously' contested, and that BA continued to support at least some of the staff, one of whom was promoted during the course of the proceedings (see *Financial Times*, November 28, 2008, 'BA Sales Chief on Price-fixing Charge to Join the Board'). For criticism in the media, see, for example, *Independent*, May 11, 2010, 'BA Price-fixing Trial Collapses after Discovery of New Evidence', and *Guardian*, May 11, 2010, 'OFT under Fire over Whistleblowers after BA Price-fixing Trial Fails'.

In November 2011 the OFT issued a statement of objections ('SO') in the context of a Chapter I Prohibition and art 101 TFEU civil investigation,[144] addressed to both British Airways and to VAA, alleging that both companies had infringed the relevant provisions. It is of interest that as early as August 2007 British Airways had agreed, as part of an early resolution agreement, that it would pay a penalty of £121.5m,[145] and that the OFT accepted that VAA would not be expected to pay a penalty 'as it currently qualifies in principle for full immunity under the OFT's leniency policy'. In its press release announcing the SO, the OFT stated that it had reviewed Virgin's leniency status following the collapse of the criminal trial, and found that its 'conduct did not amount to non co-operation such as to warrant the revocation of [its] immunity'.[146]

In December 2010 the OFT published the outcome of an internal Board Review held to review the case.[147] It is clear from this report that events moved quickly in the case in the three days to May 10, 2010. The report states that there was no 'evidence of any failure to meet the [Code for

---

[144] Case CE/7691-06 *Investigation into alleged price fixing of airline passenger fuel surcharges for long-haul passenger flights*; OFT Press Release 120/11 (November 8, 2011).

[145] See OFT press release 113/07 (August 1, 2007):

> BA has admitted that between August 2004 and January 2006 it colluded with Virgin Atlantic over the surcharges which were added to ticket prices in response to rising oil prices. Over that period, the surcharges rose from £5 to £60 per ticket for a typical BA or Virgin Atlantic long-haul return flight.
>
> . . .
>
> British Airways accepts the OFT's finding that on at least six occasions the two companies discussed and/or informed each other about proposed changes to the level of the surcharges, rather than setting levels independently as required under clear and well-established competition law principles.

In the civil case of *Reckitt Benckiser Healthcare (UK) Limited and Reckitt Benckiser Group plc* (case CE/8931/08) the undertaking also accepted an early resolution agreement, benefiting from a reduction in penalty. The undertaking did not contest the statement of objections, but was permitted to identify 'factual errors'.

[146] The OFT had earlier indicated that it was reviewing the extent to which Virgin had complied with its leniency obligations, implying that the benefit of leniency might be withdrawn (OFT Press Release 47/10, May 10, 2010).

[147] The terms of reference of the Board Review were: 'To review and report back to the Board on the facts and circumstances surrounding, and the events leading to, the decision by the OFT to offer no evidence at the criminal trial in *R v Burns and others* and, in the light of these, to make recommendations to the Board concerning the investigation and prosecution of criminal cartel cases, whether in relation to procedures, processes, policies or other matters'.

Crown Prosecutors] test before May 7, 2010', and that 'the decision not to offer evidence on May 10, 2010 was correct'.[148] The Board Review found that no one within the OFT was *negligent*, but more interesting is the very fine line trodden in the report between finding that mistakes were made, *and* that the OFT did *not* lack the capability to prosecute such a case. The wording used here is very careful indeed. The Board Review found that failings lay in 'the processes used in the case',[149] and noted that even had such failings been absent the case may still have failed as '[c]ases under the criminal cartel regime raise many legal and practical challenges and thus a proportion will inevitably fail'.[150] Problems identified include the following.

- This was a complex case, the OFT faced a 'considerable learning curve', and with hindsight this might have been the wrong case to take on as a first contentious prosecution.
- The fact that this was a two-party cartel might have brought into question the reliability of the witnesses in the eyes of both judge and jury.
- There was legal uncertainty over 'the scope of both of the OFT's obligations as a prosecuting authority to obtain, and its power to require disclosure of, documents which might be relevant to the defence'. Section 196 of the Enterprise Act, referred to above, provides, in part, that a person may not 'be required to disclose any information or produce any document which he would be entitled to refuse to disclose or produce on grounds of legal professional privilege in proceedings before the High Court. . .'. However, it appears that such material may be found, and may perhaps be compelled, in leniency applications, and that material given to secure leniency may, if a criminal trial ensues, be obtained by the defence

148 OFT, *Project Condor Board Review* (2010) at 1. Joshua has been fierce in his criticism of the OFT's procedures (Joshua, JM, note 17):

> [a]fter the trial opened, one disquieting revelation after another emerged regarding the conduct of the prosecution. The defence accused the OFT of a wholesale failure to respect the basic rules of pre-trial evidence disclosure and of farming out its prosecutorial responsibilities to VA's lawyers – whose acknowledged mission was to safeguard their client's interests. The same lawyers had also assiduously screened the prosecution's contacts with its witnesses: in the words of defence counsel, they were 'well and truly lawyered up' (internal footnotes omitted).

149 Ibid.

150 Ibid, at 2.

(see above). Thus the Board Review suggests that, in reviewing the OFT's leniency guidelines, there should be 'careful consideration of how best to ensure that immunity or leniency applicants are aware that disclosure of witness account material, including legally privileged material, may be required in criminal cases'.

- The risks of bringing the case forward were not sufficiently challenged within the OFT, and ultimate control over the case lay too far down the organisation.
- There was 'ambiguity in management responsibility'.
- The roles of lead investigator and disclosure officer were combined, when they should have been separated.
- 'Evidential material derived from electronic sources could have been imaged and/or seized at the outset' (the implication here being that they *should* have been so treated).

It did not take long for criticisms to be made of the OFT approach in applying the Cartel Offence to a situation in which there was an alleged price-fixing cartel to which there were only two parties.[151] This might have not been as significant a problem had the cartel been uncovered by a complaint, or as the result of an own-initiative investigation, but became distinctly problematic in the context of a cartel in which one party was seeking leniency and was responsible for providing the OFT with a substantial amount of the evidence that would be used against the other. It will be recalled that although the Cartel Offence is framed in such a way as to require 'dishonesty' only of the party or parties charged with committing the Offence (*R v George, Burns, Burnett and Crawley*[152]), the OFT's

---

[151] See, for example, Crowther, P, 'Opinion: Reform of Cartel Legislation Lacks Specificity', *The Lawyer* (April 11, 2011) (www.thelawyer.com):

> had the [case] got that far it would have been interesting to see what the jury would have made of BA executives potentially going to prison for doing the same thing as Virgin executives, who would walk away scot-free merely because they had confessed to their crimes. Presumably, defence counsel would also have made much of the credibility of defence witness testimony where those witnesses had agreed they were dishonest.

See also Joshua, JM, note 17:

> [w]ith jurors required to judge the defendants according to their own moral compass . . . it would have been intriguing to see how they viewed the testimony of immunised Crown witnesses who by their own admission were as deeply involved in the alleged cartel but were escaping prosecution by incriminating the defendants.

[152] [2010] EWCA Crim 1148.

no-action letter however also makes reference to the *applicant* for leniency having 'dishonestly' entered into a proscribed arrangement. The OFT's case was going to rely heavily on evidence from a party or parties who had, in effect, admitted their involvement in a breach of criminal law, and their dishonesty, who were pointing the finger at another party (which simultaneously happened to be one of its most significant competitors), and who were escaping the risk of prosecution themselves by so doing. Whether a jury would find such evidence persuasive was an important question, and it did not take the benefit of hindsight for this to be apparent. A relevant comparison may be drawn with cases in the US, and most recently with the approach of the District Court for the Eastern District of Pennsylvania in the case of *US v Stolt-Nielsen SA et al.*[153] In that case the DOJ had revoked the defendant's previously granted immunity on the grounds that the defendants had failed in their duty of continuous cooperation required as a condition of immunity. In particular it was alleged that the defendants had continued to participate in conduct falling within s 1 of the Sherman Act even after filing for leniency. The DOJ acted, in part, in response to information provided by a co-conspirator who was then offered the benefit of individual immunity, and whose employer subsequently testified that he would 'say whatever he needed to get his own release, his own immunity'.[154] Kauffman J reviewed the law relating to the credibility of witnesses, concluding that

> . . . the only testimony adduced in favour of the Division's version of [events] was the testimony of a Jo Tankers employee and a number of Odfjell employees whose accounts were fraught with contradiction and uncorroborated by documentary evidence. Each . . . witness testified in return for individual or corporate cooperation agreements that promised immunity or a reduced sentence in exchange for testimony against Defendants. Each witness had a strong motive to seek leniency from the [DOJ] and to retaliate against a competitor that had implicated him in a criminal conspiracy.

The DOJ lost its case on the grounds, in part, that the witnesses were unreliable given the dynamics of the case.[155]

---

[153] *United States v Stolt-Nielsen SA*, 2007 US Dist (E.D. Pa 2007) per Kauffman J in Criminal Action no 06-cr-466. This was the first, and so far only, case in which the DOJ has voided a corporate leniency agreement. In December 2007 the DOJ stated that it would not seek to appeal the dismissal of the indictment (December 21, 2007).

[154] Transcript, p 25.

[155] More generally it was stated in *Young As Chor v Dulles* 270 F.2d 338, 341 (9th Cir, 1959) that, in assessing the credibility of witnesses:

THE 2011 CONSULTATION AND RESPONSE

As noted in Chapter 1, in March 2011, as part of a general review of aspects of the UK competition law regime, the Coalition Government, through the Department for Business, Innovation and Skills ('BIS') published a consultation document calling for comments in a number of areas. For the purposes of this work, the key chapter in that document is Chapter 6, titled 'The criminal cartel offence'. This document, which has been referenced also above, will be quoted at some length in this section. As noted above, particular attention is paid to the 'dishonesty' element of the Offence as originally framed. Four options were presented in the document, with the Government favouring Option 4. These were, in full, as follows:

> *Option 1:* removing the 'dishonesty' element from the offence and introducing guidance for prosecutors.
> *Option 2:* removing the 'dishonesty' element from the offence and defining the offence so that it does not include a set of 'white-listed' agreements.
> *Option 3:* replacing the 'dishonesty' element of the offence with a 'secrecy' element.
> *Option 4:* removing the 'dishonesty' element from the offence and defining the offence so that it does not include agreements made openly.

Option 4 was stated as the preference on the grounds that

> this Option appears to decrease the likelihood of defendants seeking to rely on complex economic evidence that juries will find difficult to understand whilst also striking a good balance between:
>
> - excluding from the scope of the offence the kinds of agreement that might have countervailing benefits under the civil antitrust prohibitions; and
> - differentiating the offence from those prohibitions to reduce the risk that the offence would be categorised as "national competition law" in which

---

the trier of . . . fact may consider the witness' demeanour and manner while on the stand, the character of his testimony as being probable or improbable, inconsistencies, patent omissions and discrepancies in his testimony, or between the testimony of different witnesses, contradictory testimony, his interests in the outcome of the case, his relationship to the litigants, and many other factors bearing upon the truthfulness or untruthfulness of the witness' testimony.

In *United States v Sarivola* 1994 WL 613259 (SDNY November 4, 1994) it was held that factors to be taken into account in assessing credibility include 'a motive to shade the truth', and in *United States v Isaac* 134 F.3d 199, 204 (3rd Cir. 1998) the court recognised that 'a witness who has been given a reward for cooperation has also been given an incentive to shade the truth or to lie'. Both these cases were relied on by Kauffman J in *US v Stolt-Nielsen.*

> case it would not be possible to prosecute wherever there was a parallel European Commission investigation.

In addition it was noted that this would perhaps be the most straightforward option to implement, and that there was already a parallel for it in that s 188(6) of the Act, which relates to bid-rigging, includes a provision to the effect that no offence is committed where the tenderor is made aware of the arrangements by the parties.

There is necessarily much comment on the dishonesty test in the Consultation Document (some of which is referred to above). In particular criticisms of *R v Ghosh* generally are cited, but there is also a concern raised as to the application of the test to cartel activity specifically.[156] Thus, for example, Para 6.14 refers to a study published by the University of East Anglia's ESRC Centre for Competition Policy:

> . . . in the field of cartels specifically a 2007 report found that only six in ten people in Britain believe that price-fixing is dishonest and two in ten people believe that it is not. This suggests . . . that there is only moderate support for a criminal cartel offence defined around dishonesty – and that juries may not be as ready to convict for an offence based on dishonesty as was originally hoped.[157]

It also appears to be the case that pre-trial rulings in the *British Airways* case had indicated that, notwithstanding the original belief that the use of the dishonesty test would reduce the reliance on economic evidence, this would not have been the case. In the Consultation Document it is submitted that it would be possible for the defendants to argue that the arrangements allegedly entered into were not dishonest on the grounds that the arrangement was believed to have no detrimental impact on customers.[158]

The reasons for the Government not to prefer options (1) through (3) were as follows. In the case of option 1 (removing the dishonesty element from the Offence and introducing prosecutorial guidance) it was recognised that this would bring the Offence more into line with the approach in the US, but that the starting point was different from the US, in that the general law of competition in the EU and in the UK does not recognise the clear distinction made in the US between *per se* illegal anti-competitive acts, and ones to which the rule of reason applies. In the EU even price-fixing agreements may benefit from the exception provided for in art

---

156 Stephan, A, note 75. This paper has been discussed in Chapter 2, above.

157 Para 6.14, internal footnotes omitted.

158 At Para 6.13.

101(3) TFEU.[159] The need to differentiate the Offence from 'national competition' law within the terms of Recital (8) of Regulation 1/2003 was also recognised, with the concern being raised that simply removing the dishonesty requirement without further changes might make it more likely that the Cartel Offence *would* be seen as not falling within the terms of Recital (8), such that prosecutions could not, at the minimum, occur wherever there was a parallel EU Commission investigation of the same agreement. A concern was also raised that an Offence defined in part through prosecutorial guidance would be incompatible with ECHR obligations. In the case of option 2 (removing the dishonesty element and excluding from the Offence a set of 'white-listed' agreements), it was felt that the success or failure would depend on the clarity of the white list, but that there would always be room for argument. Again the spectre was raised that it would be more likely that this revision would render the Offence a 'national competition law'. Option 3 would have replaced the dishonesty test with one of secrecy. A proposed statutory definition of secrecy was put forward in the following terms:

> an agreement may be proved to have been made secretly where the persons who make the agreement take measures to prevent the agreement or the intended arrangements becoming known to customers or public authorities.[160]

Although the authors of the Consultation Document clearly saw some merit in this proposal, it was argued that requiring the prosecution to show that active steps were taken to ensure secrecy might be to create too high a burden, and that a threshold based on passive secrecy might criminalise potentially benign agreements. There also appeared, at Para 6.48, a somewhat spurious reference to the concept of 'concerted practice' which appears in art 101 TFEU, and s 2 of the CA98, but this may be discounted as a red-herring.[161]

---

159 Although this is rare there are a small number of cases in which price-fixing arrangements have been tolerated when occurring within a wider context. See, for example, *Uniform Eurocheques* (1985) OJ L35/43, and more recently *Visa International Multilateral Interchange Fee* (2002) OJ L318/17.

160 At Para 6.41.

161 At Para 6.48 it is stated that 'the notion of "secrecy" has some parallels with the concept of "concerted practice"'. This is not factually correct. The concept of 'concerted practice' has been defined by the European Court of Justice in such a way that the element of secrecy is irrelevant to the establishment of whether or not there is a concerted practice (see *Suiker Unie* (*Coöperatieve Vereniging 'Suiker Unie' UA* v *Commission* cases 40–48/73, 50/73, 54–56/73, 111/73, 113–114/73 [1976] 1 CMLR 295, paras 26–27).

In June 2011, the OFT submitted its response to the consultation exercise.[162] This has been discussed above in relation to the application of the dishonesty test. Its views on the reform of the Cartel Offence are set out at pp 84–93. The OFT favoured option 4 as set out in the consultation document ('removing the dishonesty element from the offence and defining it so as to exclude agreements made openly'), on the grounds that: (1) this would be 'the easiest to draft into legislation in clear, unambiguous language [and] does not depend on a separate set of provisions, such as prosecutorial guidance'; (2) this would, by setting a test that would 'involve relatively straightforward questions of fact', reduce uncertainty and make it easier for the prosecutor to determine which cases to proceed with; and (3) by a focus on the secrecy of the arrangement, target relevant harmful conduct.[163] Option 1 was rejected on the grounds that this would make it more likely that parallel UK criminal and EU civil enforcement would be precluded, 'significantly undermining the OFT's ability to investigate and pursue international cartels effectively'.[164] As regards option 2, the OFT argued that the construction of any 'white list' would be a difficult exercise, and would result in uncertainty, the concern being that trial courts would be 'regularly hearing legal argument as to the characterisation of the particular agreement'.[165] Option 3 would in the view of the OFT have been preferable to options 1 or 2, but it would be difficult, the OFT argued, to prove active concealment:

> . . . if option 3 were to be interpreted as requiring proof of active concealment by a defendant, this would often be difficult. Concealment often consists of omissions, for example, failing to note meetings in diaries, or failing to claim for cartel-related expenses. Also, requiring such proof creates a perverse incentive for cartel participants to minimise evidence, and destroy such evidence as is created.[166]

Not all responses to the consultation document were in agreement with the approach suggested by the OFT. Wardhaugh has made a substantial contribution to the debate,[167] and would reject option 4 for its mistaken presumption 'that the harm done by cartel activity consists in

---

162 OFT, note 33.

163 At Para 5.10. As the OFT notes, the fact that an agreement was made *openly*, and therefore not subject to prosecution, would not limit civil liability arising under the Chapter I Prohibition or Article 101 TFEU.

164 At Para 5.11.

165 At Para 5.12.

166 At Para 5.13.

167 Wardhaugh, B, note 29.

the clandestine nature of the conduct, and not its effects'.[168] This rejection does not take into account the possibility of civil enforcement and private litigation, which may be presumed to have a disciplining effect. Wardhaugh would favour option 1 as being '*by far* the most preferable'.[169] Peter Crowther, in *The Lawyer*,[170] argued that the evidence was simply insufficient to draw the conclusion that the dishonesty test was inappropriate, and that 'from the thrust of the consultation paper it seems unlikely that we will ever find out whether this element of the cartel offence was fit for purpose'. Overall BIS has noted that there was not consensus in relation to the approach to be taken to reform of the Cartel Offence.[171] As stated at Para 7.4 of the response:

> [n]early half of the formal consultation responses commented on the criminal cartel offence proposals. The views expressed formally and informally were mixed. The OFT, other prosecutors and overseas competition authorities generally favoured reform, as did a number of academics and some members of the competition bar. Businesses, members of the criminal law bar and law firms with competition practices, on the other hand, mostly did not support the proposed change.

The Government however chose to adopt a variation of option 4, and will remove dishonesty from the terms of the Offence, and allow a transitional period. The core of the argument, supporting the position taken by the OFT, is found at Para 7.8 of the response:

> [n]otwithstanding the lack of live evidence of difficulties arising during the course of a jury trial in a contested case, the Government has concluded that it is more likely than not that the inclusion of the 'dishonesty' element in the cartel offence is in fact inhibiting the OFT in prosecuting cases. 'Dishonesty' offences appear to be particularly difficult to prosecute in a white collar criminal environment. . . .

The Government will therefore bring forward legislation effecting a number of changes in the UK competition law regime. Perhaps most

---

168 At 191–92.

169 Emphasis added. See p 194:

> [o]ption one provides for legal certainty. It identifies those sorts of agreements which do harm to the economy, and prohibits them. It does not make the mistake of assuming the harm from hardcore cartel activities lies in their clandestine nature. And in the prosecution of such an offence, it would not require a jury to be confronted with complex and often contradictory economic evidence.

170 Note 151.

171 *Growth, Competition and the Competition Regime: Government Response to Consultation*, March 2012.

visibly the OFT and the Competition Commission will be merged into a new Competition and Markets Authority. As far as the Cartel Offence is concerned the legislation will remove the dishonesty rubric, and will redefine the Offence so as to exclude from its operation cartel arrangements which are made public before they are implemented.[172] In other words, a publicly disclosed cartel will escape criminal prosecution, but may of course still remain subject to civil enforcement and to actions for damages (although in the unlikely event that this actually happened there might be interesting questions relating to the duty of claimants to mitigate their damage). Crucially in the context of Regulation 1/2003 the Government takes the view – although this may again be tested before the courts – that the redefined Offence 'would remain significantly distinct and so would not be more likely to be classed as "national competition law" for the purposes of Regulation 1/2003'.[173]

---

172 See Para 7.35:

> . . . the offence is not made out if the parties agree to publish key details of the arrangements in a specified medium (which could be the London Gazette) before they are implemented. This approach has the particular advantage of simplicity. It would be straightforward to publish in the London Gazette and relatively easy for a jury to decide whether or not the defendants agreed to do this. There would be no scope for arguing that it was not reasonably practicable to publish, nor would there be any issues about identifying actual or potential customers. . . .

173 Para 7.30.

5. Criminalisation in Ireland

INTRODUCTION

The UK is a member of a fairly exclusive club. Only a minority of the EU member states operate a system within which those engaging in cartelisation may face personal criminal sanctions, whether by way of fines or imprisonment. Ireland is the most distinctive of these regimes, and a discussion of its law forms the basis of this chapter. Austria and Germany have repealed their respective criminal laws, in part to secure stronger alignment with EU competition law in the post-modernisation world. However, the UK and Ireland are not completely alone. A full survey of criminal laws operating in the EU will not be attempted here, but it is worth making some reference to the law in Greece.

Greece introduced a criminal law in March 1978,[1] and the law is currently set out in Law 359/2011, which entered into force on April 20, 2011. Article 44 of the Law is, in part, in the following terms:

> Any person who enters into an agreement, issues a decision or implements a concerted practice in breach of Article 1[2] or Article 101 of the [TFEU], shall receive a fine of between [€15,000 and €150,000]. . . . If the offence described in the first sentence involves undertakings which are actual or potential competitors, the offender shall receive imprisonment of at least two years and a fine of between [€100,000 and €1,000,000].

Specific provision is made in Article 44(1) in relation to leniency applicants who have notified, 'on their own initiative and before having been

---

[1] Law 703/1977 entered into force on March 26, 1978. Article 29 of the Law stated that:

> Any person who, independently or acting as a representative of a legal person, enters into agreements, issues decisions or implements concerted practices prohibited by Article 1(1) . . . shall receive imprisonment of at least three months and a fine of between one hundred thousand and two hundred thousand drachmas. In case of recidivism, the aforementioned amounts shall be doubled.

This provision was amended five times before being replaced, and in its original incarnation did not provide for imprisonment.

[2] Article 1 of the Law is the equivalent of art 101 TFEU.

interrogated', the practice to a competent authority. Such offenders 'shall remain unpunished'. Elsewhere the legislation forms a link between leniency and the Criminal Code, requiring that certain factors, including 'any substantial contribution' by these persons to the provision of evidence 'shall be deemed as mitigating factors under Article 84 of the Criminal Code', and may thus attract a reduced penalty under Article 83 of the Criminal Code. There has, at the time of writing, been only one case determined in Greece on the basis of the criminal law. In April 2011 the Thessaloniki Court of First Instance imposed fines of €9000 on three directors of MEVGAL, a dairy company involved in a six-party cartel, the aim of which was to compel dairy farmers to sell milk to the cartel at reduced prices. The parties had also entered into a number of agreements with major supermarket chains fixing the retail prices for milk. The low penalties reflect the fact that when the cartel was formed Article 29 of Law 703/1977 allowed for penalties up to a maximum of €30,000, and made no provision in respect of incarceration. The case does, however, at least demonstrate the willingness of the Greek authorities to apply criminal law against individuals in respect of cartel breaches.[3]

In this chapter the focus is on the criminal aspects of competition law in Ireland.[4] Ireland first criminalised aspects of its competition law in 1991, and following an amendment in 1996, the legislation was significantly enhanced in 2002, in the Competition Act 2002 ('CA 2002').[5] In the

---

3 The Slovak Republic's Criminal Code (*Trestny zakon*), 300/2005 includes, at §250 the possibility of imprisonment for a period of up to six years in respect of conduct which 'causes significant damage to its competitor or endangers the existence of business of its competitor by conduct which contravenes the rules of competition law'. The Czech Republic's criminal code of 2009 deals only with *unfair* competition, and does not extend to cartelisation. Malta also may employ criminal law in anti-cartel enforcement activity.

4 For an excellent treatment of the Irish regime see Massey, P, and Cooke, JD, 'Competition Offences in Ireland: The Regime and Its Results', in Beaton-Wells, C, and Ezrachi, A (eds), *Criminalising Cartels: Critical Studies of an International Regulatory Movement* (2011) Hart Publishing. See also Calvani, T, 'Cartel Penalties and Damages in Ireland: Criminalization and the Case for Custodial Sentences', in Cseres, KJ, Schinkel, MP, and Vogelaar, FOW, *Criminalization of Competition Law Enforcement: Economic and Legal Implications for the EU Member States* (2006) Edward Elgar at 270.

5 The Competition Act 2002, which entered into force on July 1, 2002, was amended by the Competition (Amendment) Act 2006. The amendments do not affect the provisions discussed in this chapter. In 2011 the Competition (Amendment) Bill 2011 was introduced into the Dáil. If enacted this will amend the level of the penalties specified in s 8 of the CA 2002, and I have anticipated this below.

debates in the Dáil during the passage of the latter Act it was argued, in language similar to that adopted by the framers of the Cartel Offence in the UK, that

> the assessment of such practices [hard-core cartel conduct] is clear and unambiguous. There is no evidence that they have any beneficial effects, in fact, quite the opposite – they reduce efficiency and clearly harm consumers because, effectively, they are a rip-off.[6]

As is suggested below, the experience in Ireland would appear to be a more successful one than that in the UK, although it has not been without its difficulties and failures. It may be reasonable to suppose that the wider socio-political environment, within which the specifics of competition law operate in Ireland, is not so very different to that in the UK, although we must be aware of the caution with which comparative lawyers approach different legal regimes, and the great care which they take in drawing comparisons.

CRIMINAL COMPETITION LAW IN IRELAND

The position in Ireland is distinctive. The Irish Constitution is such that, with an exception set out in Article 37, the Courts have the exclusive power to administer justice.[7] Article 37 of the Constitution permits the delegation to administrative bodies of limited powers to administer justice, but, following judgments of the Supreme Court,[8] this does not extend to powers which 'affect . . . the lives, liberties, fortunes and reputations of those' subject to the power. Thus, as Massey notes, 'the Irish Competition Authority cannot rule on whether undertakings have breached competition legislation and cannot impose fines', and '[t]he net effect of these provisions is that fines may only be imposed on individuals and undertakings convicted of a criminal offence by the Court'.[9] As we shall see, this unusual restriction may in fact have resulted in the Irish competition law regime adopting potentially a more successful approach to the criminalisation of competition law than has the UK, although the relatively low level of enforcement activity, at least as reflected in cases brought forward, might

---

6 Mr Rabbitte, Dáil Debates Official Report, February 28, 2002.

7 See Article 34.1 of the Irish Constitution. In the context of competition law see Massey, P, 'Criminal Sanctions for Competition Law: A Review of Irish Experience' (2004) *Competition Law Review* 23.

8 See *Re the Solicitors' Act 1954* [1960] IR 239.

9 Massey, P, note 7, at 24.

suggest otherwise.[10] While over 30 defendants have pleaded guilty to offences arising under the CA 2002, there have been a number of cases in which multiple parties have been prosecuted (see Table 5.1), such that the actual number of anti-competitive arrangements targeted has been well below 30. The Irish Competition Authority is able to resolve cases with settlements under civil law, such that the criminal prosecutions brought in relation to anti-competitive agreements do not reflect the totality of enforcement in Ireland.

THE LEGISLATIVE FRAMEWORK

Sections 4 and 5 of the CA 2002 create a mirror of arts 101 and 102 TFEU within Ireland (and lack therefore the requirements that trade between member states be affected). Sections 6 and 7 of the CA 2002 create offences in respect of breaches of ss 4 and 5 of the CA 2002 and of arts 101 and 102 TFEU.[11] Sections 8–15 set out various related provisions applying to penalties and procedural matters. Section 6 of the Act, which creates an offence in relation to breaches of s 4 and art 101 is given here in full, as this is central to the criminalisation of cartels, and without all the detail comparisons made to the UK system may be obscure:

> **6.** (1) An undertaking which –
> (a) enters into, or implements, an agreement, or
> (b) makes or implements a decision, or
> (c) engages in a concerted practice,
> that is prohibited by *section 4(1)* or by Article [101(1)] of the Treaty shall be guilty of an offence.
>
> (2) In proceedings for an offence under *subsection (1)*, it shall be presumed that an agreement between competing undertakings, a decision made by an

---

[10] Galbreath recognises that 'differing national traditions . . . make criminal enforcement more difficult relative to the US', while at the same time stating that the Authority 'has made an impressive start in securing criminal cartel convictions' (Galbreath, C, 'Cartel Criminalization in Ireland and Europe: Can the United States Model of Criminal Antitrust Enforcement Be Successfully Transferred to Ireland and Europe?' (2007) ABA International Section, 2007 Fall Meeting, October 1, 2007, p 3). Ms Carolyn Galbreath was appointed to the Cartels Division of the Authority in March 2006, and it is perhaps worth noting that her experience prior to this included time working as a trial attorney for the Department of Justice, Antitrust Division in San Francisco.

[11] In the legislation the older numbering of arts 81 and 82 EC is used. Consistent with the approach taken throughout this book, I have amended the numbering to reflect the current version of the Treaty.

association of competing undertakings or a concerted practice engaged in by competing undertakings the purpose of which is to –

(a) directly or indirectly fix prices with respect to the provision of goods or services to persons not party to the agreement, decision or concerted practice,

(b) limit output or sales, or

(c) share markets or customers,

has as its object the prevention, restriction or distortion of competition in trade in any goods or services in the State or in any part of the State or within the common market, as the case may be, unless the defendant proves otherwise.

(3) In proceedings for an offence under *subsection (1)* in which it is alleged that an agreement, decision or concerted practice contravened the prohibition in *section 4(1)*, it shall be a good defence to prove that the agreement, decision or concerted practice in question did not contravene that prohibition by virtue of *section 4(2)*.[12]

(4) In proceedings for an offence under *subsection (1)* in which it is alleged that an agreement, decision or concerted practice contravened the prohibition in Article [101(1)] of the Treaty, it shall be a good defence to prove that –

(a) there was in force, at the material time, in respect of the particular agreement, decision or concerted practice an exemption granted by the Commission pursuant to Article [101(3)] of the Treaty,

(b) at the material time the agreement, decision or concerted practice benefited from the terms of an exemption provided for by, or granted under, a regulation made by the Council or the Commission pursuant to that Article [101(3)], or

(c) the agreement, decision or concerted practice did not contravene that prohibition by virtue of that Article [101(3)].

(5) In proceedings for an offence under *subsection (1)*, it shall be a good defence to prove that the act or acts concerned was or were done pursuant to a determination made or a direction given by a statutory body.

(6) For the purpose of determining liability for an offence under *subsection (1)*, any act done by an officer of an employee of an undertaking for the purposes of, or in connection with, the business or affairs of the undertaking shall be regarded as an act done by the undertaking.

(7) In this section 'competing undertakings' means undertakings that provide or are capable of providing goods or services to the same applicable market and, for the purposes of this definition, 'applicable market' means a market comprising the provision of goods or services that are regarded by those to whom they are provided as interchangeable with, or substitutable for, each other by reason of the goods' or services' characteristics, prices and intended use or purpose.

---

12 Section 4(2), CA 2002 maps into Irish law the exception system of art 101(3) TFEU.

Section 6(2) of the CA 2002, above, deals with the hard-core cartels, and in effect creates a presumption whereby the conduct falling within those categories is deemed to be unlawful, unless a relevant defence applies. The effect of s 8 (set out below) is such that an individual may be arrested and held for up to 12 hours for questioning where an infringement of s 6(2) is being investigated. The Act also gives the Authority substantial investigative powers, including the rights to apply to the courts for search warrants for both businesses and private premises, to question witnesses and to require the production of documents.

The CA 2002 is unusual in that it provides a criminal offence in respect of conduct falling within art 102 TFEU (and the Irish equivalent in s 5 of the Act), but, as seen above, were this power not provided the Irish authorities would have *no* power to seek the imposition of fines in respect of those found to be in breach of art 102. This provision is not considered further in this book. The extent to which this legislation is compatible with the requirements of Regulation 1/2003, discussed in Chapter 4, above, is considered further below.

The sanction of imprisonment is available only in respect of the hard-core cartels identified in s 6(2) of the CA 2002. Fines alone may be imposed in relation to other breaches. Sections 7 and 8 of the Act set out the penalties that apply in relation to offences falling in ss 5 and 6. In the case of breaches of s 6, or art 101 TFEU, s 8 is, in part, in the following terms:[13]

> 8. (1) An undertaking guilty of an offence under *section 6* . . . shall be liable –
>
> (a) on summary conviction –
>
> (i) in the case of an undertaking that is not an individual, to a class A fine, or
>
> (ii) in the case of an individual, to such a fine or to imprisonment for a term not exceeding 6 months or to both such fine and such imprisonment,
>
> (b) on conviction on indictment –
>
> (i) in the case of an undertaking that is not an individual, to a fine not exceeding whichever of the following amounts is the greater, namely, €5,000,000 or 10 per cent of the turnover of the undertaking in the financial year ending in the 12 months prior to the conviction, or
>
> (ii) in the case of an individual, to a fine not exceeding whichever of the following amounts is the greater, namely, €5,000,000 or 10 per cent of the turnover of the individual in the financial year or to imprisonment for a term not exceeding 10 years or to both such fine (that is to say a fine not exceeding the greater of the foregoing monetary amounts) and such imprisonment.

---

13 As amended by the Competition Amendment Act, 2011.

> (2) An undertaking guilty of an offence under *section 6* (other than to one which *subsection (1)* applies) . . . shall, whether the undertaking is an individual or otherwise, be liable –
>
> (a) on summary conviction, to a class A fine, or
>
> (b) on conviction on indictment, to a fine not exceeding whichever of the following amounts is the greater, namely, €5,000,000 or 10 per cent of turnover of the undertaking in the financial year ending in the 12 months prior to the conviction.

The high level of penalty in s 8(1)(b) of up to ten years imprisonment is an uplift proposed by the Competition Bill 2011. The level specified originally was five years. The impact of this section is such that a possible range of penalties is set, up to the EU 'standard' of 10 per cent of the turnover of the undertaking in the relevant financial year. However, because fines are determined on conviction by the Court as part of a sentencing procedure, the Authority is not in the position of being able to publish guidance as to the amount of the penalty, and there is perhaps more uncertainty facing a would-be cartelist as to the level of the penalty that may be imposed on detection and punishment than is the case in the EU or in the UK. The judiciary are not constrained by any sentencing guidelines, and take into account a range of factors, including cooperation by the defendant in the course of the investigation, when assessing the level of fine. There is also not the option of plea bargaining within the sense that the term has in the United States – in fact plea bargaining in the US' sense is strictly prohibited in Ireland. It has thus been noted that:

> [w]hile a defendant may agree to plead guilty and the Director of Public Prosecutions may agree to charge only a subset of the potential available charges, this style of 'charge bargaining', if it may be so characterised, will not result in certainty about a particular sentence, except insofar as the charges pleaded to define the outer limits of range of sentence that may be imposed.[14]

Section 8(3) makes further provision in respect of the imposition of penalties in relation to ongoing infringements, such that a lower level of penalty may be applied, but for each day of infringement. Sub-sections 8(6) and (7) apply to the officers of infringing undertakings, and are in the following terms:

---

14 'Criminal Enforcement of Competition Laws in Ireland: A Look at Enforcement to Date' (2010) <http://tca.ie/images/uploaded/documents/2010-01%20Criminal%20Enforcement%20of%20Competition%20Laws%20in%20Ireland.PDF> (accessed July 30, 2011) at 8.

> (8)(6) Where an offence . . . has been committed by an undertaking and the doing of the acts that constituted the offence has been authorised, or consented to, by a person, being a director, manager, or other similar officer of the undertaking, or a person who purports to act in any such capacity, that person as well as the undertaking shall be guilty of an offence and shall be liable to be proceeded against and punished as if he or she were guilty of the first-mentioned offence.
>
> (8)(7) Where a person is proceeded against as aforesaid for such an offence and it is proved that, at the material time, he or she was a director of the undertaking concerned or a person employed by it whose duties included making decisions that, to a significant extent, could have affected the management of the undertaking, or a person who purported to act in any such capacity, it shall be presumed, until the contrary is proved, that that person consented to the doing of the acts by the undertaking which constituted the commission by it of the offence concerned. . .

The 2011 amendment to the CA 2002 introduces a new s8(11B) which states that:

> [w]here a person is convicted of an offence under this Act the court shall order the person to pay to the relevant competent authority a sum equal to the costs and expenses, measured by the court, incurred by that competent authority in relation to the investigation, detection and prosecution of the offence, unless the court is satisfied that there are special and substantial reasons for not so doing.

Unlike the position adopted in the UK, the Irish law does not shy away from the introduction of economic arguments and evidence in court, and indeed the very fact that the legislation is framed in such a way as to apply to a direct breach of art 101 TFEU throws this issue to the foreground. The distinctive Irish approach thus sits within the framework of Regulation 1/2003, the relevant provisions of which apply to the Irish criminal enforcement model, such that it has not been necessary for Ireland to draw a clear separation between the EU law-based procedure and a separate national criminal law.

Trials on indictment are held before juries in Ireland, and there are references in the legislation to the materials that may be made available for the jury, and for the use, *inter alia*, of expert witnesses. Thus, section 9(1) states that 'the opinion of any witness who appears to the court to possess the appropriate qualifications or experience as respects the matter' may be admissible. This includes, in particular, evidence relating to:

> **9.** (1)(a) the effects that types of agreements, decisions or concerted practices may have, or that specific agreements, decisions or concerted practices have had, on competition in trade,

> (b) an explanation to the court of any relevant economic principles or the application of such principles in practice, where such an explanation would be of assistance to the judge or, as the case may be, jury.

Clearly the Irish legislature has more confidence in the ability of juries to deal with economic evidence in the context of a criminal trial than does the UK legislature![15] Jurisdiction in relation to cartel offences lies with the Central Criminal Court, the highest criminal court in Ireland.

Ireland operates a *Cartel Immunity Programme* ('CIP'). This was introduced timeously on December 20, 2001, before the CA 2002 took effect. At the time of writing, a Cartel Immunity Programme Review was under way, and a consultation paper was published on July 15, 2010. No figures

---

[15] This approach has however been criticised. Thus Massey argues, *inter alia*, that:

> [t]he Irish legislation stops short of making cartels illegal *per se* and of defining a specific cartel offence. Providing a specific definition of what constitutes the offensive behaviour reduces the scope for the defence to argue that a particular activity is not caught by the offence.
>
> More importantly section 6(3) of the Irish Act provides that a defendant can claim that an agreement, which is contrary to Article [101(1)] (or Section 4(1)), satisfies the four conditions contained in Article [101(3)]. The effect of section 6(3) is that juries may be required to assess complex economic arguments and will, at the very least, greatly increase the length and complexity of cartel cases (Massey, P, note 7, at 37).

Massey, writing before the UK's Cartel Offence had been applied, was in support of the UK's approach which 'would appear to find a way around the difficulty posed by the exemption provisions in the EU Treaty' (at 38).

Gorecki and McFadden, discussing the heating oil cartel (see below), suggest that 'the one jury trial that did take place allows for at least a few observations . . . the jury seemed to have no difficulty in coming to a verdict' (Gorecki, PK, and McFadden, D, 'Criminal Cartels in Ireland: The Heating Oil Case' (2006) *European Competition Law Review*, at 631. See also Competition Authority, *Annual Report 2006*, 7 at 639). It was the case, however, that the charges were brought on the basis that the conduct was a breach 'by object', such that the jury merely had to determine whether the defendant had taken part in competitor meetings. The particulars of offence are set out at p 9 of the Competition Authority's 2009 Annual Report in the following terms:

> JP Lambe, between the 1st day of January 2001 and the 11th day of February 2002, both dates inclusive, in the County of Galway, did aid and abet Corrib Oil Company Limited, an undertaking within the meaning of section 3 of the Competition Act, 1991, to commit an offence, namely the entering into an agreement which has as its object the prevention, restriction or distortion of competition in the trade of gasoil in Galway City and County by directly or indirectly fixing the selling price of gasoil.

are available as to the number of applications made for leniency under the programme. As indicated above, the courts may in addition take into account co-operation during the course of an investigation when determining the level of any fine or penalty to be imposed, such that a party in breach of the CA 2002 who is not eligible for immunity may still benefit from a reduced fine. There will not in this latter case however be any certainty as to how big the fine is likely to be, or as to how big any subsequent reduction will be. The fact that this level of predictability is missing from the Irish system is unfortunate, but it appears not to be possible to do anything else given the structure of the Irish legal system.[16]

ENFORCEMENT

The early experience of bringing criminal prosecutions against those alleged to be breaching competition law prohibitions was not entirely successful in Ireland. In one case dealt with under the 1991 legislation it has been reported that 'the Judge in the case considered that it would be inappropriate for the defendants to be given criminal records on the basis that they may not have been aware of competition law'.[17] Writing about the Irish approach to criminalisation in 2004, Massey commented that 'the results to date have been extremely poor'.[18] Massey identified flaws in the earlier 1996 legislation, under which the investigative powers of the Authority were not sufficient to comply with the rigorous requirements of criminal prosecution. This was particularly true in relation to obtaining documentary evidence and in relation to the questioning of suspects. Thus Massey refers to one case in which 'where a file was referred to the DPP, the Gardai (police) were requested to carry out a further investigation but they reported that they had received "virtually zero cooperation"

---

16 See also Galbreath, C, note 14:

> [l]eniency for second or third co-operators, which operates in other jurisdictions to give those who offer early acceptance of responsibility and cooperation the potential of obtaining a quantifiable reduction in the level of fine or term of incarceration, is not an option under Ireland's Cartel Immunity Programme. Ireland is a signatory to the European Competition Network Model Leniency Programme but only to the extent that it does not conflict with Irish law (at p 7).

17 See 'Cartels: criminal penalties become reality in Ireland', July 18, 2006 (www.efc.ie/full-publications.php?id_publications=99) (accessed November 2, 2011).

18 Massey, P, note 7, at 27.

from the individuals that they interviewed'.[19] Writing in 2004 Massey was pessimistic as to the prospects for the success of the Irish approach:

> [i]t must be recognised that tough penalties, such as those contained in Ireland's Competition Act, 2002, by themselves, will not deter anti-competitive behaviour, if people believe that there is little likelihood of being caught. The prospect of the Competition Authority bringing in one cartel case per year suggests that the likelihood of getting caught for engaging in such behaviour is extremely remote to say the least. Far too much of the Authority's efforts have been channelled into undertaking sectoral studies rather than enforcement, which is obviously a great comfort to those engaged in cartels. In enforcement terms it's time that the Authority got off the ditch and started delivering results on the pitch.[20]

As noted above, the powers in the 2002 Act in relation to investigation are stronger than those set out in 1996, but some of the concerns raised by Massey remain pertinent today. Eight years have passed since 2004, and the Authority's website indicates that, as of the time of writing, prosecutions have been brought forward in relation to six separate cartels or anti-competitive arrangements falling within the prohibition. Not all of these prosecutions have been completely successful. While this is notably a higher level of criminal enforcement than in the UK in the same period, the fact remains that this does equate to the one case a year about which Massey was so pessimistic, and of course, unlike the position in the UK, these cases represent the totality of actions, there being no alternative mechanism of civil enforcement (other than by way of settlement). The relevant cases are: *Heating Oil*; *Irish Rail*; *Mayo Waste*; *Irish Ford Dealers Association*; *Citroën Dealers Association*; and *Grain Imports*. All of these cases related to 'home-grown' cartels, and Ireland has not yet tackled an international cartel. These are dealt with below, but Table 5.1 will allow the presentation of some key data:

It is readily apparent that the highest fine imposed to date has been €80 000. While this is substantially above the €30 000 fine imposed on Mr Manning for his participation in the Ford Dealers Association

---

[19] Ibid. In another case however, *DPP v Morgan* (Dublin Metropolitan District Court, December 22, 2005), proceedings were commenced against an individual who had refused to attend a proceeding in which he would be examined under oath. The Authority alerted the An Garda Síochána and a prosecution was commenced. While the court found that the case was established on the facts, the accused was given the benefit of a probationary sentence as he subsequently complied with the requirement (see Competition Authority, *Annual Report 2005*, at 10; and *Annual Report 2006*, at 12).

[20] Massey, P, note 7, at 39.

*Table 5.1 Irish prosecutions**

Case	Defendant	Outcome	Sentence
Heating Oil (2006)**	Michael Flanagan	Convicted	€3,500 fine
	JP Lambe	Convicted	6 months prison, suspended; €15 000 fine
	Con Muldoon	Guilty plea	€1000 fine
	Michael McMahon	Guilty plea	€1500 fine
	Sean Hester	Guilty plea	€1500 fine
	Kevin Cunniffe	Guilty plea	€1500 fine
	Three defendants	*Nolle prosequi*	
Ford Dealers Association (2006)	Denis Manning	Convicted	12 months prison, suspended; €30 000
Citroën Dealers Association (2008)	James Durrigan & Sons Ltd	Convicted	€12 000 fine
	James Durrigan	Convicted	3 months prison, suspended
	Ravenslodge Trading Limited T/A Jack Doran Motors	Convicted	€20 000 fine
	Jack Doran	Convicted	3 months prison, suspended
	Duffy Motors (Newbridge) Limited	Convicted	€50 000 fine
	Patrick Duffy	Convicted	6 months and 9 months prison, suspended
	Bursey Peppard Limited	Convicted	€80 000 fine
	James Bursey	Convicted	6 months and 9 months prison, suspended
Mayo Waste (2009)		5 individuals and 3 undertakings acquitted following deliberation by jury	
Irish Rail (2010)***		*Nolle prosequi*, with subsequent acquittal on trial	

Table 5.1 (continued)

Notes:
* This table is not complete, but is as complete as possible given the publicly available information.
** In the case of *Heating Oil* the defence argued in one case that an individual could only be convicted of an offence where a company, of which that person was a manager, had committed an offence. A case was stated to the Supreme Court. At the time of writing no date had been set for judgment. This case was brought forward under the Competition Act 1991, as amended. At that time the maximum penalties were a fine of €3m, and/or a prison term of up to two years. In addition to the details given above, a number of undertakings were also fined. The case is discussed below, and see the Authority's *Annual Report 2006* at 7–12.
*** In the case of *Irish Rail* a number of defendants were charged with breaches of s4 of the CA 2002, but a *nolle prosequi* was entered following procedural defects relating to the way in which the cases were referred to the Central Criminal Court. The DPP subsequently reinstated proceedings in the relevant court. The jury eventually returned a majority not guilty verdict.

infringement, it is well below the levels applied in the enforcement of EU competition law by the European Commission. It has been recognised that these fining levels are 'extremely modest by any standard', and that the fines have 'not reflected either the harm caused by [the cartels] or present international standards'.[21] No prison sentence has actually been served following a substantive breach (in one case a sentence was served following a failure to pay a fine), with all such terms being suspended. It is perhaps strange therefore that '[t]he Central Criminal Court has, however, made abundantly clear its antipathy for cartels and the lack of sympathy that can be expected by those involved if convicted of cartel offences'.[22] This 'antipathy' is most obviously evident in the remarks made by the judge in the case of *Duffy*, arising from the Citroën Dealers Association, discussed below.

Case History

The first case resulting in convictions on indictment in Ireland as a criminal action was brought in 2005 against participants engaged in price-fixing in relation to supplies of heating oil to residential customers in Galway.[23] The DPP took action against a total of 24 defendants. This case was, as noted above, brought under the 1991 Act (the cartel having commenced

21 Galbreath, C, note 10, at 13.
22 Galbreath, C, note 14, at 4.
23 See Gorecki, PK, and McFadden, D, note 15, at 7.

operation before the 2002 Act entered into force), as amended in 1996, at a time when the maximum penalties available were lower than is the case now. A number of defendants pleaded guilty, but Michael Flanagan, trading as Flanagan Oil, contested the charges with the result that a jury trial was held. The trial lasted three days, and the jury deliberated for a little over two hours before returning unanimous guilty verdicts on both counts. Mr Justice Raymond Groarke fined him €3500 in total. While acknowledging in the sentencing remarks that Flanagan was 'a minnow surrounded by sharks', the judge also stated that:

> [t]hose engaged in cartels and involved in the fixing of prices are doing so only with the motivation of greed, and with nothing to be gained but financial profit. That is why the legislature takes such a serious view of it . . . I could well see circumstances where persons convicted by a jury could be subjected to terms of imprisonment.[24]

Another defendant, JP Lambe, who pleaded guilty in Dublin Central Criminal Court on October 27, 2005 to aiding and abetting a price-fixing cartel in relation to home heating oil, was sentenced to 12 months imprisonment, suspended, and fined €15 000.[25] In all, at least 15 participants in the cartel were convicted.[26] It may in fact be that this was the first time that anyone in Europe – at least since the Second World War – had been sentenced to imprisonment as a result of an illegal anti-competitive act,[27] and it has been recognised that the case 'was a highly significant breakthrough for the Authority'.[28] Gorecki and McFadden point to the success of the case as being 'a practical demonstration, albeit modest, of the feasibility of bringing criminal prosecutions for hardcore offences in the EU'.[29]

Irish Ford Dealers' Association (DPP v Manning)[30] was the first case

---

24 *Director of Public Prosecutions v Michael Flanagan and others*, March 2, 2004, unreported. See Competition Authority *Annual Report 2006*, at 6–7.

25 In sentencing Lambe, Judge Delahunt stated that: 'Without your talent, acumen and knowledge of this business, the kind of distortion before the court today could not have functioned to any sort of significant level'.

26 A table, up to date as of December 31, 2006, sets out the full results in respect of all 24 defendants, at the Authority's *Annual Report 2006*, p 11.

27 This claim is made by the Authority in its *Annual Report 2006* at 9: '[t]his is the first custodial sentence received by an individual in Ireland or Europe for a competition law offence'. I am unable to verify whether this statement is accurate.

28 Geary, D, 'Irish Competition Law Update' [2007] *Competition Law Journal* 137 at 141.

29 Gorecki, PK, and McFadden, D, note 15, at 640.

30 February 9, 2007, unreported (note however that Judge McKechnie quoted from this judgment in his later judgment in *Duffy* (see below)).

to be tried before the Central Criminal Court under the 2002 Act, and the first to result in a conviction under that Act, although it has been suggested that it is evidence for the proposition that a strategy of ensuring compliance is to be preferred over one of sanctioning.[31] There were in excess of 50 members of the Irish Ford Dealers' Association ('IFDA'), and a scheme was maintained whereby price guides were distributed to the members, and whereby an enforcement system to ensure adherence to these guides was implemented. Members could be fined, and each member paid a surety to the IFDA of €1250 that could be drawn from in the event that a penalty was imposed. The scheme was managed, although not created by, Mr Manning, who was a former director of Henry Ford & Sons (Ireland) Ltd (Ford). A consultant was hired to report on competition in relation to Ford car sales in Ireland, and it was suggested at trial that this was an attempt to provide a fig-leaf for the activity, and was evidence as to a recognition of the fact that the arrangement was, in all likelihood, an unlawful one. The consultant advised that the price guidelines were lawful, but that the scheme to enforce them was not, and the sureties were repaid following his report, although deductions already levied were imposed. Mr Manning pleaded guilty in January 2007, but it was argued in his defence that he had not created the scheme, and that he was, in essence, merely following orders, and it was stressed that he had not personally benefited from the scheme (although he had been paid a salary by the IFDA). Mr Manning was sentenced by Judge McKechnie[32] to a one-year jail term, suspended, and to a fine of €30 000.[33] The relatively light sentence imposed

---

[31] See Curtis, ME, and McNally, J, 'The Classic Cartel – Hatchback Sentence?' (2007) 4:1 *Competition Law Review* 41. For a brief case comment see Geary, D, note 28, at 141–42.

[32] It has been noted that 'Ireland does not have a specialist competition court; therefore it is significant that the judge who imposed the prison sentence in relation to the motor dealers' cartel, McKechnie J, is the same judge who oversees the Civil High Court Competition List' (Geary, D, note 28, at 142).

[33] See Curtis, ME, and McNally, J, note 31, at 45:

> [t]o put the sentence in context, Lambe [in *Heating Oil*] received a six month suspended sentence out of a possible two years imprisonment (25%) while Manning received a twelve month suspended sentence out of a possible five years imprisonment (20%). Both men were of similar age and both were considered as the facilitator of the cartel. However despite Manning having a longer involvement in the operation of a cartel, he received a more lenient sentence. The same can more or less be said of the fines imposed, in Lambe's case €15,000 out of a possible €3,810,000 (£3,000,000) while Manning was fined €30,000 out of a possible €4,000,000. The sentence does not appear to reflect the increased teeth provided for in the 2002 Act (internal footnotes omitted).

on Mr Manning has been criticised as being 'a cause for concern',[34] but it may be significant that the same judge was involved also in the case of *Duffy*, discussed below, in which a somewhat more robust approach was taken. Mr Manning was the only person to be prosecuted in relation to this price-fixing arrangement for reasons that are somewhat opaque. It is notable that the only person to be convicted was not himself a car dealer at the time of the cartel, and that the car dealers themselves who were benefiting directly from the higher fixed prices were not charged or convicted.

By far the most significant case brought to date under the CA 2002 is that of *The Citroën Dealers Association*,[35] with proceedings being brought by the DPP against 15 undertakings and individuals, all of whom were members of the Citroën Dealers Association ('CDA'). It was alleged that the defendants had engaged in illegal price-fixing. Some defendants were charged on the basis of the 1991 statute, and were convicted in the circuit criminal courts. Eight defendants, of whom five were individuals, pleaded guilty and were convicted before the Central Criminal Court. One defendant became the first person to serve a prison sentence when he was sentenced to a term of 28 days following his failure to pay an €80 000 fine imposed on him for his participation in the cartel. The case of *Duffy*[36] is particularly important:

> [f]irstly, it is the first case involving the criminal conviction of a breach of Irish competition legislation where the judgment has been made available. Secondly, it outlines how seriously the court views such anti-competitive behaviour. Finally, in his judgment the [judge] gave a very clear signal that the next individual before the Court on such a charge could expect a term of imprisonment and, while so doing, outlined some sentencing guidelines for consideration in cases involving white-collar crime.[37]

---

34 Ibid, at 47. At 50 Curtis and McNally argue further that '[t]he reality is, however, that white collar criminals do not face the same punishment as the traditional criminal.' It has also been noted by Riley that:

> [t]here is a real whiff in *Manning* of the first modern criminal antitrust cases in the US; the *Lysine Cartel* where Federal Judges found it difficult to jail individuals. (Riley, A, 'Editorial – Developing Criminal Cartel Law: Dealing with the Growing Pains' (2007) *Competition Law Review* 1 at 4)

35 For a substantial case comment see McNally, J, 'Case Comment: *D.P.P. v. Duffy and Duffy Motors (Newbridge) Limited*' (2010) 1(2) *Irish Journal of Legal Studies* 116.

36 *Director of Public Prosecutions v Patrick Duffy and Duffy Motors (Newbridge) Limited* [2009] IEHC 208.

37 McNally, J, note 35, at 116.

The CDA was established in March 1995. A sophisticated and wide-ranging scheme to fix the prices of new cars, and various services and accessories, was created, with regular meetings being held to achieve and monitor compliance. In particular the CDA established a monitoring mechanism whereby 'mystery shoppers', employed by independent companies, would monitor prices. If these shoppers were quoted prices that were not in line with the agreed fixed price this would be reported to the CDA Secretary, and a fine of up to £1000 would be imposed on the infringing party. One party who was 'fined' by the CDA having been found to be in breach of the agreement became the primary whistle-blower, and provided significant evidence of the unlawful arrangement to the Authority. Patrick Duffy played a key role in the CDA, in that he was its treasurer and was responsible for the costs incurred by the Secretary, and for the costs of the 'mystery shoppers'. In 2004 Mr Duffy was interviewed under caution. Subsequently both his company, Duffy Motors (Newbridge) Ltd, and Mr Duffy personally, were charged on a number of counts in respect of breaches of the Competition Acts 1991 and 1996. Mr Duffy pleaded guilty to four of the charges in January 2009. Judge McKechnie was in no doubt as to the evil of cartelisation, referring to cartels as '"hard-core" infringements of competition law . . . involving odious practices'.[38] While some have been critical of language which demonises cartels and cartelists, McKechnie had previously stated in *Manning* that:

> [t]his type of crime is a crime against all consumers and is not simply against one or more individuals. To that extent it is different from other types of crime: and while society has an interest in preventing, detecting and prosecuting all crimes, those which involve a breach of the Competition Act are particularly pernicious.[39]

The judge placed cartelisation in the category of crimes against property, likening it to 'burglary or larceny'[40] but accepted further, quoting Werden, that:

---

38 *Duffy*, Para [22].

39 *DPP v Manning*, February 9, 2007, High Court, unreported; quoted in *Duffy*, at Para [23].

40 At Para [24], quoting from Werden, GJ, 'Sanctioning Cartel Activity: Let the Punishment Fit the Crime' (seminar presentation of November 22, 2008, later published at (2009) 5:1 *European Competition Journal* 19). As argued in Chapter 2, a more appropriate analogy is with the offence of fraud, rather than of theft, and it is notable that McKechnie himself, in *Manning*, drew on the language of fraud: '[i]n effect, every individual who wished to purchase, for cash, a vehicle from these dealers over the period which I have mentioned were liable to be de-frauded, and

> cartel activity inflicts far greater economic harm. Cartel activity robs consumers and other market participants of the tangible blessings of competition. Cartel activity is never efficient or otherwise socially desirable; cartel participants can never gain more than the public loses. Cartel activity, therefore, is not like tortious conduct. . . . Like other property crimes, cartel activity should be prohibited rather than merely taxed. As Judge Richard Posner explained of criminal sanctions generally, they 'are not really prices designed to ration the activity; the purpose so far as possible is to extirpate it'.[41]

Mr Duffy was not the only individual to be prosecuted in relation to the operation of the CDA, but cases involving Mr Durrigan and Mr Doran were heard in the Circuit Criminal Court as the change effected in the CA 2002 under which cases were to be brought before the Central Criminal Court had not taken effect at the time of those prosecutions. Mr Durrigan was sentenced to three months imprisonment, suspended for two years, and Mr Doran also to three months, suspended for five years.

In the case of *Duffy* the judge commented at length on appropriate sentencing, citing both from other judgments, including his own sentencing remarks in *DPP v Manning*, and from academic work.[42] He also referenced EU law and practice, and the judgment of Hallett LJ in *R v Whittle, Alison and Brammar*,[43] the latter being more relevant to the Irish context. McKechnie J quoted with approval from his own judgment in the earlier case of *Manning*:

> [i]n my view, there are good reasons as to why a court should consider the imposition of a custodial sentence in such cases. Firstly, such a sentence can operate as an effective deterrent in particular where if fines were to have the same effect they would have to be pitched at an impossibly high figure.[44] Secondly, fines on companies might not always guarantee an adequate incentive for

---

many surely were by the scheme and by the practices which unashamedly this cartel operated' (quoted in *Duffy* at Para [23]); see also Para [47] of *Duffy* describing the offence as a 'wanton criminal conspiracy against the greater public with the intention of defrauding them for financial gain'.

41 At Para 24. The source of the quote is Posner, RA, 'An Economic Theory of Criminal Law' (1985) 85 *Columbia Law Review* 1193 at 1215.

42 See, for example, Werden, GJ, 'Sanctioning Cartel Activity: Let the Punishment Fit the Crime' (2009) 5:1 *European Competition Journal* at 19, and Whelan, PM, 'A Principled Argument for Personal Criminal Sanctions as Punishment under EC Cartel Law' (2007) 4:1 *Competition Law Review* 7 (note that McKechnie J mis-cites the latter as 'A Principal (*sic*). . .'.

43 [2008] EWCA Crim 2560 (see Chapters 4, above, and 6, below); cited by McKechnie J at Para [33].

44 See Chapter 2, and the discussion of the arguments advanced, *inter alia*, by Elzinga and Breit for a different view.

individuals with those firms to act responsibly. This particular point may not, in some circumstances, have the same force where individuals are concerned. Thirdly, knowledge within undertakings that courts will regularly make use of a custodial sentence may act as an incentive to people to offer greater cooperation in cartel investigations against [others], and quite frequently against their employers. Fourthly, prison, in particular for those with unblemished pasts, for those who are respected within the community, and for those who are unlikely to re-offend can be a very powerful deterrent and finally, the imposition of the sentence for the type or category of persons above described can carry a uniquely strong moral message. Accordingly, they are in my view some very powerful reasons to custodise an individual who has been found guilty under the Competition Acts.[45]

At Para 44 of his judgment McKechnie J held that he would, at least, have to take into account the following factors when considering the appropriate sentence: (1) the gravity of the offences; (2) the circumstances in which they were carried out; (3) the nature of the offences; (4) their duration; (5) the role played in the offences by Mr Duffy; (6) Mr Duffy's circumstances; (7) Duffy Motors (Newbridge) Ltd's circumstances; (8) aggravating and mitigating factors; and (9) the principles of proportionality and totality. In relation to mitigating factors the defence argued that it was relevant that Mr Duffy had a previously spotless reputation, and that he was unlikely to re-offend. The judge took a firmer position than that adopted by the English Court of Appeal, Criminal Division, in *R v Whittle, Allison and Brammar*:

[a]lthough it may be true that the offence is unlikely to be repeated; as stated above, the on-going and continuous nature of the cartel crimes would tend to suggest that the acts complained of were not, in fact, out of character. The accused was not a man of generally good character who committed an unfortunate, foolish or impulsive act. Whatever his public *persona*, which I have no doubt was a positive one, he was, in private, deliberately engaging in wanton criminal conspiracy against the greater public with the intention of defrauding them for financial gain. For five years, being the period of the indictment (in fact the Association had operated for almost nine), he involved himself in the significant ongoing efforts which are required by the operators of criminal cartels. Operating a cartel is not a once off criminal act. It is not done on the spur of the moment. It is continuous and requires high levels of planning and organisation. A person seeking to successfully implement a price fixing agreement decides every day to go into work and therein to commit and conceal a criminal conspiracy. That person, typically will be well educated, businessly astute, either owns the business or has risen to senior management, and almost certainly will have done a value benefit/detection appraisal. He then proceeds, indefinite as to duration, ceasing only when confronted. For that person

[45] *Director of Public Prosecutions v Patrick Duffy and Duffy Motors (Newbridge) Limited*, per Mr Justice McKechnie at Para [42].

> whose *persona* is representative of carteliers, it is very difficult to say that such behaviour is out of character.[46]

Judge McKechnie also commented on the extent to which cooperation during the course of an investigation could be taken into account in sentencing. The CIP is, like the US' programme, based around total immunity for the first eligible applicant and does not introduce a graduated scale of penalty reduction for later applicants. The judge stated that, even if a defendant was not part of the CIP, courts could grant leniency in respect of both fines and imprisonment where defendants had cooperated with the Authority and where the effect was to increase the efficacy of the law.[47] The judge was not persuaded that Mr Duffy's sentence should be the same as was the case in relation to Mr Doran and Mr Durrigan, notwithstanding the similarity in some of the charges. While he accepted that 'a genuine sense of grievance could follow if I were to impose a sentence and demand its service by Mr Duffy',[48] he drew a distinction in that Mr Duffy had 'implemented' the arrangement, and considered this to be more serious, in that it ensured the success of the arrangement, than the counts of 'entering' into the arrangement. McKechnie J actually went as far as to say that, had he been dealing with the first two cases, 'the results would not necessarily have been as they were'.[49] At Para 67 of the judgment McKechnie J stated that 'if the first generation of carteliers have escaped prison, the second and present generation almost certainly will not'.[50]

---

46 Ibid, Para [47].

47 See Para 57: '[f]or co-operation to count, when either considering a prosecution or when passing sentence, it would have to have far greater beneficial value. An obvious example is the way in which the existence of the [CDA] came to light; even if those who contacted or co-operated with the Competition Authority were not granted general or qualified immunity, the giving of such information would have to be reflected by the Court. Co-operation must be judged by its utility whether in the impending investigation or otherwise. How useful has it been to prevent, detect, halt or disrupt the illegal activity? Its value as measured in this way can then be arrived at. Finally, the Authority's [CIP] could usefully be referred to in this context.'

48 At Para [69].

49 At Para [68].

50 'I pointed out in *Manning*, more than two years ago, that this type of activity, of which price fixing is probably one of the more heinous examples, has been unlawful since 1991 (and generally potentially punishable by imprisonment since 1996), which is now almost 20 years. I warned that, because of the activity's harmful effects on the public, those involved would have to take note that any lead-in period for leniency could not be prolonged. I anticipated that the serving of a custodial sentence was near at hand' (at Para [67]).

The Competition Authority has only lost one prosecution, when in June 2009 the jury found that a number of defendants were not guilty of breaching ss 4 and 6 of the Competition Act 2002. The case was economically complex, and it has been suggested that the case was perhaps more suited to a summary trial in a District Court before a judge.[51]

CONCLUSION

McNally has suggested that the outcome of the *Duffy* case was disappointing, in that 'yet another blatant cartelier has received a fine and a suspended sentence', but appears to take comfort in his expectation that 'the case illustrates that future breaches of competition law will be punished with incarceration'.[52] At the time of writing, the position remains that no-one has been sent to jail in Ireland for a breach of the substantive provisions of the Competition Act 2002, and in fact the most recent cases prosecuted have resulted in acquittals.

Whether the experience in Ireland is one to which the UK should turn as a reference point is not entirely clear. Ireland has, unlike the UK, been successful in obtaining convictions entirely through its own efforts. Also, like the UK, cases have been unsuccessful. Ireland is a smaller economy than the UK, and the Authority does not have the resources which are available to the OFT (it does not have the OFT's workload either). It is at least arguable that the Irish experience has been more successful than has the UK's. If it has, we must focus on the differences between the two. Most striking is the fact that Ireland has not sought to separate the criminal prosecution of individuals from the general law of competition applicable to undertakings. The Irish constitution has forced Ireland to align its criminal enforcement with the general scheme, and with Regulation 1/2003. This does have some small negative consequences. Ireland, for example, is not able to adopt fully the ECN model leniency programme as this would unduly fetter judicial and prosecutorial discretion.[53] This however would seem to be a relatively small price to pay if its application of criminal law sanctions in general, and incarceration in particular, were to prove successful in the longer run in deterring cartel conduct in Ireland.

---

51 Massey, P, and Cooke, JD, note 4, at 126.

52 At 141.

53 For example, Para III(5) of the ECN Model Leniency Programme (discussing type 1A leniency) states that: 'The [Competition Authority] will grant an undertaking immunity from any fine which would otherwise have been imposed. . .'.

One aspect though causes particular problems in Ireland. It is notable that all of the cartel cases discussed here have focused on national cartels. At no point has Ireland sought to apply its law to an international cartel, and it is also likely that in none of the cases was there an effect on trade between member states sufficient to bring into play the requirement to apply art 101 TFEU. It has been suggested that it would be difficult for Ireland to apply its law to a cartel in respect of which the procedural requirements of art 3 of Regulation 1/2003 would apply.[54] If this is the case, then Ireland is somewhat adrift in the sea of EU competition law, able to apply domestic law to domestic cartels, but unable to play a positive role within the ECN. This suggests that it may not be straightforward to align a national criminal law targeting cartelisation with the wider EU civil regime, and to retain efficacy in operating both.

[54] See, for example, Massey, P, and Cooke, JD, note 4, at 128.

6. Case studies

INTRODUCTION

In this chapter a small number of cases are discussed in more detail than has been permitted in the previous chapters. I hope by doing so to give a fuller picture of how cartels operate, and how enforcement proceeds.[1] This treatment should also make clear the extent to which international cooperation in enforcement is important, and the extent to which differences in the operation of particular regimes, in particular the US and the UK, shape the enforcement response, and perhaps the enforcement results. The reader should be aware that by the time formal decisions are taken, or trials are held, the amount of information available may be vast. In the case of the *Marine Hose* cartel, for example, there are approximately 100 documents available on the Department of Justice, Antitrust Division website (by way of contrast the material available from DG Competition seems positively impoverished, at a mere nine documents). Particular attention is paid to the story of this cartel here, given that it to date represents the only case prosecuted at the criminal level both in the US and in the UK, and it also resulted in an infringement decision at the EU level. This case thus illustrates like no other the ways in which these different regimes may interact. The cases discussed here are presented in chronological order, although it should be noted that given the length of time it may take for a case to work its way through different legal systems, these may overlap. Further, a particular case may continue to be important in setting an enforcement path long after it has itself been resolved. This will be the situation, for example, where an investigation in one case leads to leniency applications in others, and where *those* cases in turn might generate further leniency applications. This pattern will be discussed in relation to the lysine cartel involving Archer Daniels Midland, which may perhaps be taken as the case which (re)invigorated criminal enforcement. The vitamins cartel is considered on the basis that, more than any other,

[1] It is beyond doubt that the best work to give detailed case studies of cartels is Connor, JM, *Global Price Fixing* (2009, 2nd edn), Springer. Connor also discusses, as I do below, the lysine and vitamins cartels.

it generated enforcement activity in multiple jurisdictions, with at least the following mounting formal investigations: Australia, Brazil, Canada, the EU, Japan, Mexico, Switzerland, and the US. This chapter concludes with a discussion of enforcement in relation to the *Marine Hose* cartel.

LYSINE

Just as the *General Electric* case reinvigorated criminal enforcement in the early 1960s, the lysine prosecutions had a similar effect in the mid-1990s, and generated a wave of international enforcement efforts against cartels that continues to produce results (lysine is an amino acid derived feed additive used in livestock feeds).[2] For Connor there are four reasons why the case is of importance: it 'represented the US government's first completely successful conviction of a global cartel in more than four decades';[3] it 'was the first public manifestation of a sea change in enforcement priorities';[4] it 'demonstrated the government's intention to employ tough "blue-collar" criminal investigative techniques to what had formerly been treated as gentle "white-collar" misdemeanours';[5] and it showed that although penalties had 'escalated enormously' in recent years 'they may still be inadequate to suppress recidivism'.[6]

In the US, enforcement efforts in the lysine cartel led to the first imposition of a fine on a corporation of more than the standard Sherman Act maximum of $10m. Using the alternative penalty provisions of 18 USC §3571, which allows for the recovery of up to twice the cartel profit, or

---

[2] See also Connor, JM, note 1, at Chapters 7–9; and 'Global Cartels Redux: The Lysine Antitrust Litigation (1996)', in Kwoka, JE Jr, and White, LJ, *The Antitrust Revolution: Economics, Competition and Policy* (2009, 5th edn) Oxford University Press (which is drawn from the former work), and '"Our Customers Are Our Enemies": The Lysine Cartel of 1992–1995' (2001) 18 *Review of Industrial Organization* 5; White, LJ, 'Lysine and Price Fixing: How Long? How Severe?' (2001) 18 *Review of Industrial Organization* 23; and Taylor, CR, 'Indirect Damages from Price Fixing: The Alabama Lysine Case' (2001) 18 *Review of Industrial Organization* 33. Extensive extracts of transcripts of tape recordings of meetings are available in Griffin, JM, 'An Inside View of a Cartel at Work: Common Characteristics of International Cartels', in Konkurrensverket (Swedish Competition Authority), *Fighting Cartels – Why and How?* (2001) Konkurrensverket at 29.

[3] Connor, JM, 'Global Cartels Redux: The Lysine Antitrust Litigation (1996)', in Kwoka, JE Jr, and White, LJ, *The Antitrust Revolution*, note 2, at 301.

[4] Ibid, at 302.

[5] Ibid, at 302.

[6] Ibid, at 303.

twice the loss to consumers (see Chapter 3, above), the DOJ secured a fine of $70m from Archer Daniels Midland ('ADM') in relation to its participation in the lysine cartel and simultaneously a further $30m in relation to its participation in the citric acid cartel. In September 1998 the jury returned guilty verdicts on all three executives who had been subject to a ten-week trial in Chicago. Prison sentences ranged from 24 to 30 months, and two were fined $350 000 each.[7] In the EU the Commission took action culminating in an infringement decision, in which further significant financial penalties were imposed.[8] The cartel participants acted at a time when competition between them had previously been robust, divided the market on a worldwide basis, and fixed prices. The DOJ stated that as a result prices rose by approximately 70 per cent in the first three months of the operation of the conspiracy.

The following is a complete list of all the lysine cases in the US:[9]

- *United States v Ajinomoto Co, Inc* (Japanese firm, defendant agreed to $10m fine in plea agreement);
- *United States v Kyowa Hakko Kogyo Co Ltd* (Japanese firm, $10m fine);
- *United States v Sewon America, Inc* (US subsidiary of Korean company, $328 000 fine);
- *United States v Kanji Mimoto* (Japanese citizen, $75 000 fine);
- *United States v Masaru Yamamoto* (Japanese citizen, $50 000 fine);
- *United States v Jhom Su Kim* (Korean citizen, $75 000 fine);
- *United States v Archer Daniels Midland* (US firm, $100m fine – $70m for lysine and $30m for citric acid);
- *United States v Cheil Jedang Ltd* (Korean company, $1.25m fine);
- *United States v Michael D Andreas; Mark E Whitacre; Terrance S Wilson; and Kazutoshi Yamada* ('Andreas, Whitacre and Wilson, all US citizens, convicted at trial; Andreas and Wilson each sentenced to serve 24 months incarceration and to pay fines of $350 000; Whitacre sentenced to serve 30 months incarceration . . . Yamada, a Japanese citizen, did not appear at trial and remains a fugitive').

---

[7] Two books have been written about this case: Eichenwald, K, *The Informant: A True Story* (2000) Broadway, and Lieber, JB, *Rats in the Grain: The Dirty Tricks and Trials of Archer Daniels Midland, the Supermarket to the World* (2000) Basic Books. See (literally) also Soderbergh, S, *The Informant!* (2009).

[8] Commission Decision 2001/418/EC *Amino Acids* (2001) OJ L152/4.

[9] See DOJ, Antitrust Selected Criminal Cases April 1, 1996 through September 30, 1999. All cases were brought in the Northern District for Illinois in 1996.

The investigation into the lysine cartel in the US became a matter of public knowledge on June 27, 1995, when the FBI, on the basis of subpoenas issued by a Chicago federal grand jury, raided the Decatur, Illinois, headquarters of ADM. This action was widely reported, and led very quickly to the launch of a number of private damages actions, the outcomes and dynamics of which have been analysed by, *inter alia*, White,[10] and Taylor.[11]

There was, and remains, a limited number of companies forming a global oligopoly in the market for the supply of lysine. It has been noted that '[b]eing a chemical compound, lysine is as close as we can get to a homogenous product'.[12] Lysine suitable for livestock feedstuffs had been produced since the early 1970s, and the growth in demand was 'remarkable'.[13] In 1979 some 30000 tonnes were sold worldwide, and by 2000 demand stood at some 250000 tonnes. While prices almost doubled between 1981 and 1988, they began to fall after that point as production increased, and as entrants penetrated the market. Until ADM and Cheil Jedang Corporation ('Cheil') began to invest in the development of lysine production capacity, the only participants were Ajinomoto Company Inc (Ajinomoto), Kyowa Hakko Kogyo Company Limited ('Kyowa'), and Daesang Corporation ('Daesang'), all of whom also operated European subsidiaries. In 1989 ADM determined to build a major plant for the production of lysine in Decatur, at a scale sufficient to double the world's production capacity. The European Commission stated in its infringement decision that it was unable to prove the existence of an Asian/European cartel before July 1990, although the Commission had 'indications' that the three producers had co-operated in price and volume fixing in the 1970s and 1980s.[14] In July 1990 a meeting took place between Ajinomoto and Sewon, part of the Daesang group of companies. A letter from Sewon to Ajinomoto of December 6, 1990, obtained by the EU Commission, recorded the meeting, and it was stated that Sewon was 'able to raise sharply the price of lysine "with the help of [Ajinomoto]"'.[15] A further

---

10 White, LJ, note 2.

11 Taylor, CR, note 2.

12 de Roos, N, 'Examining Models of Collusion: The Market for Lysine' (2006) 24 *International Journal of Industrial Organization* 1083.

13 Commission Decision 2001/418/EC *Amino Acids* (2001) OJ L152/4.

14 Ibid, at Para 50. Connor states that the oligopoly 'colluded successfully at least three times prior to 1992. It fixed prices in Japan in the 1970s and 1980s and in Europe in the 1980s. From 1986 to 1990, Ajinomoto and Kyowa Hakko fixed prices and divided the US lysine market' (Connor, JM, note 3, at 307).

15 Commission Decision 2001/418/EC *Amino Acids* (2001) OJ L152/4, at Para 52.

meeting was held between the companies on September 20, 1990 at which Ajinomoto informed Sewon that its US subsidiary had announced a new price, and that this would become the world standard price. All three parties had discussed the price rises on the telephone. A chain of further discussions and meetings were held.[16]

When ADM entered the market it did so with significant scale, and the effect was to double the global capacity for the production of lysine. Even before it was fully active in the market it had 'sent signals to the incumbent producers that, though it intended to be a big player in the lysine market, it preferred to achieve its part of the market by coordination, rather than by a price war'.[17] Ajinomoto and Sewon agreed between themselves in March 1992 that co-operation with ADM was the best strategy, and a meeting in Mexico between ADM, Ajinomoto and Kyowa representatives was held on June 23, 1992, with the results being passed on to Sewon after the meeting.[18] There followed a series of meetings and discussions between the participants, with the global arrangement persisting through to June 27,

---

16 Ibid, at Paras 52–68.

17 Ibid, at Para 69.

18 A discussion between cartel participants in April 1995 was recorded by Mark Whitacre, the FBI informant, and reported in Eichenwald, K, note 7, at 156:

> Crouy leaned in. 'Let's not forget that if prices went up in Europe, it's because we talked in Mexico first.'
> 'That's right,' Wilson agreed.
> 'Then because we talked in Europe a lot after.'
> 'I mean, it didn't just go up like that.'
> 'You made it happen,' Wilson repeated.
>
> Whitacre tried not to breathe. Crouy and Wilson had just confessed: Lysine prices went up because competitors met in Mexico. *They made it happen* (emphasis in original).

See Commission Decision 2001/418/EC *Amino Acids* (2001) OJ L152/4 at Para 73:

> ADM's primary goal was to have the same production share as that of the largest competitor, which would result in one third of total world demand for ADM, one third for the Ajinomoto group, and one third for Kyowa and the Korean producers. Kyowa and Ajinomoto expressed their disagreement with this proposal at least as far as timing was concerned. ADM then suggested that it would implement its quota proposal over the second year, by allocating to it all extra market growth until it has reached Ajinomoto's market share. For 1992, the proposed quota scheme was: Ajinomoto 66,000t; ADM 48,000t; Kyowa 34,000t; Sewon 18,000t and Cheil 6,000t. Ajinomoto was prepared to accept 48,000t for ADM in 1992 with the prospect of growth over time. ADM indicated that it would, in any event, implement the proposal on quantity as from 1 October 1992.

1995,[19] when the FBI agents searched the offices of ADM, Ajinomoto's American subsidiary, and Sewon America.

The story of the uncovering of the lysine cartel, and the DOJ/FBI investigation, is a remarkable one that no novelist would have the temerity to fabricate.[20]

The EU and US enforcement authorities did not cooperate in the investigation into this cartel, although there can be no doubt that the US enforcement action had a significant impact in easing the path for EU and Canadian enforcement efforts. The European Commission published its first leniency notice on July 18, 1996;[21] Ajinomoto applied for leniency 'immediately' after the publication of the Notice, and 'offered . . . its full cooperation in establishing the existence of a cartel in the lysine market and its effect in the EEA'.[22] The EU Commission thereafter had exclusive jurisdiction over the case until its conclusion.[23] Not only the structure of the EU system, but also the fact that at the time of the infringement the UK had not introduced an *ex ante* prohibitive competition law, precluded the UK from acting. While the EU competition law regime accepts the principle of *non bis in idem*, it has been made clear that in the calculation of

---

A disagreement as to the allocation of market shares destabilised the cartel briefly in 1993 when

> a brief price war broke out among the conspirators, mainly because of ADM's insistence that the participants had to agree to global market shares. After a top-level meeting in October 1993 resolved the issue, the cartel displayed a high level of harmony and consensus. Cheating was restrained in part by largely accurate monthly reporting of each company's lysine sales volume to all the members of the cartel (Connor, JM, note 3, at 309).

[19] See Commission Decision 2001/418/EC *Amino Acids* (2001) OJ L152/4, Paras 72–165.

[20] The fate of Mark Whitacre is wryly summed up with unintentional humour at Para 179 of Commission Decision 2001/418/EC *Amino Acids* (2001) OJ L152/4:

> [o]n 4 November 1992 the former President of ADM's Bioproducts Division, who served this undertaking during the relevant period, began working with the FBI. He agreed to follow all directions given by FBI agents. Currently, the former President of ADM's Bioproducts Division is serving a nine-year prison term for the theft of nearly $10m from ADM.

See also Soderbergh, S, *The Informant!* (2009).

[21] *Notice on the Non-Imposition or Reductions of Fines in Cartel Cases* (1996) OJ C207/4.

[22] Commission Decision 2001/418/EC *Amino Acids* (2001) OJ L152/4 at Para 167.

[23] The EU procedure is set out at Paras 167–176 of Commission Decision 2001/418/EC *Amino Acids* (2001) OJ L152/4.

penalties the Commission should, where appropriate, take into account the global turnover of the parties concerned, and that the penalty itself reflects the enforcement of the law in respect of conduct having an effect within the territory of the EU, and that the principle of *non bis in idem* is not infringed by the proper operation of this principle.[24] The penalties imposed in the EU totalled €109 900 000, with ADM being fined €47 300 000.

The Canadian authorities also responded to the cartel, and on May 27, 1998 it was announced that ADM had pleaded guilty to having participated in an unlawful price-fixing and market-sharing cartel, and would pay a penalty of C$16m. Ajinomoto was fined C$3.5m, and Sewon was fined C$70 000. Kyowa benefited from the operation of the leniency regime in Canada and was granted immunity. ADM also paid penalties to the Mexican competition authorities.

While the total penalties imposed in the US on the lysine cartel were significant, Connor and Lande have suggested that they fell well below the amount that would have been required *ex ante* to constitute the optimal penalty: the optimal penalty was calculated to be $514–$719m; the total sanctions imposed (including a financial assessment of the cost of imprisonment on those incarcerated) was $263 million, leaving a substantial

---

[24] See, for example, *Daiichi Pharmaceutical Co Ltd v Commission* case T-26/02 [2006] 5 CMLR 3at Para 78, and *Showa Denko KK v Commission* case C-298/04 P [2006] 5 CMLR 14 at Para 16. ADM had argued before the Commission that the penalty imposed in the EU should take into account the fact that a deterrent element was not necessary given that the cumulative effect of the penalties imposed in other jurisdictions was that 'it has been sufficiently deterred from further infringement in the USA, Europe or indeed anywhere else in the world' (Commission Decision 2001/418/EC *Amino Acids* (2001) OJ L152/4 at Para 306). The Commission's response to these arguments is set out at Para 311 of its decision:

> [t]he Commission does not consider that, in the present case, fines imposed elsewhere, especially in the USA, on ADM, Ajinomoto or any other undertaking to which the present Decision is addressed, have any bearing on the fines to be imposed for infringing European competition rules. Nor does the possibility that undertakings may have been obliged to pay damages in civil actions have any relevance. Payments of damages in civil law actions which have the objective of recouping the damages caused by cartels to individual companies or consumers cannot be compared with public law sanctions for illegal behaviour. The Commission also notes that according to information provided by the authorities of the USA and Canada, the criminal fines imposed by those authorities on the undertakings concerned by this Decision only took account of the anti-competitive effects that the collusion under scrutiny in this Decision produced in the area of their jurisdictions. Finally, criminal fines imposed on individuals cannot in any event be taken into account because the present proceedings do not address natural persons.

shortfall.[25] There has been some criticism of Connor's calculation of the damages inflicted by the cartel – White has argued that his assumption of a 'but for' price failed to take into account the fact that the industry was highly concentrated in terms of production, and highly fragmented in terms of the customer base, such that the analyst 'must enter the world of oligopoly speculation'.[26] White has argued that the price absent the cartel would have been substantially above the amount estimated by Connor.

VITAMINS[27]

The vitamins cartel has been described as 'the most pervasive and harmful criminal antitrust conspiracy ever uncovered by the [DOJ]',[28] and as exemplifying 'the durability, breadth, and harm of international cartels'.[29] In the US it resulted in what was then, and remains at the time of writing, the largest fine, $500m, ever imposed by the DOJ under antitrust law,[30] as well as a number of criminal prosecutions, leading to European executives for the first time serving prison terms in the US following a s 1 prosecution.[31] Action against the cartel was taken up in the EU by the Commission, resulting in an infringement decision[32] requiring that penalties be paid by eight parties, with F Hoffmann-La Roche AG ('HLR')

---

25 Connor, JM, and Lande, RH, 'Optimal Cartel Deterrence: An Empirical Comparison of Sanctions to Overcharges' (2011) AAI Working Paper No. 11-08 at 47–48.

26 White, LJ, note 2, at 28.

27 For other treatments of this cartel see in particular Connor, JM, note 1, chapters 10–12, and Clarke, JL, and Evenett, SJ, 'The Deterrent Effects of National Anticartel Laws: Evidence from the International Vitamins Cartel' (2003) 48 *The Antitrust Bulletin* 689, at 696–701; and Shaffer, GC, and Nesbitt, NH, 'Criminalizing Cartels: A Global Trend?' (2011) 12 *Sedona Conference Journal*; *Minnesota Legal Studies Research Paper No 11-26* (2011) University of Minnesota, School of Law at 13ff.

28 DOJ, 'Statement of Assistant Attorney General Joel I Klein', May 20, 1999. See also Connor, JM, note 1, at Chapters 10–12.

29 Schmidt, JT, 'Keeping US Courts Open to Foreign Antitrust Plaintiffs: A Hybrid Approach to the Effective Deterrence of International Cartels' (2006) 31 *Yale Journal of International Law*, 211 at 212.

30 Until *Vitamins* the record stood at $135m, paid by SGL following its participation in the graphite electrodes conspiracy.

31 Although Mr Yamada was sentenced to a period of imprisonment for his part in the lysine cartel (see above), he declined to visit the United States, and 'remains a fugitive'.

32 Commission Decision 2003/2/EC, *Vitamins* (2003) OJ L6/1.

being fined a further €462m to add to the $500m paid in the US. There was no enforcement action in the UK, and no UK participants were involved in the cartel. There has been some civil litigation by customers of the cartel launched in the UK. The cartel is significant in that its complexity provides proof positive that cartelists are able to agree and implement complicated arrangements.[33] The record of the enforcement action shows how the work of different jurisdictions' authorities becomes mutually supportive and mutually reinforcing, and the different level of punishment meted out on the cartelists in the US and in the EU, with the limitations of the latter, is clearly demonstrated.

In the US the first public notice of the action came in late 1997, when it was reported that the DOJ had convened a Federal Grand Jury to investigate possible criminal violations of s 1 in relation to the market for vitamins. This was followed by the issuing on May 8, 1998 by the District Court of Northern Texas of a subpoena on HLR's US subsidiary. On May 20, 1998 an information was filed in the same court charging HLR and BASF with criminal violations of the Sherman Act, s 1. At the same time a number of individuals were also charged.

Joel Klein, then Assistant Attorney General, had this to say about the cartel when the US cases were first filed:

> [t]he cartel was truly extraordinary. It lasted almost a decade and involved a highly sophisticated and elaborate conspiracy to control everything about the sale of these products. These companies fixed the price; they allocated sales volumes; they allocated customers; and in the United States they even rigged bids to make absolutely sure that their cartel would work. The conspirators actually held 'annual meetings' to fix prices and to carve up world markets, as well as frequent follow-up meetings to ensure compliance with their illegal scheme. The enormous effort that went into maintaining this conspiracy reflects the magnitude of the illegal revenues it generated as well as the harm it inflicted on the American economy.[34]

The fact that the DOJ sought prison sentences in respect of foreign nationals may flow from the fact that fines alone were shown, through the participants in this case, to be an insufficient deterrent. Hoffmann-La Roche had previously been fined $14m in March 1997 for its participation

---

[33] See, for example, Clarke, JL, and Evenett, SJ, note 27, at 690: '. . . these cartels [including vitamins] tended not to collapse under the weight of their own incentive problems . . . [this] suggests that market forces alone may be unable to quickly undermine attempts to fix prices, rig bids, allocate quotas and market shares'.

[34] DOJ, 'Statement of Assistant Attorney General Joel I Klein', May 20, 1999.

in the citric acid cartel, and had also previously been sanctioned by the EU Commission. As noted in Chapter 3, although recidivism has been found to be present in EU cases, there has been no recidivism in detected cartels in the US since the first convictions in the vitamins cases.[35]

The following, taken from the Information[36] in the case of HLR,[37] is typical of the charges brought in relation to the vitamins prosecutions in the US courts:

> [t]he charged combination and conspiracy:
> (a) consisted of a continuing agreement, understanding and concert of action among the defendant and co-conspirators regarding certain vitamins manufactured by the corporate conspirators and sold by them in the United States and elsewhere, the substantial terms of which were to:
> (i) fix, increase, and maintain prices and to coordinate price increases for the sale of such vitamins in the United States and elsewhere;
> (ii) allocate among the corporate conspirators the volume of sales and market shares of such vitamins in the United States and elsewhere; and
> (iii) allocate among corporate conspirators all or part of certain contracts to supply vitamin premixes to various customers located throughout the United States and to refrain from submitting bids, or to submit collusive, non-competitive and rigged bids, therefore;
> (b) involved a changing group of conspirators and affected a changing group of vitamins at various points in time during the period covered by this Information, its scope adjusting over time to the manufacturers producing certain vitamins and participating in the combination and conspiracy . . .

The charges in the US related to five vitamins, to beta-carotene, and to certain vitamin pre-mixes, with the alleged unlawful activity occurring, depending on the relevant product, from January 1990 to at least December 1998. It was alleged that in order to achieve these aims the participants in the cartel met regularly and held conversations regarding their arrangements, agreed prices during those meetings and conversations, agreed

35 Werden, GJ, Hammond, SD, and Barnett, BA, 'Recidivism Eliminated: Cartel Enforcement in the United States since 1999' (2011) Georgetown Global Antitrust Enforcement Symposium, September 22, 2011 at 6.

36 It was noted in Chapter 3 that, notwithstanding that the legal effect of indictments and informations is precisely the same, executives prefer to be charged by way of an information, and the presentation of the charge in this way may form part of a plea agreement.

37 *US v F. Hoffmann-La Roche Ltd*, criminal case no. 3:99-CR-184-R ND Texas, filed May 20, 1999.

approximate volumes to be supplied by each participant, exchanged 'sales and customer information for the purpose of monitoring and enforcing adherence' to the agreements, issued price announcements in accordance with the agreements, and sold their vitamins at the agreed prices. The cartel affected at least eight markets,[38] and encompassed 13 participants, with not all participants being involved in all aspects of the cartel at all times. HLR and BASF entered into a plea agreement with the DOJ, and two of the members of HLR's executive board also pleaded guilty, and agreed to serve prison terms of four and five months, in addition to paying personal fines.[39] On September 9, 1999 a further three firms, Takeda Chemical Industries Ltd ('Takeda'), Eisai Co Ltd ('Eisai'), and Daiichi Pharmaceutical Co Ltd ('Daiichi') pleaded guilty and paid fines of respectively \$72m, \$40m and \$25m. Rhône-Poulenc[40] benefited from conditional leniency under the DOJ's leniency programme, having cooperated with the US authorities.

The Canadian authorities also acted against the cartel, and on September 22, 1999 five of the six parties prosecuted in the US pleaded guilty in the Federal Court of Canada (Trial Division) to indictments brought forward under the Competition Act 1985, s 45. HLR was fined C\$48m.

Following the initial steps in the US action, Rhône-Poulenc applied for leniency to the EU Commission on May 12, 1999.[41] It is a curious feature of the case that HLR and BASF AG had already contacted the Commission ahead of Rhône-Poulenc informing the Commission of 'their intention to cooperate with any investigations, but without at the time providing any statement or documentary evidence'.[42] Both HLR and

---

[38] For a description of the relevant products and markets see Commission Decision 2003/2/EC, *Vitamins* (2003) OJ L6/1 at paras 22–68.

[39] The DOJ has maintained since these prosecutions a policy of insisting wherever possible that at least one foreign executive implicated in the cartel serves time in a US prison. The interrelationships between plea agreements entered into with firms and with individuals are such that there is an incentive to firms pleading guilty to incentivise their employees or officers to accept such a sentence. There is strong anecdotal evidence in Korea that executives of Korean firms who serve prison sentences in the US may be compensated for doing so, and that their 'personal' fines may be repaid by the firms. If such arrangements do exist, the evidence does not suggest that they undermine the deterrent effect of such personal sentences.

[40] Rhône-Poulenc became Aventis SA during the course of the cartel and subsequent proceedings.

[41] At the time the relevant programme was set out in the *Commission Notice on the Non-imposition or Reduction of Fines in Cartel Cases* (1996) OJ C207/4.

[42] Commission Decision 2003/2/EC, *Vitamins* (2003) OJ L6/1, Para 127.

BASF confirmed to the Commission that they had committed infringements of art 101 TFEU in relation to products which were the subject of the US enforcement action, but did not admit to infringements in relation to other products.

In a similar trajectory to that existing in the lysine cartel, the vitamins cartel came into existence following a period of intense competition in some of the affected markets. During the late 1980s the prices of vitamins A and E fell 'significantly'[43] in response to aggressive pricing by Eisai and Rhône-Poulenc. This led to a series of meetings being organised, with HLR and BASF holding a first meeting in June in Basel, Switzerland, and a follow-up meeting involving also Rhône-Poulenc was held in Zurich later that summer. A two-day meeting was then held in September 1989, again in Zurich. Here the parties struggled to reach agreement on market shares: the EU Commission stated that HLR was 'satisfied' with its 50 per cent market share, that BASF sought an increase from its 30 per cent share, and that Rhône-Poulenc would have liked to expand its 15 per cent market share, but realised that this was not possible. Significantly, the parties were able to reach agreement, a process described in the EU infringement decision:

> [o]n the first day senior executives responsible for vitamin marketing in each company, together with some product managers, identified the size of the market for vitamins A and E and then agreed the allocation between the four producers of the world and regional markets on the basis of their respective achieved sales in 1988.
>
> In summary, the underlying objective was to stabilise the world market shares of each producer. Market shares were frozen at 1988 levels; as the market expanded, each company could increase its sales only in accordance with its agreed quota and in line with market growth and not at the expense of a competitor.
>
> On the second day, the chairmen of the fine chemicals division or the equivalent and the heads of vitamins marketing of each company joined the meeting to approve the agreed quotas and to establish 'confidence' between the participants that the arrangements would be respected. The maxim 'price before volume' was accepted as the underlying principle of the cartel. Specific pricing levels were also discussed.[44]

As the cartel developed, regular meetings were held and a complex, but effective, managerial mechanism was created. At regular meetings participants exchanged sales data, set targets, determined prices, and determined

---

43 Ibid, Para 160.
44 Ibid, Paras 163–65.

who was to act as price leader (usually, but not always, HLR). The majority of meetings were held in Switzerland, outwith the jurisdiction of the US or the EU. In 1991, following a 'summit' meeting held in Japan, Eisai agreed to join the cartel.[45] Over time the cartel expanded both in terms of membership and in terms of the products covered by its operation. In addition to setting generalised market-share targets for different regional markets, the cartel participants also agreed their responses to particularly significant customers, including the Coca Cola Corporation, one of the largest customers for vitamin C (ascorbic acid), and Pfizer.

Clarke and Evenett have demonstrated the very significant impact of the cartel on global prices, notwithstanding the impact of Chinese competitors. They find that the value of imports of vitamins affected by the cartel rose by over 50 per cent in Africa, Europe and Latin America (where countries did not have an effective anti-cartel law in place), and even in Western European economies in the EU the value of imports rose by over 17 per cent; Brazil might well have paid an overcharge in excess of $183m.[46] The overcharge across 90 economies was estimated to be $2709.87m.[47] On the other hand the 'unprecedented fines'[48] paid by the participants globally amounted to $3bn (with further damages, the amounts of which are unknown, paid to defendants). It is therefore possible that, significant as the overcharges were, the vitamins cartel was not profitable.

The actions of the companies engaged in the cartel throughout demonstrate clearly that all were aware of the illegality of their acts; following the parties' becoming aware of the DOJ investigation they sought to minimise their contacts, and took steps to create the public impression that the cartel had been abandoned.[49]

In the EU, where the only punishment for cartelists is the imposition of

---

45 Ibid, Para 218: 'Eisai appears to have rationalised the discussions with competitors in terms of antitrust law by meeting each of the three separately for 20 minutes each; it disingenuously calls these meetings "courtesy calls".'

46 Clarke, JL, and Evenett, SJ, note 27, at 717–25 (see Tables 6 and 7).

47 Ibid, at 725.

48 Shaffer, GC, and Nesbitt, NH, note 27, at 14.

49 See, however, Commission Decision 2003/2/EC, *Vitamins* (2003) OJ L6/1, Para 231:

> [h]owever, whatever formal or official instructions may have been given, the reality was otherwise: senior executives from all three companies decided to continue the cooperation in a modified form and on a 'more discreet basis', as BASF put it.

penalties in accordance with Regulation 1/2003,[50] the 'very serious' nature of the infringements was spelt out in the infringement decision (resulting in a higher penalty than would apply were the infringement merely a 'serious' one), HLR and BASF had their penalties uplifted to take into account their 'capacity to cause significant damage to competition',[51] and the Commission raised the penalties on both parties by 100 per cent to take into account the need for deterrence. Further increases to the basic amounts of the penalties were determined by the duration of the existence of the cartel arrangements in relation to each individual product market.[52] A further uplift, introduced under the 'aggravating circumstances' rubric of the Commission Notice on fines, followed based on the fact that HLR and BASF were the 'joint leaders and instigators of the collusive arrangements'.[53] Rhône-Poulenc was found to have met the requirements set out in the Commission's leniency programme to the extent that it was able to benefit from 100 per cent leniency (although this did not extend to a finding of an infringement in respect of the market for vitamin D3).

The public enforcement also exposed the participating cartel members to third-party liability, with a number of settlements of actions, and an amount of litigation arising in several jurisdictions. The most significant consequence of the vitamins cartel on enforcement however is that it 'spurred greater attention to anti-cartel enforcement around the globe, and spurred the DOJ to increase international anti-cartel cooperative efforts'.[54]

---

50 Formerly the rules relating to penalties were set out in Regulation 17/62. The basic provision has not changed. Article 23(2) of Regulation 1/2003 is in the following terms:

> The Commission may by decision impose fines on undertakings and associations of undertakings where, either intentionally or negligently:
> (a) they infringe art [101] or art [102] of the Treaty;
>
> . . .
>
> For each undertaking and association of undertakings participating in the infringement, the fine shall not exceed 10 per cent of its total turnover in the preceding business year.

The Commission has published guidance relating to the calculation of penalties: see *Guidelines on the Method of Setting Fines Pursuant to Art 23(2)(a) of Regulation 1/2003* (2006) OJ C217/02; see also Commission Press Release IP/06/857, June 28, 2006.

51 See Commission Decision 2003/2/EC, *Vitamins* (2003) OJ L6/1, Para 678.

52 Ibid, Paras 700–10.

53 Ibid, Para 712.

54 Shaffer, GC, and Nesbitt, NH, note 27, at 14.

MARINE HOSE[55]

The marine hose cartel, prosecuted successfully in the US and in the UK, and the subject of an EU Commission infringement decision,[56] is a textbook example of the way in which a cartel and its participants may be subject to different enforcement actions in different jurisdictions, and of ways in which those jurisdictions may interact. It has been noted that the most remarkable feature of the cartel 'was that rigorous collusion between the participants had almost totally replaced competition'.[57]

It is an exquisite irony that the cartel appears to have been formed on April Fools' Day, 1986, and it was not until 21 years later that a member lodged leniency applications with a number of competition authorities. As noted above, particular attention is being paid to this cartel here, as it is the only one at the time of writing to be prosecuted successfully in the UK. Various elements of the UK case, and in particular the arguments relating to sentencing, have been discussed in Chapter 4, above. Given the complexity of the case, and the number of interlocking procedures, a basic timetable (with many steps omitted) is set out at Table 6.1.

The description of the relevant product given here is taken from the EU infringement decision:

> . . . Marine hoses are used to load sweet or processed crude oil and other petroleum products from offshore facilities (for example buoys, floating production storage and offloading systems) onto vessels and to offload them back to offshore or onshore facilities (for example buoys or jetties). Hence marine hoses are used mainly in the context of oil transportation from remote places of exploitation not linked to major oil consuming countries by pipelines. Marine

---

55 The correct citation for this case in the UK is *R v Whittle, Allison and Brammar* [2008] EWCA Crim 2560 [2009] UKCLR 247, but given that the cartel was subject to action in the US and in the EU, as well as in the UK, under a number of different references, it will be referred to here by its subject matter, unless the context requires otherwise.

56 Case COMP/39406 – *Marine Hoses*, Commission Decision of January 28, 2009, relating to a proceeding under Article [101] of the Treaty and Article 53 of the EEA Agreement. There are a considerable number of redactions from the Commission Decision in its published form. Note that the case was also investigated by the Japanese Fair Trade Commission, and that this was the first case in which the JFTC cooperated with the US and EU authorities in the conducting of raids (see Matsushita, M, 'Reforming the Enforcement of the Japanese Antimonopoly Law' (2009) 41 *Loyola University Chicago Law Journal* 521 at 524).

57 Lucraft, M, Payne, T, and Rawlings, D, 'Case Comment: The Dunlop Three: The Cartel Offence Makes Its Debut' (2009) *Archbold News* 7.

Table 6.1 Marine Hose *timeline*

April 1, 1986	At least five companies enter into a memorandum of understanding
December 20, 2006	Yokohama applies for leniency to DG Competition, the DOJ, and the JFTC
May 2, 2007	DG Competition launches surprise inspections; OFT launches investigations; arrest and search warrants executed in the United States
March 2007	Various plea agreements entered into in the United States; further guilty pleas entered, and indictments made over following months
February 22, 2008	JFTC issues 'cease and desist' orders
March 24, 2008	Consolidated class action filed in the Southern District of Florida
April 29, 2008	EU Commission issues Statement of Objections
November 14, 2008	UK Court of Appeal confirms convictions of Whittle, Allison and Brammar
January 28, 2009	EU Commission makes infringement decision, imposing fines in total of €131 510 000
June 1, 2009	Australian Competition and Consumer Commission institutes proceedings in Melbourne Federal Court
April 13, 2010	Australian Court orders penalties of AUS$8 242 500, along with costs, and injunctions

hoses are used offshore, that is near or in the water, while onshore or industrial hoses are used on land.

Marine hoses are usually composed of an inner elastomere layer (lining), a steel helix and textile or wire layers to reinforce the hose, an outer cover composed of elastomere, and an end fitting allowing connection to another hose. Marine hoses can be composed of one or two carcasses (single or double carcass hoses). Marine hoses usually have an internal diameter of 4 to 24 inch and a length of up to 40 feet. Marine hoses include floating hoses, which rest on the surface of the water, and submarine hoses, which provide a connection between seabed pipelines and floating facilities. Marine hoses almost invariably comply with the 1991 industry standard 'OCIMF' (Oil Companies International Marine Hoses Forum).

Each marine hoses installation is composed according to the clients' specific needs of a number of standard hoses, specific hoses at the connections at both ends, and ancillary equipment (for example, valves, end gear, floating equipment).[58]

[58] Commission Decision, Paras 4–6.

The geographic market was a global one; although technical requirements differed from site to site these were not determined at a wider geographic level, and there were no significant regulatory differences which would have given rise to segregated national markets. At least 11 undertakings were involved, at various stages, in the cartel: Bridgestone Corporation; Bridgestone Industrial Limited; The Yokohama Rubber Company Limited; Dunlop Oil & Marine Limited; ContiTech AG; Continental AG; Trelleborg Industrie SAS; Trelleborg AB; Parker ITR Srl; Parker Hannifin Corporation; and Manuli Rubber Industries SpA. In the US the investigation (discussed below) focussed on the activities of six manufacturers and Peter Whittle. It was in relation to the activities of Dunlop that the three UK defendants were prosecuted. At the time of the enforcement action Dunlop was a UK registered company, and part of the Continental Group. On December 12, 1997, it acquired the marine hose assets of a business which is unnamed in the Decision.[59]

It would appear that the cartel was in operation since '*at least*' 1986.[60] On April 1, 1986, at least five parties entered into a memorandum of understanding, reproduced as follows in the Commission Decision:

> *MEMORANDUM OF UNDERSTANDING 1/4/86*
> 1 Quotations for new business to be on the basis of:
> Original Equipment: Dunlop [. . .] list prices dated 1st January, 1986 less 25% less 18%
> Replacement Sales: Dunlop [. . .] list prices dated 1st January 1986 less 25%
> 2 'Favoured' bidder to bid prices 4% below second lowest bidder. Band of prices between second lowest and highest bidder to be 4%, varied by items, to avoid identical individual prices.
> 3 Target market shares for the period 1/2/86 to 1/4/87 to be as follows: [. . .][61]

Although not named in the Decision, it is likely that this document was found, by the OFT, in the house of Mr Peter Whittle. The Decision states that: 'this document is evidence of a cartel . . . (i) Mr [cartel coordinator], in whose house this document was found, was exclusively involved in consultancy activities regarding one product, marine hoses'.[62]

---

[59] The full, and complicated, history of the company is set out at Paras 17–24 of the Decision.

[60] Commission Decision, Para 71. In the US investigation the focus was on activity occurring since 'at least 1999 through at least 2006' (*US v Peter Whittle and others*, Case no 07-2553 – PRP, Southern District of Florida, Criminal Complaint (April 24, 2007) at Para 6).

[61] Commission Decision, Para 75. Redactions as in original.

[62] Commission Decision, Para 76.

Peter Whittle played a key role in the maintenance and management of the cartel. He was the sole proprietor of PW Consulting (Oil & Marine) Limited, the principal business of which, as set out in the plea agreement he entered into in the United States, was 'to coordinate a bid-rigging, price-fixing and market share allocation conspiracy among manufacturers of marine hose'.[63] In effect Mr Whittle's sole occupation was to manage, on behalf of its members, an international cartel. The full role Mr Whittle played is spelt out in further detail at Para 4(b) of the plea agreement:

> [d]uring the relevant period, the defendant participated in a conspiracy with other persons and entities engaged in the manufacture and sale of marine hose, the primary purpose of which was to suppress and eliminate competition by rigging bids, fixing prices and allocating market shares for sales of marine hose sold in the United States. In furtherance of the conspiracy, the defendant attended meetings and engaged in discussions with executives from marine hose manufacturers. During such meetings and discussions, the defendant and co-conspirators agreed to rig bids, fix prices and allocate market shares for the sale of marine hose in the United States. Each of the conspiring manufacturers jointly funded the defendant who acted as coordinator for the cartel and provided him with information about upcoming marine hose jobs. The defendant then designated, based on rules agreed to by the co-conspirators and preferences expressed by the co-conspirators, which of the conspiring manufacturers would win the job, referring to the winning conspirator as the 'champion'. After the champion had been designated, the defendant provided the other conspirators with instructions regarding how much to bid on the job for the purpose of ensuring that the designated champion would win the job.[64]

Peter Whittle was paid approximately $50,000 a year by each cartel member for his work in managing the arrangements; between October 2001 and April 2004, for example, he sent invoices to Yokohama totalling approximately £140,000.

The investigation in the United States, which followed Yokohama's leniency application, was under the oversight of a grand jury in the Southern District of California, and was conducted by the Department of Defense Criminal Investigative Service ('DCIS'), the Naval Criminal Investigative Service, ('NCIS'),[65] and the Antitrust Division of the DOJ.

---

63 Case H-07-487-03, *US v Peter Whittle,* District Court, Southern District of Texas, entered on March 12, 2007, Para 4(a).

64 In the EU Commission Decision it is stated that the Japanese and European arms of the cartel operated under different coordinators until the mid-1990s, when a single firm took over the management. From some time in 1999 until late in 2001 the role was taken by Parker ITR, but was then transferred to Mr Whittle who continued to operate the cartel until its exposure (see Paras 239–41).

65 The involvement of DCIS and NCIS is explained by the fact that a number of contracts affected by the cartel related to Department of Defense contracts.

Yokohama had submitted substantial documentation relating to the cartel to the DOJ. Following the application, the DCIS interviewed Yokohama executives who were involved in the conspiracy. These confirmed the involvement of Yokohama in the cartel, and described the arrangements to an agent of the DCIS. The evidence gathered by the investigation team, prior to the making of the application for arrest warrants, indicated that a number of meetings between participants had taken place, with at least four 'general meetings' held between 1999 to 2002. Thus, for example, there is a reference to a

> general meeting . . . in December 2000 in Bangkok, Thailand. Defendants Whittle, Brammar and Cognard, as well as the conspirator living in Broward County, attended this meeting, at which the conspirators discussed how to keep the cartel running smoothly. They reviewed and agreed to the market shares allotted to each conspiring manufacturer and discussed and agreed to price lists for marine hose and related equipment, including those for use in the United States.[66]

Other meetings were held in Key Largo and London. Throughout this time the cartel members took careful efforts to conceal the existence of the cartel from the authorities, and the members cannot but have known that their activity was illegal under the laws of a number of jurisdictions. Participating companies were referred to by code names, for example, 'B1' stood in for Dunlop. The cartel was referred to by the conspirators as 'the club', or as the 'Technical Committee – Marine Hose'. When arrest warrants were sought in respect of the three UK defendants (and, in the same procedure, in respect of a French suspect, Jacques Cognard[67]), the link with a particular meeting, and with international enforcement efforts was made clear. Again, it is worth quoting fully from the Criminal Complaint:

> [26] The United States is seeking warrants in the Southern District of Texas to search the defendants and their hotel rooms, and to seize items, including records, documents and materials relating to marine hose bids and prices, during the defendants' anticipated upcoming stay in Houston, Texas, for the

---

[66] *US v Peter Whittle and others*, Case no 07-2553 – PRP, Southern District of Florida, Criminal Complaint (April 24, 2007) at Para 20.

[67] Mr Cognard, who was an executive of Trelleborg Industrie SA, a subsidiary of the Swedish corporation Trelleborg AG (which was named in the EU Commission decision) subsequently entered into a plea agreement under which he was required to serve a period of imprisonment of 14 months, and to pay a criminal fine of $100 000 (as well as a 'special assessment' of $100) (case 07-cr-60269-KAM, *US v Jacques Cognard*, District Court, Southern District of Florida, entered on November 15, 2007).

> Offshore Technology Conference ('OTC'). The OTC is an annual worldwide conference of engineers, scientists and managers associated with the ocean resources industry. This year, the OTC is scheduled for April 30 to May 3, 2007. Corporate members of the conspiracy are regularly represented at the OTC, and documents I have reviewed suggest that defendants Whittle, Brammar, Allison and Cognard each have attended the OTC at least once from at least 2001 through 2006. I have reviewed emails between Whittle and other cartel members in which Whittle has tried to organise in-person meetings during or immediately after the OTC to discuss the marine hose conspiracy, including with co-conspirators from Dunlop, Trelleborg and the marine hose manufacturer with operations in Broward County. At these meetings, according to documents I have reviewed, Whittle planned to discuss with these co-conspirators, among other things, upcoming prices to quote for marine hose.
>
> [27] DCIS has learned through its investigation that the defendants will be staying in hotels in Houston during the time of this year's OTC. A private meeting including Whittle, Brammar, Allison and Cognard and other co-conspirators is planned during the OTC. Documents I have reviewed show that Whittle intends to discuss future understandings about the marine hose conspiracy during this meeting.
>
> [28] The United States plans to arrest the defendants on the requested warrants soon after this meeting in the Southern District of Texas. The United States anticipates executing these arrest warrants simultaneously with the execution of the search warrants. The United States is coordinating the execution of its planned searches with the execution of warrants and/or other searches in locations across the United States and in several foreign countries. The foreign jurisdictions have determined that they must begin their searches as early as 5:00am Central Daylight Time in the United States. Once the searches begin abroad, there is a risk that individuals in foreign locations will contact the defendants in the United States. This would give the defendants an opportunity to flee and/or destroy or remove evidence sought before daylight or otherwise obstruct the investigation before warrants can be executed in the United States. Due to these potential exigent circumstances, and given the difficulty of coordinating execution with foreign law enforcement, the United States may need to execute these arrest warrants as early as 5:00am Central Daylight Time.

The meeting in Houston was bugged by the NCIS, and following the meeting arrests were duly made on May 2, 2007 in Houston and San Francisco. It will be noted that this is the same day on which the EU Commission, operating under its civil enforcement powers conferred by Regulation 1/2003, first carried out its 'unannounced' inspections at premises in France, Italy and the United Kingdom. In each case Commission officials were accompanied by counterparts from relevant national competition authorities. Given that the JFTC had also been involved in the investigation, this means that by early May 2007 enforcement activity was being coordinated across at least six countries, under four different laws (Japanese, United States, EU, and the UK's Cartel

Offence). The investigations carried out by DG Competition in the UK with the cooperation and assistance of OFT officials were part of the investigation by DG Competition into breaches of art 101 TFEU, which were separated out from the investigation of a potential Offence in the UK. The legal relationship between the competition law of the EU and of the UK (discussed in part in Chapter 4, above) is of such a nature that the OFT was *not* investigating whether the conduct was in breach of the Chapter I Prohibition of the Competition Act 1998, as the EU Commission had taken control of the case within the framework of the operation of the European Competition Network. In the case of the EU Commission's investigation, it is also worth noting that this was the first time, since the power was given in Regulation 1/2003, art 21, that a private home was inspected. Again, although the name of the occupier of the premises is redacted in the Commission Decision, it is stated that this was 'the private home of Mr [cartel coordinator]', so most likely this was Mr Whittle's home in Lincolnshire. Mr Whittle's home was the first private residence to be raided, on May 2, 2007, by the OFT in the course of an investigation into a competition law violation.

Following the arrests in the US, the three UK defendants, Bryan Allison and David Brammar (directors of Dunlop Oil & Marine Ltd), and Peter Whittle entered into plea agreements with the DOJ.[68]

It is worth quoting from the plea agreement entered into by Peter Whittle, which very strongly connects the US and UK enforcement, '*[n]otwithstanding* that the recommended sentence is based solely on effects in the United States and that the UK cartel offence relates only to effects in the United Kingdom'.[69] The information presented would charge the defendant with:

> participating in a conspiracy to suppress and eliminate competition by rigging bids, fixing prices and allocating market shares for sales of marine hose sold in the United States, beginning at least as early as 1999 and continuing until as late as May 2007 in unreasonable restraint of foreign trade and interstate trade and commerce in violation of the Sherman Antitrust Act. . . .

Mr Whittle first 'voluntarily and knowingly' waived various rights set out in the Agreement, and similarly waived any right to appeal against any

---

[68] See generally DOJ Press Release of December 3, 2007, 'Three United Kingdom Nationals Charged with Participating In Worldwide Bid-Rigging Conspiracy in the Marine Hose Market'.

[69] Case H-07-487-03, *US v Peter Whittle*, District Court, Southern District of Texas, entered on March 12, 2007, at Para 16, emphasis added.

sentence imposed by the Court as long as that sentence was that as set out in the Agreement, or less than that set out. The defendant agreed to the imposition of a fine of $100 000 and a period of imprisonment of 30 months, the latter 'subject to the potential reduction set out in Paragraph 16'. Paragraph 16 is, in part, in the following terms:

> . . . the United States and the defendant agree to recommend to this Court, if this Court permits the defendant to return to the United Kingdom and defers sentencing . . . and a sentence of imprisonment is imposed upon conviction for the UK cartel offence, that the period of imprisonment recommended [above] be reduced by one day for each day of the total term of the sentence imposed upon the defendant following his conviction for the UK cartel offence; however, a term of imprisonment that is suspended shall not be included in the reduction of the period of imprisonment recommended [above]. The defendant agrees not to seek from the UK court a sentence of imprisonment less than that set out [above].

Under the US Sentencing Guidelines the adjusted level for the offence would have given rise normally to a prison sentence of between 41 to 51 months' imprisonment, and the level of the financial penalty would have been between $1.15m to $5.75m, both significantly higher than that agreed to in the plea agreement. As part of the Agreement the US prosecuting authorities undertook to make a motion for a downward adjustment from the figures suggested by the guidelines 'because of the defendant's substantial assistance in the United States' investigation'.[70] A further advantage of such agreements, and one which DOJ officials appear to believe is an important one in securing such arrangements, is that the defendant would remain eligible for non-immigration visas should he need to travel to the US in the future. This is spelt out in Mr Whittle's case at Para 23 of the Agreement. It is clear that the agreement was constructed with close cooperation of the relevant UK authorities; Para 11 spelt out what would happen in the event that the Agreement was to be accepted:

> [i]f the Court permits the defendant to return to the United Kingdom . . . the defendant understands that, in connection with the investigation and prosecution of the UK cartel offence, he will initially be returned to the United Kingdom in custody to Heathrow Airport in London where, on arrival, he will be arrested by uniformed officers of the London Metropolitan Police. He will then be interviewed by officials of the OFT. The defendant will then be released on police bail subject to the following conditions:
>
> (a) he surrenders his passport and agrees not to apply for any travel documents;

[70] At Para 18.

(b) he remains in the jurisdiction of the UK court;
(c) he secures a surety in an amount specified by the London Metropolitan Police;
(d) he resides at his home address in Lincolnshire, United Kingdom; and
(e) he reports regularly to the Lincolnshire police station.

The DOJ itself stated that the 'proposed plea agreements represent the results of the Antitrust Division's extensive cooperation with foreign jurisdictions'.[71] Like Whittle, Allison agreed to pay a fine of $100,000, and Brammar to pay a fine of $75,000. The DOJ noted at the time that the jail terms were the longest to be agreed to by foreign defendants at that point. More importantly from the UK perspective the DOJ gave a ringing endorsement of the new UK criminal regime:

> [t]his investigation has not only netted record-setting jail sentences but has involved unprecedented coordination with the United Kingdom . . . The United Kingdom's Enterprise Act, which provides for criminal sanctions for individuals who engage in cartel offences, is an important new weapon in the fight against international cartels. The fact that other governments are now prosecuting cartels criminally, using jail time as a deterrent, shows that the stakes are rising for antitrust violators.[72]

This was the first occasion in which the US government allowed defendants to defer sentencing in the US if they agreed to be returned to another jurisdiction and plead guilty. It is impossible to conclude that this was anything other than an attempt to bolster criminal enforcement in the UK.[73] If Mr Whittle was not convicted by a UK court, or was convicted but to a lesser sentence than that specified in the Plea Agreement, such that his return to the United States to serve the remainder of his US sentence was required, provision was made in the Agreement should he be reluctant to do so. The defendant agreed not to fight any extradition request, and, just in case, also agreed that the statement of facts contained in the Agreement 'provide[d] a sufficient basis for any possible future extradition request'.[74] It was further agreed that a charge in the UK under the Cartel Offence

---

[71] DOJ Press Release, note 68.

[72] Note 26, above.

[73] Indeed, it was suggested by Scott D Hammond, Deputy Assistant Attorney General, Antitrust Division, that one of the considerations taken into account by the DOJ was that it was important to the creation of the global challenge against cartels that the OFT be able to secure convictions against cartelists ('Remarks at ABA International Cartel Workshop, February 1, 2008, cited in ABA, *2008 Annual Review of Antitrust Law Developments* (2009), at 198–99).

[74] At Para 13.

would not provide a double jeopardy or due process defence in the US, and that the same was true in reverse.

It is particularly noteworthy that in the one case to go to trial in the US the Government was unsuccessful. In *United States v Northcutt (Marine Hose)*,[75] after a four-week trial which included testimony from other cartel participants, the jury found a junior executive not guilty after only two hours deliberation. However, of the other cartel participants arrested at the same time as Whittle, Allison and Brammar in 2007, at least two pleaded guilty and agreed to jail terms of 14 months.

The civil EU Commission investigation, coordinated over a number of member states, was meanwhile proceeding. Like the DOJ, the Commission had access to documentation submitted by Yokohama, and then used the various powers conferred under Regulation 1/2003 to supplement this. Three further undertakings make applications under the EU leniency programme once the investigations were under way, but two of these were subsequently informed that their applications did not meet the relevant criteria. A Statement of Objections was adopted on April 28, 2008, and following hearings the final decision was adopted on January 28, 2010. The Commission imposed fines on five undertakings, with Manuli Rubber Industries SpA benefiting from a 30 per cent reduction in penalty (valued at €2 100 000) as its leniency application had been accepted. Yokohama would have faced a penalty calculated to be in the amount of €14 400 000 had it not been granted full leniency. Article 3 of the Decision adopted the familiar rubric in requiring that the 'undertakings listed in Article 1 shall immediately bring to an end the infringements referred to . . . [and] shall refrain from repeating any act or conduct described in Article 1, and from any act or conduct having similar effect'. It is, given Mr Whittle's role, a matter of interest that the EU Commission did not include him as an addressee of the Decision.[76]

The operation of the cartel was, as indicated above, highly sophisticated, and it was clear throughout that the participants knew of the illegality of their actions. While the arrangements were, in a perverse sense, admirable, it has been pointed out that the 'sheer volume and detail of the

[75] SD Fla, 2008.

[76] Although EU competition law is applicable *only* to undertakings, with the single exception that a natural person not being part of an undertaking may be questioned under Regulation 1/2003 (but may decline to answer, and cannot be punished for so doing, or if answers are misleading or inaccurate), an individual may simultaneously be an undertaking if the relevant criteria are fulfilled.

contact between each company and the coordinator [Whittle] exposed the cartel to detection'.[77]

It was reported by a number of sources in 2008 and 2009 that private actions seeking damages were underway, and it was generally believed that these might be relatively straightforward. Purchasers were businesses, or public sector agencies (such as the US Department of Defense, and the UK Ministry of Defence). If settlements have been reached they have not been made public.

Action in the UK – *R v Whittle, Allison and Brammar*[78]

In the UK the cartel controlled contracts worth some £17.5m; at trial the OFT alleged that the damage caused was assessed at £2.6m, equating to a price rise of some 15 per cent.

On June 10, 2008 Peter Whittle, Bryan Allison and David Brammar were convicted and sentenced in the UK for their participation in the marine hose cartel, having pleaded guilty, the first two receiving prison terms of 3 years, and Mr Brammar receiving a term of 2½ years. Bryan Allison's sentence reflected in part his role as Managing Director of the company. Thus Rivlin QC, Honorary Recorder of Westminster, stated in his remarks on sentencing that:

> [y]ou were higher up in the company than Mr Brammar. Indeed, you were at the very top of the company. Even though you may not have been as deeply involved as he was in the everyday workings of the cartel, I have no doubt that your responsibility in the dishonest management of your company was greater than his. I have come to the conclusion that, in all the circumstances, in terms of your culpability in relation to this indictment, you should be seen as being on the same level as Mr Whittle. The sentence, therefore, in your case, is one of three years' imprisonment.

On appeal these sentences were reduced to 2½ years, 2 years, and 20 months respectively. Director disqualification orders were made in respect of all three under s 2 of the Company Directors Disqualification Act 1986,[79] and Mr Allison was ordered to bear prosecution costs of £25 000. The plea-bargaining arrangement entered into in the US, which constrained the arguments made in court by the appellants, led to the Court

---

77 Lucraft, M, Payne, T, and Rawlings, D, note 57, at 7.

78 [2008] EWCA Crim 2560 [2009] UKCLR 247.

79 Whittle and Allison were both disqualified for seven years, and Brammar for five years.

of Appeal expressing 'considerable misgivings' about its disposal of the applications of appeal.[80]

On July 1, 2008, in the course of confiscation proceedings at Southwark Crown Court, Whittle was ordered to pay £649 636 within six months, or face another four years in jail. Whittle was, in effect, deprived of the income he had received in his role as cartel coordinator, which had been his only source of income over the relevant period. Brammar was ordered to pay £366 354, which reflected the money he had personally received in 'kickbacks', within 28 days; failure to pay would expose him to the risk of a further three years in jail.

The case, which was viewed as 'an important legal milestone',[81] received a significant amount of attention in the legal media, although analyses tended to be short, with the focus of pieces being to alert corporate executives and employees that a new legal threat faced them were they to engage in cartelisation.[82] Whether the case should be considered as significant, other than in providing an interesting and unique point of reference, remains to be seen. If it had the effect of encouraging the OFT to be over-confident in bringing forward the prosecution in the *British Airways* case (and it is impossible to verify whether this was the case), then it will have been important. It is unlikely, following the criticism made of the plea-bargaining process in the US, that the OFT, or any other successor prosecuting agency, would be party to similar plea agreements in the future. The case does however, demonstrate clearly the rewards that flow to competition law enforcement agencies from international cooperation, and the resultant increase in risk faced by cartel participants.

Very unusually, Mr Allison allowed himself to be interviewed after he had served his prison sentence, by Michael O'Kane, who was involved in the litigation,[83] and I have quoted a number of extracts from the interview

---

80 *R v Whittle and others* [2008] EWCA Crim 2560 [2009] UKCLR 247. See Chapter 4, above.

81 Lucraft, M, Payne, T, and Rawlings, D, note 57, at 8.

82 See, for example, ibid; 'Case Comment' (2008) *Global Competition Litigation Review* R63; Cleary Gottlieb, 'UK Imposes First Criminal Sentences on Cartel Participants' (July 2, 2008) (Cleary Gottlieb website); Simpson Thacher, 'Landmark US Cartel Case: UK Nationals Agree Plea with Record Sentences' (December 13, 2007) (Simpson Thacher and Bartlett LLP website); News (2008) *European Competition Law Review* N165; Tassopoulou, L, 'Case Comment' (2009) *European Competition Law Review* N41.

83 O'Kane, M, 'Does Prison Work for Cartelists? – the View from Behind Bars: An Interview of Bryan Allison by Michael O'Kane' (2011) 56:2 *Antitrust Bulletin* 483.

in this text (see Chapter 2). I will close this chapter however with a further quote:

> . . . I would not put myself out in such a risky and precarious position personally in order to achieve [survival in the market]. The personal damage, be it money, be whatever it is, is too great to allow yourself to worry about what will happen to other people. That's a terrible sentence to come out with, it really is. *I would never ever do it again*, and I wouldn't recommend to anyone that they do it. The loss to you in terms of your life is too great.[84]

---

84 Ibid, at 498, emphasis added.

7. Conclusion

It is not novel to argue that the problem with the UK's Cartel Offence, as originally framed, lies not in the specific language of the legislation, but with the deliberately constructed separation between the civil regime enshrined in the Competition Act 1998 and in the TFEU and the criminal regime set out in s 188 of the Enterprise Act 2002. Before the EA02 was introduced the Competition Law Association ('CLA') had argued, in its response to the Government consultation process, that there should be links between the civil and criminal regimes. As noted by Parkinson, the CLA 'thought that the government's approach would lead to unnecessary complication between the position of an individual defendant and a company which was the subject of an investigation by the competition law authorities'.[1] The Opposition proposed an amendment which would have required the prosecution to prove that the defendant knew that their act would be a breach of the CA98 or art 101 TFEU. This amendment was probably not the right way forward.

It is unfortunate that it is difficult to make an assessment of the operation of the criminal enforcement regime in the UK in isolation. The Office of Fair Trading, responsible for both criminal and civil enforcement until such time as criminal enforcement responsibility is moved to another agency, has been subject, properly, to serious criticism in recent years.[2] It is hard to escape the conclusion that the OFT has, at best, struggled, or at worse failed, in its civil enforcement since the CA98 took effect on March 1, 2000. The OFT's record of enforcement of the Chapter I and II Prohibitions is weak, and far too much time and resource has been

---

[1] Parkinson, S, 'The Cartel Offence under the Enterprise Act 2002' [2004] *Company Lawyer* 187 at 188.

[2] See, for example, reports by the National Audit Office which have been critical of the OFT's work (National Audit Office, *The Office of Fair Trading – Maintaining Competition in Markets* (2005) HC 593 session 2005–2006; and *Progress Report on Maintaining Competition in Markets* (2009) HC 127 session 2008–2009). The Serious Fraud Office ('SFO') has also been subject to general criticism and internal reorganisation following a critical report prepared by a senior US prosecutor (de Grazia, J, *Review of the Serious Fraud Office, Final Report* (2008) (www.sfo.gov.uk)).

devoted to a limited number of cases. In particular, the OFT became bogged down in cases relating to retail tobacco sales,[3] dairy products,[4] and construction[5] and struggled to find a way through these. In *Bid Rigging in the Construction Industry in England*, where at one point criminal actions were being touted, the OFT took action against 103 undertakings, selecting in respect of each a limited number of infringements, and produced a decision which ran to approximately 2000 pages. The OFT was first alerted to possible infringements on April 1, 2004, such that the final Decision was not made until nearly five and a half years later. The OFT faced a large number of appeals, in which notwithstanding the adoption of an early resolution procedure, the appellants were significantly successful in challenging the method of calculation of the penalty and the amounts imposed. There were then a number of further actions relating to costs, with the OFT being required to pay a substantial proportion of the costs of the partially successful appellants. The OFT may have been surprised (although it should not have been) by the extent to which targets of its investigations are prepared to devote resources to their defence. That there have been wider faults in OFT enforcement activity generally has, in effect, been accepted by the OFT and is evidenced in its own consultation paper published in March 2012.[6] It is something of a surprise to find

---

[3] OFT Decision, *Tobacco*, CA98/01/2010 (April 15, 2010). This case originated in January 2003 (see Para [2.88] of the Decision), and therefore took some seven years to complete. The final Decision ran to over 650 pages (including appendices). On December 12, 2011, the Competition Appeals Tribunal quashed the Decision when the OFT sought to defend its position on the basis of a refined case (*Imperial Tobacco Group plc and others v Office of Fair Trading* [2011] CAT 41). On February 23, 2012, the OFT's Chief Executive, John Fingleton, resigned (OFT Press Release 10/12, February 23, 2012).

[4] See OFT Decision in Case CE/3094-03, July 26, 2011. At the time of writing this Decision is the subject of an appeal brought before the CAT by Tesco Stores Limited and others (case number 1188/1/1/11).

[5] See, for example, OFT Decision, *Construction Recruitment Forum*, CA98/01/2009 (May 24, 2011). This case originated in response to an application for leniency made in late 2005, and was therefore resolved in a relatively timely manner. On appeal the CAT upheld the substance of the Decision, but reduced the amount of the penalties (*Eden Brown Limited and others v Office of Fair Trading* [2011] CAT 8). See also *Bid Rigging in the Construction Industry in England*, CA98/02/2009 (September 21, 2009).

[6] OFT, *Review of the OFT's Investigation Procedures in Competition Cases – A Consultation Paper* (OFT 1263con2, March 2012). The consultation has as its aim 'increasing the speed of CA98 investigations, enhancing the level of engagement with parties to investigations, and at improving robustness of the OFT's decision-making processes'. In *The Impact of Competition Interventions on Compliance and Deterrence: Final Report* (OFT 1391, December 2011) it is stated that '[t]he

therefore that in March 2012 the Global Competition Law Review named the OFT as 'agency of the year: Europe'.

In an ideal world the study of the Cartel Offence in this book would be of historical rather than current interest – I am not alone in suggesting that the failure in enforcement has fundamentally damaged the criminalisation project in the UK. Stephan, for example, has argued that the evidence as of 2011 raised 'a question of whether the current cartel offence has irreparably damaged our appetite and capacity for criminalisation altogether; causing us to eventually revert back to a purely civil cartel enforcement regime'.[7] The starting point in the 2011 consultation document on competition reform in relation to the Cartel Offence was that an amendment of some sort was required. It is surprising that the Government did not consider simply the abandonment of the Offence – the Conservative Party in opposition had strongly resisted its introduction. Unfortunately it did not do so, and, as others have pointed out, 'the criminal prosecution of individuals involved in cartels remains very much alive and likely to remain so for some time at least'.[8] As should be clear from my comments throughout this text, I find the case for personal sanctioning of cartelists persuasive, and it is with a degree of sadness that I suggest that the UK should abandon definitively its present position, and should in its place act as an advocate of reform within the EU structures.

In 2005, Wils[9] suggested that whether a criminal competition law

---

OFT's effectiveness in merger cases is generally rated more favourably by legal professionals than the effectiveness in competition law cases' (Para 1.33), and that 'legal professionals suggest that . . . the probability of detection is relatively low in competition cases' (Para 1.31).

[7] Stephan, A, 'How Dishonesty Killed the Cartel Offence' (2011) *Criminal Law Review* 446 at 455.

[8] Purnell, N, Bellamy, C, Kar, N, Piccinin, D, and Sahathevan, P, 'Criminal Cartel Enforcement – More Turbulence Ahead? The Implications of the BA/Virgin Case' (2010) *Competition Law Journal* 313 at 314 (although the authors anticipated a transfer of prosecutorial power from the OFT to a new agency – a plan since abandoned). Contrast this comment with Joshua: '[t]here may, however, be no more cartel offence prosecutions anyway: after this debacle, it could be destined for the new coalition government's "bonfire" of futile legislation' (Joshua, JM, 'DOA: Can the UK Cartel Offence Be Resuscitated?', in Beaton-Wells, C, and Ezrachi, A (eds), *Criminalising Cartels: Critical Studies of an International Regulatory Movement* (2011) Hart Publishing at 130).

[9] Wils, WPJ, 'Is Criminalization of EU Competition Law the Answer?' (2005) 28:2 *World Competition* 117 (also reproduced in Cseres, KJ, et al (eds), *Remedies and Sanctions in Competition Policy: Economic and Legal Implications of the Tendency to Criminalize Antitrust Enforcement in the EU Member States* (2005) Edward Elgar, at 60–132). See also Morgan, EJ, 'Criminal Cartel Sanctions under

regime was effective could be determined with reference to five criteria: (1) whether the regime was enforced by a 'sufficiently well-resourced and sufficiently dedicated body', which need not necessarily be *exclusively* dedicated to criminal enforcement; (2) whether investigatory powers were sufficient; (3) that those charged with determining guilt must be prepared to convict those charged where the evidence supported the allegations; (4) the support of politicians and the public for the regime; and (5) the continued existence of penalties in respect of breaches of competition law not falling within the hard-core criminal category. Baker has argued that the relative success enjoyed by the US in advancing criminal prosecutions flows from six factors: (1) the 'expansion to antitrust of traditional criminal prosecutorial and investigative techniques by the [DOJ] and the [FBI]'; (2) the strong leniency programme operated by the DOJ; (3) 'a grand jury system that tends to strongly favour the investigators'; (4) substantial funding for criminal enforcement; (5) courts' willingness increasingly to impose jail terms; and (6) a 'broad political consensus that cartels are bad and Sherman Act enforcement is good'.[10] That the US system *is* effective would appear to be beyond doubt.[11] It may be true however that the success of the US approach 'is based on some politics and public psychologies that others may regard as peculiarly American'.[12] The question becomes that of whether these peculiar features can be transplanted into other regimes. As suggested in Chapter 3, above, the US approach did not emerge overnight: it took nearly 90 years for the criminal regime to find its place as a vigorous part of the US system of antitrust enforcement.

There is substantial overlap between Wils' and Baker's analyses, and

---

the UK Enterprise Act: An Assessment' (2010) 17:1 *International Journal of the Economics of Business* 67, who critiques the UK regime (before the *British Airways* case collapsed) in light of the Wils' criteria.

[10] Baker, DI, 'The Use of Criminal Law Remedies to Deter and Punish Cartels and Bid-Rigging' (2000–2001) 69 *George Washington Law Review* 693 at 693–94.

[11] Although there has been criticism of a tendency in commentators and analysts to be insufficiently critical in assessments of the US regime. See, for example, Beaton-Wells, C, and Fisse, B, 'US Policy and Practice in Pursuing Individual Accountability for Cartel Conduct: A Preliminary Critique' (2011) 56:2 *Antitrust Bulletin* 277 at 278–79:

> . . . with only a handful of exceptions, the DOJ's contemporary policy and performance record with respect to criminal cartel enforcement have escaped critical scrutiny from US commentators. Indeed, most tend to lionise the Antitrust Division's efforts to eradicate cartels from the US and global economies.

[12] Baker, DI, 'Punishment for Cartel Participants in the US: A Special Model?', in Beaton-Wells, C, and Ezrachi, A (eds), *Criminalising Cartels*, at 27.

if we are to consider the operation of the UK regime within a similar framework the conclusions will not be positive. In particular it would appear that the OFT simply does not have the resources available to it to adequately fulfil a role as criminal investigator and prosecutor, although as I argue here the very structure of the UK regime results in an over-complex enforcement environment, which imposes costs that would be better avoided, but which cannot be avoided. It seems clear in particular that the OFT may feel somewhat aggrieved that, in relation to civil enforcement, the fines it recovers from infringers do not flow to its budget, whereas all costs incurred in enforcement and in appeals (including costs recovered by successful or partially-successful appellants) flow *from* its budget.[13] Morgan's analysis of the UK's criminal regime in light of Wils's benchmarks leads her to a pessimistic conclusion, and while she accepts the view that '[p]ersonal sanctions are required to ensure that individuals who organise cartels bear the risk of breaking the law',[14] she suggests that 'alternative sanctions such as director disqualifications which do not require criminal proceedings appear to deserve much more attention'.[15] Support for this position may be found in more general literature. Ogus, for example, has argued that as an alternative to the imposition of criminal law in regulatory contexts, 'consideration ought to be given to . . . making greater use of the deprivation of the right lawfully to undertake a profitable activity as a sanction'.[16] In fact it became clear even before the collapse of the *British Airways* case that the OFT *was* putting greater emphasis than it previously had on the exploitation of its power to seek competition director disqualification orders (CDOs).[17] In the OFT 2011 report, *The Impact of Competition Interventions on Compliance and Deterrence: Final Report*,[18] it is stated that director disqualification orders are less effective in driving deterrence than is the threat of personal criminal sanctions, but

---

13 In a chain of costs decisions in 2011 and 2012 the Competition Appeals Tribunal was unsympathetic to arguments about the impact of its costs decisions on the capacity of the OFT to fulfil its functions.

14 Morgan, EJ, note 9, at 82.

15 Ibid, at 82.

16 Ogus, A, 'Enforcing Regulation: Do We Need the Criminal Law?', in Sjögren, H, and Skogh, G (eds), *New Perspectives on Economic Crime* (2004) Edward Elgar, at 54.

17 In *Applications for Leniency and No-action in Cartel Cases. OFT's Detailed Guidance on the Principles and Process: A Consultation on OFT Guidance* (OFT 803con, October 2011) the OFT stated that the possibility that CDOs might be granted were 'a key incentive to apply for leniency' (at Para 5.5(b)).

18 OFT 1391, December 2011.

that they 'may be a relatively more effective deterrent for small companies than for large companies'.[19]

The UK's experience in enforcing the Cartel Offence does *not* cast light on how criminalisation might develop were the EU to adopt a criminal law of competition, although it does provide examples of what *not* to do. The primary difficulty in the UK's introduction of, and implementation of, the Cartel Offence stems from the coexistence of civil and criminal regimes, and the complex interactions between EU and UK law which arise. Neelie Kroes, former Commissioner for Competition Policy in the EU, argued in 2009 that there was no need for 'an artificial debate about criminal *versus* administrative cartel systems',[20] and pointed to the fact that the ECN provided a 'living example of how criminal and non-criminal systems can work together'. If so, the example is not one that should be embraced as an example of good practice.[21] Were the EU to adopt a criminal standard in respect of certain 'hard-core' cartel conduct, it would be possible to avoid these difficulties (allowing them to be replaced by different difficulties) by adopting a US-style approach in which public enforcement was directed at an early stage to *either* a criminal *or* a civil enforcement mode, but never with the two operating simultaneously. Some have argued that it is unrealistic to anticipate such a development,[22] but I am not so pessimistic.

Wils has argued that 'the idea that article [101 TFEU] is somehow inherently non-criminal, and could not be enforced by penalties on individuals, including penalties of a criminal law nature, is mistaken, and contradicted by Regulation No 1/2003, as well as by the practice of other Member States',[23] and that there would be 'three or four advantages in criminalising the enforcement of EU antitrust law in all Member States, through

---

19 At Para 6.9.

20 Kroes, N, 'Tackling Cartels – a Never-ending Task' (2009) Speech, Brasilia, October 8, 2009.

21 Kroes went on to say: '[w]e have no choice. We are bound to implement the same EU laws, and yet some Member States work additionally with criminal penalties and others not'. That she made no comment on the view of the Commission as to the desirability of these two systems being maintained is only to be expected.

22 See, for example, Massey, P, 'Criminal Sanctions for Competition Law: A Review of Irish Experience' (2004) *Competition Law Review* 23 at 32: '[o]bviously an EU criminal code is some way away as this is an area where member States guard their powers jealously. It is therefore unrealistic to expect that such provisions would be put in place to deal with cartels'.

23 Wils, WPJ, note 9, at 132; see also Cseres, KJ, Schinkel, MP, and Vogelaar, FOW, *Criminalization of Competition Law Enforcement: Economic and Legal Implications for the EU Member States* (2006) Edward Elgar, at 60–109.

EU harmonisation'.[24] It is perhaps unfortunate that Wils envisaged that the UK's experience in enforcing the Cartel Offence would be a positive one,[25] but based on that assumption, information exchange problems that arise at present within the ECN would be eliminated were criminal enforcement to be standard; sanctions would be more effectively managed (including, for example, by way of intra-EU extradition); and the burdens of competition law enforcement could be more evenly shared.[26]

There remain strong national sensitivities that limit the EU's ability to act in bringing criminal law forward. The Commission has recognised that 'criminal law is a sensitive policy field where differences amongst the national systems remain substantial, for example regarding sanction types and levels as well as the classification of certain conduct as an administrative or criminal offence'.[27] It is unlikely, but not inconceivable, that the EU could move towards the adoption of criminal law at the EU level in respect of cartelisation. The Commission takes the view, justifiably, that 'where the enforcement choices in the Member States [with respect to Union policies] do not yield the desired result and levels of enforcement itself remain uneven, the Union may itself set common rules on how to ensure implementation, including, if necessary, the requirement for criminal sanctions for breaches of EU law'.[28] The EU has, for example, enacted a directive in relation to environmental law which included provisions relating to criminal sanctions.[29] The EU has been given some scope in Chapter 4 of the TFEU, 'Judicial cooperation in criminal matters', to introduce measures

---

24 Wils, WPJ, note 9, at 154.

25 'I would personally expect that criminal cartel enforcement for instance in the United Kingdom will prove to be effective' (Wils, WPJ, note 9, at 154).

26 I am not entirely persuaded of a fourth 'advantage' postulated by Wils, who argues that at present even while information may not be exchanged freely around the ECN with differential civil and criminal standards applying, the impact of criminal regimes may be to deter undertakings from applying for leniency in those which do *not* apply criminal law, or that information may be less forthcoming in the course of investigations in those member states.

27 *Towards an EU Criminal Policy: Ensuring the Effective Implementation of EU Policies through Criminal Law*, Communication from the Commission to the European Parliament, the Council, the European Economic and Social Committee and the Committee of the Regions, COM(2011) 573 final, October 20, 2011, at 2.

28 Ibid, at 3.

29 Directive 2008/99/EC on the protection of the environment through criminal law (2008) OJ L328/28. See also Directive 2009/123/EC amending Directive 2005/35/EC on ship-source pollution and on the introduction of penalties for infringements (2009) OJ L280/52, and Directive 2009/52/EC providing for minimum standards on sanctions and measures against employers of illegally staying third-country nationals (2009) OJ L168/24.

relating to substantive criminal law and to criminal law procedures.[30] The list of areas in respect of which substantive law may be introduced under the procedure set out in art 83 TFEU does not at present include matters relating to the enforcement of competition law, but a power is reserved to the Council, acting unanimously, to add to that list. The most likely basis on which criminal laws in respect of cartelisation could be promulgated by the EU is that set out in art 83(2) TFEU:

> [i]f the approximation of criminal laws and regulations of the Member States proves essential to ensure the effective implementation of a Union policy in an area which has been subject to harmonisation measures, directives may establish minimum rules with regard to the definition of criminal offences and sanctions in the area concerned.

Given that the approach to cartel agreements entered into by undertakings *has* been harmonised at the EU level through Regulation 1/2003, and arguably through the existence of art 101 TFEU itself, it is open to the EU to introduce criminal cartel law. That this is, in the medium term, unlikely, is more than hinted at in the omission of competition law from a list of areas in which criminal law might be necessary, put forward by the Commission in its 2011 communication, *Towards an EU Criminal Policy*.[31]

---

[30] Article 83(1) of the TFEU (ex art 31 TEU), provides that:

> The European Parliament and the Council may, by means of directives adopted in accordance with the ordinary legislative procedure, establish minimum rules concerning the definition of criminal offences and sanctions in the areas of particularly serious crime with a cross-border dimension resulting from the impact of such offences or from a special need to combat them on a common basis.
>
> These areas of crime are the following: terrorism, trafficking in human beings and sexual exploitation of women and children, illicit drug trafficking, illicit arms trafficking, money laundering, corruption, counterfeiting means of payment, computer crime and organised crime.
>
> On the basis of developments in crime, the Council may adopt a decision identifying other areas of crime that meet the criteria specified in this paragraph. It shall act unanimously after obtaining the consent of the European Parliament.

[31] See note 27, where the Commission makes reference to 'measures to fight serious damaging practices and illegal profits in some economic sectors in order to protect activities of legitimate businesses and safeguard the interest of taxpayers' (at p 10). Areas highlighted are: the financial sector, 'concerning market manipulation or insider trading'; 'the fight against fraud'; the prevention of fraud relating to the euro. A number of 'indicative examples' of areas in which the introduction of criminal law could be reflected on are also set out: road transport, data protection, customs rules, environmental protection, fisheries policy, and internal market policies 'to fight serious illegal practices such as counterfeiting and corruption', but *not*, notably, illegal anti-competitive agreements.

Simonsson has argued that rather than seeking EU harmonisation in the short term, 'we should use the best aspects of the existing decentralisation of competition law to look for an efficient, although geographically uneven, criminalisation system. This would be achieved when a few resourceful Member States step forward and take the lead regionally by criminalising cartels, and by ensuring credible and sustainable enforcement.'[32]

Ingeborg Simonsson is an acute commentator, and is a judge at the Stockholm City Court with experience in handling competition cases from the bench; her *Legitimacy in EU Cartel Control*[33] is excellent. I do not agree, however, with her conclusions quoted above, and not only because the key example of what might be a 'resourceful' state – the UK – has, in its attempts to introduce criminal cartel law, failed spectacularly to ensure 'credible and sustained enforcement'; surely the UK example will deter other member states from taking a similar approach. More importantly it is the very lack of harmonisation and control at the EU centre that is responsible, significantly, for difficulties and limitations encountered in the operation of national criminal laws, at least in the UK, and Ireland.

There is no doubt that harmonising or controlling the creation of criminal laws pertaining to cartelisation would be a difficult project, and I do not mean here to suggest that it is an exercise that could be undertaken lightly. This book however, is not the place in which to explore the feasibility of such a project in detail.

Many of the problems seen in the UK's operation of the Cartel Offence in the 'first period' may perhaps be ascribed to institutional failure, and more charitably perhaps simply to the existence of a steep learning curve.

---

32 Simonsson, I, 'Criminalising Cartels in the EU: Is There a Case for Harmonisation?', in Beaton-Wells, C, and Ezrachi, A (eds), *Criminalising Cartels*, at 216. Simonsson is not alone in advancing this argument; see also Reindl, AP, 'How Strong Is the Case for Criminal Sanctions in Cartel Cases?', in Cseres, KJ, et al, *Criminalization of Competition Law Enforcement*, at 127:

> . . . those who favour the use of criminal sanctions against individuals in anti-cartel enforcement should not be too concerned if substantial criminal enforcement efforts first develop in individual member states, and if only then a serious debate starts as to whether criminal enforcement powers should be conferred on the European Commission. Member states would be a good place to focus on the discussion of criminal sanctions, experiment with different regimes as well as institutional and procedural set-ups to obtain better cost-benefit outcomes, develop expertise in criminal enforcement, and build public support for a criminal enforcement system.

33 (2010) Hart Publishing.

It is clear, as discussed in Chapter 3 above, that the apparently effective criminal regime in the US was not put in place overnight. Rather a *century* was required to achieve this result. As Baker notes, it may be the case that 'the United States is simply a few years ahead of the other major countries in using criminal enforcement remedies this way'.[34] Blame for OFT failure cannot be entirely laid at its own door, although perhaps it was unwise for the OFT to advocate for the introduction of the Offence; the criminal regime should not have been introduced when the OFT was barely getting to grips with civil enforcement of a prohibitory regime. Unfortunately, the fact that the Cartel Offence was introduced at that time may have fatally damaged the credibility of the criminalisation project in the UK.

Finally, I hope that events prove me wrong. Cartelisation is undoubtedly harmful, and the harms are often borne by those with no power to mitigate that harm, even were its existence to be identified by them. Vigorous, well-directed and well-managed enforcement of a criminal law under which cartelists face personalised sanctions should be the aim of EU and UK policy. That the Government has chosen to continue with the project in the UK shows at least some determination to this end. The task now will be for the OFT to improve its enforcement procedures and expertise, and to make better case selections than was the case, certainly, with the British Airways prosecution. Juries need to convict (and as discussed in Chapter 2 the evidence shows that the public does not wholeheartedly support this law), and judges need to sentence appropriately. This may take some time to achieve – the first ten years of the project have given us only failure.

---

[34] Baker, DI, note 12, at 694.

Bibliography

Books, Articles and Speeches

ABA Section of Antitrust Law, *Handbook on Antitrust Grand Jury Investigations* (2002) 3rd edn, American Bar Association

ABA Section of Antitrust Law, *Criminal Antitrust Litigation Handbook* (2006) 2nd edn, American Bar Association

ABA Section of Antitrust Law, *Antitrust Law Developments (Sixth)* (2007) American Bar Association

Aubert, C, Rey, P, and Kovacic, WE, 'The Impact of Leniency and Whistle-blowing Programs on Cartels' (2006) 24 *International Journal of Industrial Organization* 1241

Bailin, A, 'Doing Away with Dishonesty' (2011) *Competition Law Journal* 169

Baker, DI, 'The Use of Criminal Law Remedies to Deter and Punish Cartels and Bid-Rigging' (2000–2001) 69 *George Washington Law Review* 693

Beaton-Wells, C, and Ezrachi, A (eds), *Criminalising Cartels: Critical Studies of an International Regulatory Movement* (2011) Hart Publishing

Beaton-Wells, C, and Fisse, B, 'US Policy and Practice in Pursuing Individual Accountability for Cartel Conduct: A Preliminary Critique' (2011) 56:2 *Antitrust Bulletin* 277

Beckenstein, AR, and Landis-Gabel, H, 'Antitrust Compliance: Results of a Survey of Legal Opinion' (1982) 51 *Antitrust Law Journal* 459

Becker, GS, 'Crime and Punishment: An Economic Approach' (1968) 76 *Journal of Political Economy* 169

Bennett, DJ, 'Killing One Bird with Two Stones: The Effect of *Empagran* and the Antitrust Criminal Penalty Enhancement and Reform Act of 2004 on Detecting and Deterring International Cartels' (2004–2005) 93 *Georgetown Law Journal* 1421

Benson, BL, and Zimmerman, PR (eds), *Handbook on the Economics of Crime* (2010) Edward Elgar

Blake, S, 'Criminal and Civil Cartel Enforcement: Issues and Challenges for Advisors and Authorities – Perspective of the Authority' (2008) *Competition Law Journal* 9

Block, M, and Sidak, JG, 'The Cost of Antitrust Deterrence: Why Not

Hang a Price Fixer Now and Then?' (1980) 68 *Georgetown Law Journal* 1131
Bos, I, and Wandschneider, F, 'Cartel Ringleaders and the Corporate Leniency Program' (2011) Centre for Competition Policy, CCP Working Paper 11–13
Braithwaite, J, 'Challenging Just Deserts: Punishing White-Collar Criminals' (1982) 73:2 *Journal of Criminal Law and Criminology* 723
Bryant, PG, and Eckard, EW, 'Price Fixing: The Probability of Getting Caught' (1991) 73:3 *Review of Economics and Statistics* 531
Clark, JD, *The Federal Trust Policy* (1931) Johns Hopkins University Press
Clarke, JL, and Evenett, SJ, 'The Deterrent Effects of National Anticartel Laws: Evidence from the International Vitamins Cartel' (2003) 48 *Antitrust Bulletin* 689
Combe, E, and Monnier, C, 'Fines against Hard Core Cartels in Europe: The Myth of Overenforcement' (2011) 56 *Antitrust Bulletin* 235
Combe, E, Monnier, C, and Legal, R, 'Cartels: The Probability of Getting Caught in the European Union' (2008) *Bruges European Economic Research Papers*, Paper 12
Conklin, JE, *"Illegal but Not Criminal": Business Crime in America* (1977) Prentice-Hall
Connor, JM, 'Forensic Economics in Action: The Lysine Cartel' (2001) 18 *Review of Industrial Organization* 1
Connor, JM, '"Our Customers Are Our Enemies": The Lysine Cartel of 1992–1995' (2001) 18 *Review of Industrial Organization* 5
Connor, JM, 'Effectiveness of Antitrust Sanctions on Modern International Cartels' (2006) 6 *Journal of Industrial Competition and Trade* 195
Connor, JM, *Global Price Fixing* (2009, 2nd edn) Springer
Connor, JM, 'Global Cartels Redux: The Lysine Antitrust Litigation (1996)', in Kwoka, JE Jr, and White, LJ, *The Antitrust Revolution: Economics, Competition and Policy* (2009, 5th edn), Oxford University Press
Connor, JM, 'Recidivism Revealed: Private International Cartels 1990–2009' (2010) 6:2 *Competition Policy International* 101
Connor, JM, 'Problems with Prison in International Cartel Cases' (2011) 56 *Antitrust Bulletin* 311
Connor, JM, and Bolotova, Y, 'Cartel Overcharges: Survey and Meta-analysis' (2006) 24 *International Journal of Industrial Organization* 1109
Connor, JM, and Lande, RH, 'The Size of Cartel Overcharges: Implications for US and EU Fining Policies' (2006) 51:4 *Antitrust Bulletin* 983
Connor, JM, and Lande, RH, 'Optimal Cartel Deterrence: An Empirical

Comparison of Sanctions to Overcharges' (2011) AAI Working Paper No. 11-08
Craycraft, C, Craycraft, JL, and Gallo, JC, 'Antitrust Sanctions and a Firm's Ability to Pay' (1997) 12 *Review of Industrial Organization* 171
Cseres, KJ, Schinkel, MP, and Vogelaar, FOW, *Criminalization of Competition Law Enforcement: Economic and Legal Implications for the EU Member States* (2006) Edward Elgar
Curtis, ME, and McNally, J, 'The Classic Cartel – Hatchback Sentence?' (2007) 4:1 *Competition Law Review* 41
Dannecker, G, and Jansen, O, *Competition Law Sanctioning in the European Union* (2004) Kluwer Law International
de Roos, N, 'Examining Models of Collusion: The Market for Lysine' (2006) 24 *International Journal of Industrial Organization* 1083
Ehlermann, CD, and Atanasiu, I (eds), *European Competition Law Annual 2006: Enforcement of Prohibition of Cartels* (2007) Hart Publishing
Eichenwald, K, *The Informant: A True Story* (2000) Broadway
Elzinga, KG, and Breit, W, *The Antitrust Penalties: A Study in Law and Economics* (1976) Yale University Press
Ermann, MD, and Lundman, RJ, *Corporate and Governmental Deviance: Problems of Organizational Behavior in Contemporary Society* (1978) Oxford University Press
Evenett, SJ, Levenstein, MC, and Suslow, VY, 'International Cartel Enforcement: Lessons from the 1990s' (2001) 24 *World Economy* 1221
Feinberg, RM, 'The Enforcement and Effects of European Competition Policy: Results of a Survey of Legal Opinion' (1985) 23:4 *Journal of Common Market Studies* 373
Fisse, B, 'The Cartel Offence: Dishonesty?' (2007) 35 *Australian Business Law Review* 235
Fleming, P, and Zyglidopoulos, SC, *Charting Corporate Corruption: Agency, Structure and Escalation* (2009) Edward Elgar
Fraas, AG, and Greer, DF, 'Market Structure and Price Collusion: An Empirical Analysis' (1977) 26 *Journal of Industrial Economics* 21
Frazer, T, 'Big Boys' Games, Big Boys' Rules: Compliance, Competition Law and the Criminology of the Corporation', Paper for Socio-Legal Studies Association Annual Conference, Leeds, March 1995 (unpublished)
Frazer, T, 'Monopoly, Prohibition and Deterrence' (1995) 58 *Modern Law Review* 846
Frezal, S, 'On Optimal Cartel Deterrence Policies' (2006) 24 *International Journal of Industrial Organization* 1231
Furse, M, 'The Cartel Offence – "Great for a Headline but Not Much Else"?' (2011) *European Competition Law Review* 223

Furse, M, and Nash, S, *The Cartel Offence* (2004) Hart Publishing

Galbreath, C, 'Cartel Criminalization in Ireland and Europe: Can the United States Model of Criminal Antitrust Enforcement be Successfully Transferred to Ireland and Europe?' (2007) ABA International Section, 2007 Fall Meeting, October 1, 2007

Galbreath, C, 'Criminalization of Cartel Offences in Ireland: Implications for International Cartels' (2010) ABA Spring Meeting Cartel Panel

Galbreath, C, 'Criminal Enforcement of Competition Laws in Ireland: A Look at Enforcement to Date' (2010) <http://tca.ie/images/uploaded/documents/2010-01%20Criminal%20Enforcement%20of%20Competition%20Laws%20in%20Ireland.PDF> (accessed July 30, 2011)

Garoupa, N (ed), *Criminal Law and Economics* (2009) Edward Elgar

Geary, D, 'Irish Competition Law Update' (2007) *Competition Law Journal* 137

Green, SP, 'Moral Ambiguity in White Collar Criminal Law' (2004) 18 *Notre Dame Journal of Law, Ethics and Public Policy* 501

Ghosal, V, 'The Law and Economics of Enhancing Cartel Enforcement: Using Information from *Non*-Cartel Investigations to Prosecute Cartels' (2011) CESifo Working Paper No 3506 (www.ssrn.com)

Gibbons, DC, 'Crime and Punishment: A Study in Social Attitudes' (1969) 47 *Social Forces* 391

Gorecki, PK, and McFadden, D, 'Criminal Cartels in Ireland: The Heating Oil Case' (2006) *European Competition Law Review* 631

Hammond, SD, 'Cornerstones of an Effective Leniency Program', ICN Workshop on Leniency Programs, November 22–23, 2004 (www.justice.gov/atr/public/speeches/206611.htm)

Hammond, SD, 'Measuring the Value of Second-In Cooperation in Corporate Plea Negotiations', 54th Annual ABA Section of Antitrust Law Spring Meeting, March 29, 2006 (www.justice.gov/atr/public/speeches/215514.htm)

Hammond, SD, 'The U.S. Model of Negotiated Plea Agreements: A Good Deal with Benefits for All' (2006) OECD Competition Committee, Working Party 3

Hammond, SD, 'Recent Developments Relating to the Antitrust Division's Corporate Leniency Program', 23rd National Institute on White Collar Crime, March 5, 2009 (www.justice.gov/atr/public/speeches/speech-criminal.html)

Harding, C, 'Cartel Deterrence: The Search for Evidence and Argument' (2011) 56 *Antitrust Bulletin* 345

Harding, C, and Joshua, J, 'Breaking Up the Hard Core: The Prospects for the Proposed Cartel Offence' (2002) *Criminal Law Review* 933

Harrison, G, and Bell, M, 'Recent Enhancements in Antitrust Criminal

Enforcement: Bigger Sticks and Sweeter Carrots' (2005–2006) 6 *Houston Business and Tax Law Journal* 206

Hay, GA, and Kelley, D, 'An Empirical Survey of Price Fixing Conspiracies' (1974) *Journal of Law and Economics* 13

Heilbroner, RL, et al, *In the Name of Profit* (1972) Doubleday

Joshua, JM, 'The UK's New Cartel Offence and Its Implications for EC Competition Law: A Tangled Web' (2003) *European Law Review* 620

Joshua, JM, 'Extradition: The DOJ's New Foreign Policy Weapon' (2005) June, *Competition Law Insight* 12

Joshua, JM, 'Shooting the Messenger: Does the UK Criminal Cartel Offense Have a Future?' (2010) *theantitrustsource*, August (www.antitrustsource.com)

Konkurrensverket (Swedish Competition Authority), *Fighting Cartels – Why and How?* (2001) Konkurrensverket

Kriesberg, SM, 'Decisionmaking Models and the Control of Corporate Crime' (1976) 85 *Yale Law Journal* 1091

Kroes, N, 'Tackling Cartels – a Never-ending Task' (2009) Speech, Brasilia, October 8, 2009

Landes, WM, 'Optimal Sanctions for Antitrust Violations' (1983) 50 *University of Chicago Law Review* 652

Lawrence, J, et al, 'Hardcore Bargains: What Could Plea Bargaining Offer in UK Criminal Cartel Cases?' (2008) *Competition Law Journal* 17

Leslie, CR, 'Antitrust Amnesty, Game Theory and Cartel Stability' (2006) 31 *Journal of Corporation Law* 453

Lester, M, 'Prosecuting Cartels for Conspiracy to Defraud' (2008) *Competition Law Journal* 134

Letwin, WL, 'Congress and the Sherman Antitrust Law: 1887–1890' (1955–1956) 23 *University of Chicago Law Review* 221

Letwin, WL, *Law and Economic Policy in America: The Evolution of the Sherman Act* (1967) Edinburgh University Press

Levenstein, MC, and Suslow, VY, 'What Determines Cartel Success?' (2006) 44 *Journal of Economic Literature* 43

Lever, J, and Pike, J, 'Cartel Agreements, Criminal Conspiracy and the Statutory "Cartel Offence": Part 1' (2005) *European Competition Law Review* 90

Lever, J, and Pike, J, 'Cartel Agreements, Criminal Conspiracy and the Statutory "Cartel Offence": Part 2' (2005) *European Competition Law Review* 164

Lieber, JB, *Rats in the Grain: The Dirty Tricks and Trials of Archer Daniels Midland, the Supermarket to the World* (2000) Basic Books

Lopatka, JE, and Page, WH, 'Indirect Purchaser Suits and the Consumer Interest' (2003) 48 *Antitrust Bulletin* 531

Low, DM, and O'Carroll, S, 'Added Complexity – Recent Developments in Criminal Cartel Law' (2008) 4 *Competition Law International* 30

Lucraft, M, Payne, T, and Rawlings, D, 'Case Comment: The Dunlop Three: The Cartel Offence Makes Its Debut' (2009) *Archbold News* 7

MacCulloch, A, 'The Cartel Offence and the Criminalisation of United Kingdom Competition Law' (2003) *Journal of Business Law* 616

MacCulloch, A, 'Honesty, Morality and the Cartel Offence' (2007) *European Competition Law Review* 355

MacCulloch, A, 'The Cartel Offence: Is Honesty the Best Policy?', in Rodger, BJ (ed), *Ten Years of Competition Law Reform* (2010) Dundee University Press

MacCulloch, A, 'The Cartel Offence: Defining an Appropriate "Moral Space"' (2012) 8:1 *European Competition Journal* 73

McNally, J, 'Case Comment: *D.P.P. v. Duffy and Duffy Motors (Newbridge) Limited*' (2010) 1:2 *Irish Journal of Legal Studies* 116

Mason, C, *The Art of the Steal: Inside the Sotheby's–Christie's Auction House Scandal* (2004) Putnam

Massey, P, 'Criminal Sanctions for Competition Law: A Review of Irish Experience' (2004) *The Competition Law Review* 23

Matsushita, M, 'Reforming the Enforcement of the Japanese Antimonopoly Law' (2009) 41 *Loyola University Chicago Law Journal* 521

Morgan, EJ, 'Criminal Cartel Sanctions under the UK Enterprise Act: An Assessment' (2010) 17:1 *International Journal of the Economics of Business* 67

Neal, PC, and Goldberg, P, 'The Electrical Equipment Antitrust Cases: Novel Judicial Administration' (1964) 50 *ABA Journal* 621

O'Kane, M, *The Law of Criminal Cartels* (2009) Oxford University Press

O'Kane, M, 'Does Prison Work for Cartelists? – the View from behind Bars: An Interview of Bryan Allison by Michael O'Kane' (2011) 56 *Antitrust Bulletin* 483

Ormosi, P, 'How Big Is the Tip of an Iceberg? A Parsimonious Way to Estimate Cartel Detection Rate' (2011) Centre for Competition Policy, CCP Working Paper 11-6

Parker, C, and Nielsen, VL, 'Deterrence and the Impact of Calculative Thinking on Business Compliance with Competition and Consumer Regulation' (2011) 56 *Antitrust Bulletin* 377

Parkinson, S, 'The Cartel Offence under the Enterprise Act 2002' (2004) *Company Lawyer* 187

Peretz, G, and Lewis, J, 'Go Directly to Jail: Losing Badly in "Monopoly"' (2003) *New Law Journal* 99

Peritz, RJR, *Competition Policy in America 1888–1992: History, Rhetoric, Law* (1996) Oxford University Press

Porter, RH, 'A Study of Cartel Stability: The Joint Executive Committee, 1880–1886' (1983) 14:2 *Bell Journal of Economics* 301

Posner, RA, 'An Economic Theory of Criminal Law' (1985) 85 *Columbia Law Review* 1193

Purnell, N, Bellamy, C, Kar, N, Piccinin, D, and Sahathevan, P, 'Criminal Cartel Enforcement – More Turbulence Ahead? The Implications of the BA/Virgin Case' (2010) *Competition Law Journal* 313

Ramage, S, 'Criminal Cartels' (2008) *Criminal Lawyer* 5

Richardson, GB, 'The Pricing of Heavy Electrical Equipment: Competition or Agreement?' (1966) 28:2 *Bulletin of the Oxford University Institute of Economics & Statistics* 73

Riley, A, 'Editorial – Developing Criminal Cartel Law: Dealing with the Growing Pains' (2007) *Competition Law Review* 1

Riley, A, 'Modernising Cartel Sanctions: Effective Sanctions for Price-fixing in the European Union' (2011) *European Competition Law Review* 551

Rosati, F, and Ehmer, C, 'Science, Myth and Fines: Do Cartels Typically Raise Prices by 25%?' (2009) 4 *Concurrences* no 28832

Shaffer, GC, and Nesbitt, NH, 'Criminalizing Cartels: A Global Trend?' (2011) 12 *Sedona Conference Journal*; *Minnesota Legal Studies Research Paper No 11-26* (2011) University of Minnesota, School of Law

Schmidt, JT, 'Keeping US Courts Open to Foreign Antitrust Plaintiffs: A Hybrid Approach to the Effective Deterrence of International Cartels' (2006) 31 *Yale Journal of International Law* 211

Simonsson, I, *Legitimacy in EU Cartel Control* (2010) Hart Publishing

Simpson, S, *Corporate Crime, Law and Social Control* (2002) Cambridge University Press

Sjögren, H, and Skogh, G (eds), *New Perspectives on Economic Crime* (2004) Edward Elgar

Smith, RA, 'The Incredible Electrical Conspiracy' (1961) *Fortune*, April, at 132, and May, at 161

Snow, TG, 'The Investigation and Prosecution of White Collar Crime: International Challenges and the Legal Tools Available to Address Them' (2002–2003) 11 *William & Mary Bill of Rights Journal* 209

Stephan, A, 'Survey of Public Attitudes to Price-Fixing and Cartel Enforcement in Britain' (2008) *Competition Law Review* 123

Stephan, A, 'How Dishonesty Killed the Cartel Offence' (2011) *Criminal Law Review* 446

Stigler, GJ, 'A Theory of Oligopoly' (1964) 72:1 *Journal of Political Economy* 44

Stucke, ME, 'Morality and Antitrust' (2006) *Columbia Business Law Review* 443

Taylor, CR, 'Indirect Damages from Price Fixing: The Alabama Lysine Case' (2001) 18 *Review of Industrial Organization* 33

Thorelli, HB, *The Federal Antitrust Policy* (1955) Johns Hopkins University Press

Utton, MA, *Cartels and Economic Collusion: The Persistence of Corporate Conspiracies* (2011) Edward Elgar

Veljanovski, C, 'The Economics of Cartels' (2006) *Finnish Competition Law Yearbook*

Walton, C, and Cleveland, F, *Corporations on Trial: The Electric Cases* (1964) Wadsworth Publishing

Wardhaugh, B, 'Closing the Deterrence Gap: Individual Liability, the Cartel Offence and the BIS Consultation' (2011) *Competition Law Journal* 175

Watkins, MW, 'Electrical Equipment Antitrust Cases: Their Implications for Government and for Business' (1961) 29:1 *University of Chicago Law Review* 97

Werden, GJ, 'Sanctioning Cartel Activity: Let the Punishment Fit the Crime' (2009) 5:1 *European Competition Journal* 19

Werden, GJ, Hammond, SD, and Barnett, BA, 'Recidivism Eliminated: Cartel Enforcement in the United States since 1999' (2011) Georgetown Global Antitrust Enforcement Symposium, September 22, 2011

Werden, GJ, Hammond, SD, and Barnett, BA, 'Deterrence and Detection of Cartels: Using All the Tools and Sanctions' (2011) 56 *Antitrust Bulletin* 207

Werden, GJ, and Simon, MJ, 'Why Price Fixers Should Go to Prison' (1987) 32 *Antitrust Bulletin* 917

Whelan, PM, 'A Principled Argument for Personal Criminal Sanctions as Punishment under EC Cartel Law' (2007) 4:1 *Competition Law Review* 7

Whelan, PM, 'Contemplating the Future: Personal Criminal Sanctions for Infringements of EC Competition Law' (2008) 19:2 *King's College Law Journal* 364

Whelan, PM, 'Resisting the Long Arm of Criminal Antitrust Laws: *Norris v The United States*' (2009) 72:2 *Modern Law Review* 272

White, LJ, 'Lysine and Price Fixing: How Long? How Severe?' (2001) 18 *Review of Industrial Organization* 23

Whiting, RA, 'Antitrust and the Corporate Executive' (1962) 48:1 *Virginia Law Review* 1

Wils, WPJ, 'Is Criminalization of EU Competition Law the Answer?' (2005) 28:2 *World Competition* 117

Official Publications

Department of Justice, Antitrust Division, *Antitrust Division Manual*, 4th edn (www.justice.gov/atr/public/divisionmanual)
Department of Justice, Antitrust Division, 'Frequently asked questions regarding the Antitrust Division's leniency program and model leniency letters' (2008) (www.justice.gov/atr/public/criminal/239583.pdf)
Department for Business, Innovation and Skills, *A Competition Regime for Growth: A Consultation on Options for Reform* (March 2011)
Department for Business, Innovation and Skills, *Growth, Competition and the Competition Regime: Government Response to Consultation* (March 2012)
Department of Trade and Industry, *Productivity and Enterprise: A World Class Competition Regime* (July 2001) Cm 2533
The Law Commission, *Legislating the Criminal Code: Fraud and Deception* (1999) Consultation Paper No 1555
The Law Commission, *Criminal Liability in Regulatory Contexts: A Consultation Paper* (2010) Consultation Paper No 195
Office of Fair Trading, *The Proposed Criminalisation of Cartels in the UK – a Report Prepared for the Office of Fair Trading by Sir Anthony Hammond QC and Roy Penrose OBE QPM* (OFT 365, November 2001) [2002] UKCLR 97
Office of Fair Trading, *The Cartel Offence: Guidance on the Issue of No-action Letters for Individuals* (OFT 513, April 2003)
Office of Fair Trading, *Powers for Investigating Criminal Cartels* (January 2004)
Office of Fair Trading, *Covert Surveillance in Cartel Investigations: Code of Practice* (OFT 738, August 2004)
Office of Fair Trading, *Covert Human Intelligence Sources in Cartel Investigations: Code of Practice* (OFT 739, August 2004)
Office of Fair Trading, *The Deterrent Effect of Competition Enforcement by the OFT* (OFT 962, November 2007)
Office of Fair Trading, *Leniency and No-action: OFT's Guidance Note on the Handling of Applications* (OFT 803, December 2008)
Office of Fair Trading, *Memorandum of Understanding between the Office of Fair Trading (OFT) and the National Casework Division (NCD), Crown Office, Scotland* (OFT 546, June 2009)
Office of Fair Trading, *Drivers of Compliance and Non-Compliance with Competition Law* (OFT 1227, May 2010)Office of Fair Trading, *Project Condor Board Review* (OFT, December 2010)
Office of Fair Trading, *A Competition Regime for Growth. A Consultation*

on Options for Reform: The OFT's Response to the Government's Consultation (OFT 1335, June 2011)

Office of Fair Trading, *Applications for Leniency and No-action in Cartel Cases. OFT's Detailed Guidance on the Principles and Process: a Consultation on OFT guidance* (OFT 803con, October 2011)

Office of Fair Trading, *The Impact of Competition Interventions on Compliance and Deterrence: Final Report* (OFT 1391, December 2011)

Office of Fair Trading, *Review of the OFT's Investigation Procedures in Competition Cases – a Consultation Paper* (OFT 1263con2, March 2012)

OECD, *Recommendation of the Council Concerning Effective Action against Hard Core Cartels*, March 25, 1998 [C/M(98)7/PROV]

OECD, *Hard Core Cartels* (2000)

OECD, *Cartel Sanctions against Individuals* (2003) DAF/COMP(2004)39

Other Media

Rossiter, N (dir.), *Sotheby's and Christie's: A Crime amongst Gentlemen* (2002) BBC (Documentary)

Soderbergh, S (dir.), *The Informant!* (2009) Warner Brothers Pictures

Index